W0091304

Beyond Code

AI-powered coding tools are revolutionizing software development, transforming programming from a specialized skill into an accessible educational practice across disciplines. This book investigates how tools such as Cursor AI, GitHub Copilot, and Replit's Ghostwriter are dismantling traditional barriers to entry for learners—particularly those from non-STEM backgrounds—by enabling natural language code generation, intelligent debugging, and interactive, project-based learning. Bridging the gap between theoretical instruction and practical application, the book serves as both a guide and a critical framework for integrating generative AI into curricula. It highlights how these tools expand the boundaries of programming education by supporting interdisciplinary applications, from literary analysis to creative writing, thereby making coding relevant and actionable for students in the humanities and beyond. The book equips educators with the tools and strategies necessary to incorporate AI-assisted programming into diverse academic contexts by offering lesson plans and adaptable project models. This resource is essential for instructors seeking to demystify coding, promote inclusivity in technical learning, and reimagine the role of software literacy in the twenty-first-century classroom.

Daniel Plate, a preeminent scholar in the field of educational technology, focuses his research and pedagogy on the integration of generative artificial intelligence in pedagogical methodologies. Educated with a Bachelor of Arts in English and Philosophy from Taylor University, a Master of Fine Arts in Creative Writing from the University of Arkansas, and a PhD in Literature from Washington University in St. Louis, Plate presently serves as a faculty member at Lindenwood University. There, he instructs courses in creative writing, literature, and composition. Beyond his contributions to poetry, he has co-authored numerous case studies that explore the nuanced applications of AI in classroom settings. These scholarly works not only contribute to the existing body of literature but also offer practical insights for educators interested in leveraging generative AI to enrich the learning experience. Plate's scholarly endeavors straddle the intersection of technology and pedagogy; he divides his professional time between developing code to augment teaching methods and conducting empirical research to better understand the symbiotic relationship between AI and innovative pedagogy. A prolific author in the field of AI in education, his latest publication is *Generative AI in the English Composition Classroom: Practical and Adaptable Strategies* (2024).

James Hutson specializes in multidisciplinary research that encompasses artificial intelligence, neurohumanities, neurodiversity, immersive realities, and the gamification of education. Earning a Bachelor of Arts in Art from the University of Tulsa, a Master of Arts in Art History from Southern Methodist University, and a PhD in Art History from the University of Maryland, College Park, he later acquired additional Master's degrees in Leadership and Game Design from Lindenwood University and additional PhD in Artificial Intelligence at Capitol Technology University (2023). Over the span of his academic career since 2006, Hutson has held various pedagogical and administrative positions across five universities, including Chair of Art History, Assistant Dean of Graduate and Online Programs, and most recently, Lead XR Disruptor and Department Head of Art History, AI, and Visual Culture. Notably, his scholarly portfolio includes several books on the application of artificial intelligence in education and cultural heritage, such as *Creative Convergence: The AI Renaissance in Art and Design* (2024), as well as numerous articles and case studies.

Beyond Code

Redefining Programming Education Beyond STEM

Daniel Plate and James Hutson

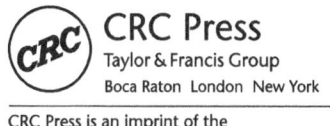

CRC Press
Taylor & Francis Group
Boca Raton London New York

CRC Press is an imprint of the
Taylor & Francis Group, an **informa** business

A CHAPMAN & HALL BOOK

First edition published 2026
by CRC Press
2385 NW Executive Center Drive, Suite 320, Boca Raton FL 33431

and by CRC Press
4 Park Square, Milton Park, Abingdon, Oxon, OX14 4RN

CRC Press is an imprint of Taylor & Francis Group, LLC

ISBN: 9781041069003 (hbk)
ISBN: 9781041068969 (pbk)
ISBN: 9781003637738 (ebk)

DOI: 10.1201/9781003637738

Typeset in Palatino
by Deanta Global Publishing Services, Chennai, India

Dedication

This manuscript is dedicated to our families, whose unwavering support and encouragement have been the cornerstone of our journey. To our parents, we express deep gratitude for instilling in us a thirst for knowledge and the determination to pursue our passions. Your belief in our abilities and unwavering support have propelled us forward.

To our spouses and partners, we extend heartfelt appreciation for standing by our side throughout the long hours of research and writing. To our children, we are grateful for your inspiration and the joy you bring to our lives. Your presence reminds us of the importance of our work and motivates us to strive for excellence. To our extended families, friends, and loved ones, we thank you for your encouragement, words of wisdom, and unwavering belief in our abilities. In particular, James Hutson would like to thank his wife Piper and children Bishop and Aurora.

Your support has been a source of strength and inspiration. We acknowledge the sacrifices you have made and the understanding you have shown, allowing us the time and space to pursue our scholarly endeavors. This manuscript stands as a testament to your love and support. With deepest appreciation and heartfelt gratitude, we dedicate this work to our families.

Epigraph

The purpose of abstraction is not to be vague, but to create a new semantic level in which one can be absolutely precise.

—Edsger W. Dijkstra

Contents

Preface

Programming has conventionally existed as a technical discipline, mostly confined to the domains of computer science, engineering, and mathematics. The conventional approach to teaching coding prioritizes syntax mastery—students spend months, even years, learning the foundational structures of programming languages before creating anything tangible. This approach parallels early writing pedagogy: grammar and sentence structure precede composition and critical argumentation. As generative AI reshapes how students engage with writing, coding tools reshape programming education, lower barriers to entry, and make computational thinking more accessible across disciplines. The carefully enforced boundaries between STEM and the humanities—once maintained through distinct methodologies and disciplinary priorities—now dissolve, challenging established assumptions about education.

This book examines both coding instruction and the broader rethinking of software literacy in our AI-augmented world. These evolving tools now enable non-STEM educators to incorporate programming elements into their teaching without extensive technical expertise. The landscape has changed for researchers in qualitative disciplines as well—computational methods once restricted to those with technical training have become widely accessible. A new reciprocity has emerged: humanities scholars leverage the technology to analyze large datasets and automate research tasks, while computer scientists and quantitative experts use applications to produce clearer documentation, explain code conversationally, and embrace qualitative reasoning that was previously beyond their scope.

In the past, coding education followed a strict hierarchy: learn syntax, practice problem sets, and eventually build complex full programs. This approach, though rigorous, led to high attrition rates, particularly among students who struggled to see its immediate relevance. Similarly, writing was taught with an emphasis on grammatical precision before students were encouraged to develop their own voice and arguments. Both models assumed that mastery of the micro-level—whether in syntax or sentence structure—had to precede engagement with the macro-level of organization and meaning-making. AI-assisted tools challenge this assumption, offering students an alternative pathway: starting with the big picture and working back toward the technical details as needed.

For instance, tools like GitHub Copilot, Windsurf, and Cursor provide coding assistance that allows users to describe what they want in natural language and receive functioning code in return. This is analogous to how generative writing tools help students generate structured essays based on prompts or fragmented ideas. These technologies remake the memorization of syntax and procedural rules into a process of refining, curating, and troubleshooting machine-generated content. The conventional sequence—memorization before application—becomes obsolete when AI can provide support throughout the learning journey.

The lowering of technical barriers is already being felt in interdisciplinary research. Even before the most recent advances, literary scholars were gaining the ability to analyze vast corpora of texts using Python's Natural Language Toolkit (NLTK) or SpaCy without the requirement of a background in computational linguistics. And with the advances from generative tools, historians can use AI-powered data visualization to map historical trends. Similar rapid changes have shown up in computer science instruction, where AI-assisted code explanations allow programmers to engage in qualitative, natural language reasoning about their own work. This convergence of skills forces educators to reconsider the artificial boundary between disciplines, opening the door for hybrid approaches to problem-solving that integrate computational precision with humanistic inquiry.

This is particularly important for general education courses. In the past, general education students from diverse academic backgrounds did not have time to learn enough about programming to use code in these courses. Because of the historical necessity of progressing from basic syntax and coding exercises to basic programs with only minimal practical application during first-semester courses, it would never be possible for educators to bring coding into general education classes. It is possible now with assistive programming to introduce students to project-based programming, allowing students to see immediate results and develop confidence before diving into the technical specifics. In a first-year sociology class, for example, students might use these solutions to generate data visualizations that analyze social trends, while literature students could employ LLMs to generate thematic mappings of complex texts. These applications make programming feel less like an isolated technical skill and more like a methodological tool applicable across fields.

At the same time, students in conventional STEM programs benefit from the contributions of these tools to writing and qualitative analysis. Previously, computer science students beginning their coding education were evaluated primarily on producing efficient, well-structured code, with less emphasis on explaining thought processes or documenting decisions. Enhanced tools now enable programmers to craft clear explanations of their work, structure documentation effectively, and engage in deeper qualitative reasoning. This capability proves especially valuable in fields like data science, where narrative-building and interpretive analysis hold equal importance to statistical modeling.

Educators confront a complex challenge: they must incorporate these tools into classrooms while reconceptualizing assessment methods entirely. When smart systems instantly generate polished essays or functional code, established evaluation metrics lose relevance. Assessment now requires evidence of students' analytical capabilities and their critical engagement with generated material. Writing instructors must emphasize curation over creation, guiding students to evaluate and reshape generated content rather than rewarding mere production. Programming courses similarly prioritize students' ability to validate and debug generated code while understanding its broader significance within software systems.

The emergence of assisted coding brings both opportunities and challenges, particularly in how it reshapes domain expertise, pedagogical strategies, and assessment models. While these tools expand access to programming, they also disrupt traditional coding instruction by rethinking the balance between conceptual understanding and automation. Similar concerns have emerged in writing-intensive disciplines, where generative tools have raised questions about plagiarism, intellectual integrity, and the erosion of deep engagement with texts. In both spheres of academia, this technology challenges longstanding assumptions about skill acquisition, authorship, and expertise, forcing educators to reconsider how foundational knowledge is taught, assessed, and validated. The potential overreliance on the resource risks diminishing essential problem-solving and critical thinking skills, as students may bypass core learning processes in favor of generated solutions. Additionally, as AI blurs the boundaries of original work and collaborative computation, questions arise about authorship, attribution, and the integrity of student output. This book will explore strategies for mitigating these risks, ensuring that these applications serve as an augmentative tool that enhances learning rather than replacing the development of essential competencies. Addressing these concerns requires rethinking pedagogical approaches, adapting assessment methods, and cultivating "AI Literacy" that emphasizes critical engagement with technology rather than passive dependence.

Therefore, this book is about preparing educators and students for a world where AI is not just an occasional assistant but an integral part of both writing and coding workflows. It offers practical strategies for integrating assisted programming into non-STEM curricula, providing examples of how coding can enrich research and teaching across disciplines. At the same time, it presents a vision for a more integrated approach to education—one where technical and humanistic expertise are not at odds but mutually reinforcing.

As these tools continue to evolve, the ability to navigate these interdisciplinary intersections will be one of the most valuable skills students can develop. Whether they are writing essays, building software, or conducting research, the key competency of the future will not be technical mastery alone but the ability to work fluidly between natural language and structured computation, between creative ideation and algorithmic execution. This book serves as a guide to that future, helping educators and students alike embrace the possibilities of AI-enhanced learning while remaining critical, ethical, and intellectually engaged.

Acknowledgments

The authors express profound appreciation to the myriad individuals and institutions whose contributions and unwavering support have been pivotal in the genesis and fruition of this tome. At the vanguard of acknowledgment stands Dr John Porter, whose innovative leadership in aligning the adoption of emergent technologies like AI with educational initiatives has left an indelible mark on this work's evolution.

Acknowledgment is due to Dr Kathi Vosevich, Dean of the College of Arts and Humanities, for her steadfast encouragement and support of the research culminating in this publication. Vosevich's guidance and confidence in the authors' academic endeavors have been fundamental in sculpting the contours of this volume.

The authors extend their gratitude to the research team responsible for composing this manuscript and acknowledge the critical insights and contributions of various colleagues and co-authors from ancillary projects. James Hutson extends thanks to Professors Ben Fulcher, Jeremiah Ratican, Joe Weber, Ben Scholle, and Dr Trent Olsen. Additionally, Dr Emily Barnes was instrumental in shaping many of the sections and the direction.

The authors also convey their deep appreciation to the administrative leaders at all of the institutions that participated in the study for their relentless support and dedication to creating an environment conducive to academic excellence and scholarly exploration. The leadership, encompassing Presidents, Provosts, and Deans at these institutions, has been instrumental in providing the necessary guidance and resources for this research and writing project.

To those who provided insight into their experiences as leaders in industry and education, we are indebted and thank you for your invaluable time and efforts in helping others navigate this unpredictable time. Finally, the authors are thankful for the insights and constructive feedback from colleagues and fellow researchers throughout this project. Their contributions have significantly enriched the work and helped to refine the ideas encapsulated within this volume.

1

Introduction: The Paradigm Shift—From Syntax to Software Literacy

Historically, programming instruction has emphasized a bottom-up approach, demanding that students become fluent in the detailed rules of a language before tackling broader design or architectural issues. A comprehensive education in programming naturally incorporates larger program structures, deployment awareness, and purpose-driven development—yet syntax mastery has remained the principal requirement. This syntax-first methodology has characterized computer science education for decades, simultaneously contributing to high attrition rates, particularly among non-STEM students struggling to connect with its immediate relevance. The emergence of AI-powered coding assistants is reshaping this landscape. These tools prioritize a holistic understanding of software development, enabling learners to explore programming through high-level design, logical reasoning, and project structure—not just rote memorization. AI-powered editor tools such as GitHub Copilot and Cursor provide in-context assistance, allowing students to work at higher levels of abstraction while refining technical details as needed. This evolution in tooling dissolves long-established academic boundaries, creating opportunities for collaborative projects and research spanning science, technology, engineering, mathematics, and the humanities. Contemporary generative tools enable scholars outside computer science to incorporate programming and computational methods into their research while equipping STEM professionals with powerful capabilities for qualitative analysis, writing, and interpretation. This increased accessibility of programming skills elevates computational thinking beyond the exclusive domain of technical experts into a core competency across diverse disciplines. However, the traditional syntax-first approach in programming education also falls short in preparing students for the collaborative nature of modern software development, the complexities of real-world codebases, and the importance of design thinking before implementation. This book will explore how assistive tools can address these broader shortcomings, supporting not only technical proficiency but also essential design, collaboration, and problem-solving skills.

DOI: 10.1201/9781003637738-1

1.1 Traditional Syntax-Focused Approaches and Their Evolution

What is coding, and how does it differ from programming or scripting? These terms are used interchangeably in everyday conversation. Each describes a distinct layer within software creation. Coding involves converting instructions into computer-comprehensible language and primarily centers on command entry and syntactic accuracy. Programming has a broader scope: planning, designing, and testing complete software systems through logical structuring and progressive refinement. Scripting occupies a middle ground between simple code fragments and comprehensive applications by automating tasks within existing frameworks. All three share a foundation in problem-solving and algorithmic thinking—skills increasingly vital in our digital world. For many years, writing code has remained mostly confined to those earning specialized technical training. The rise of AI-driven tools and more inclusive teaching approaches is now likely to open these technical domains to new audiences. This chapter explores how reimagined coding education can make computational literacy available beyond conventional computer science programs. A university is now possible in which disciplinary boundaries do not keep students cordoned off, and technical skills can grow as needed for particular courses or projects.

Programming education has been shaped by a combination of cognitive, pedagogical, and technological factors. For decades, instruction has featured a grammar-first method, where students must first master programming syntax before engaging with more sophisticated problem-solving. And this method was required in the early days of computing. It reflected the realities of programming at a time when languages like Fortran, COBOL, and Assembly demanded meticulous attention to syntax and structure. But programming languages (Figure 1.1) evolved into more human-readable forms, including C, Java, and Python, and the emphasis on syntax mastery persisted. This reinforced the belief that foundational knowledge of the grammar of a programming language was an essential part of a meaningful application (Lau, 2018). Educational researchers began to challenge this model as new programming methodologies emerged, questioning whether strict adherence to syntax-first teaching was the most effective approach for developing computational thinking and problem-solving abilities among all learners (Edwards et al., 2020). Even before the more radical ability to sidestep coding altogether came into view with current coding assistants, conceptual understanding before implementation gained traction as a competing pedagogical approach. The goal emerged, at least, of teaching algorithmic thinking and systems design before students could master the minutiae of language-specific syntax. Though this goal remained necessarily unrealized without these tools that could code "at the sentence level," the way was starting to be

```
4    import os
5    try:
6        from pyunpack import Archive
7    except:
8        os.system("pip install pyunpack")
9        os.system("pip install patool")
10       from pyunpack import Archive
11
12   logs = os.listdir('logs/')
13   logs = [[x, x[:7]] for x in logs if '.gz' in x] # list of dates
14
15   for i,x in enumerate(logs, 0):
16       try:
17           Archive(f'logs/{x[0]}').extractall(f'history/{x[1]}')
18       except:
19           os.makedirs(f'history/{x[1]}')
20           Archive(f'logs/{x[0]}').extractall(f'history/{x[1]}')
21       os.remove(f'logs/{x[0]}')
22
23
```

FIGURE 1.1
Python Code File Extractor

cleared for planning and conceptualizing without knowing the particular details of implementation.

Research in computer science education reveals that too much emphasis on grammatical precision can impede learning in programming beginners. While students generally possess adequate logical reasoning abilities, many abandon programming courses because syntactic correctness creates an insurmountable barrier (Lister, 2011). This departure affects introductory courses the most, with non-STEM students leaving at especially high rates. Traditional teaching methods, with their insistence on syntactic accuracy, frequently fail to illustrate programming's practical value in solving real-world problems. In response, educators and researchers now advocate application-driven pedagogies that introduce computational thinking concepts before syntax rules, decreasing the burden on novice programming students (Nelson, 2017). Table 1.1 examines these syntax-first pedagogical challenges and proposes new directions.

Grammar and structure errors, a frequent source of frustration for students, prevent concentration on problem-solving and algorithmic reasoning. Studies indicate that novice programmers struggle considerably with syntax-related mistakes, leading to discouragement and elevated dropout rates in introductory computer science courses (Denny et al., 2011). A significant number of students give up on programming early in their education because of difficulties with syntax and not necessarily an inability to grasp computational concepts. The conventional foregrounding of grammatical rules also misaligns with programming's application in professional and

TABLE 1.1

Limitations of Syntax-First Programming Education and Proposed Solutions

Issue with Syntax-First Approach	Why This Is a Problem	Proposed Solution
High Cognitive Load	Syntax memorization requires significant mental effort, often before students understand the purpose of their code.	Integrate AI-driven tools to provide real-time syntax correction, allowing students to consider logic.
Lack of Immediate Application	Students do not see tangible results early, reducing motivation and making programming feel irrelevant.	Introduce project-based learning early, using HTML, JavaScript, and AI-assisted coding for immediate application.
High Attrition Rates	Many students drop out due to frustration with syntax rather than difficulty in understanding logic or problem-solving.	Use AI-enhanced, adaptive learning models to provide personalized feedback and reduce frustration.
Disconnection from Professional Use	Real-world programming considers logic, design, and algorithms, not rote syntax memorization.	Reframe programming education to prioritize problem-solving, debugging strategies, and project planning.
Barrier to Non-STEM Students	Many introductory courses have math prerequisites that filter out students who could excel in logic-based problem-solving.	Expand coding education to broader audiences by reducing technical prerequisites wherever possible.
Delayed Engagement with Problem-Solving	Students are often required to complete syntax drills before working on meaningful projects, which delays engagement.	Encourage early coding projects, leveraging assistants to handle syntax corrections while students learn logic.
Similarity to Outdated Pedagogical Models	Similar to how Latin instruction focuses on grammar before practical use, this approach detaches programming from real-world applications.	Implement pedagogies inspired by modern language learning, where students engage with real-world tasks early.
Fails to Integrate Computational Thinking Early	Computational thinking involves breaking problems into steps, yet syntax-first models delay this crucial skill.	Use coding assistants like GitHub Copilot to structure computational thinking from the beginning.
Hinders Interdisciplinary Applications	Programming could be widely used in business, humanities, and sciences, but syntax-heavy approaches alienate non-CS students.	Embed coding environments into non-CS fields, demonstrating immediate interdisciplinary benefits.
Rigid Assessment Models	Assessment models prioritize the correctness of syntax over the understanding of logic and problem-solving techniques.	Design assessments that evaluate coding logic, problem-solving, and project development rather than rote syntax.

interdisciplinary contexts, where breaking down problems, algorithm creation, and logical thinking take precedence over memorizing language conventions. In professional environments, software development prioritizes design thinking and conceptual modeling far more than flawless syntactic recall. This produces a significant gap between education and practice. The capacity to envision software architecture, comprehend system components, and conceptually model solutions distinguishes effective software engineers from those who merely write code.

Addressing these challenges, some educators have explored alternative frameworks that prioritize problem-solving, postponing syntax mastery to later learning stages (Hill, 2016). Such approaches concentrate on what should be built rather than just how to build it, encouraging students to develop a comprehensive understanding of computational solutions before tackling implementation specifics. All of this means that any tools (such as coding assistants) that can give students the ability to write code earlier in the process will help educators implement pedagogical practices they already know would be better—if only they could be achieved. Until very recently, the suggestion that students be allowed more opportunities to focus on planning and program conceptualization might have been applauded, but the stubborn fact has remained that the code still has to be written, and without syntactic correctness, even well-conceived code would not run. Mathematical prerequisites also function as a significant entry barrier for students interested in learning programming, especially in disciplines outside STEM fields. Numerous computer science programs require minimum competency in algebra or calculus before students may enroll in foundational coding courses, essentially filtering out individuals who might excel in logic and problem-solving but lack strong mathematical backgrounds. For instance, universities commonly establish calculus as a prerequisite for introductory computer science classes, even when many practical coding applications—such as web development or data visualization—require minimal advanced mathematics.

First-year programming courses, such as CS101 or Introduction to Computer Science, are typically structured as rigorous, grammar-heavy experiences that eliminate students who struggle with technical minutiae rather than providing progressive guidance for various learning approaches. This arrangement disproportionately excludes learners from non-conventional backgrounds, including those pursuing humanities, business, or education degrees. There are similarities in how this structuring of knowledge acquisition compares to other disciplines. For example, the traditional method of teaching programming is strikingly similar to how Latin has been taught as a classical language. In both cases, instruction has been structured around grammar and syntax mastery before engaging with more meaningful applications of the language (Zhou et al., 2016). Latin students, much like programming novices, first memorize extensive grammar rules, including verb conjugations and noun declensions, comparable to how programming students learn loops, variables, and data types. And as Latin learners study grammatical structures quite painfully through charts and textbooks, they naturally wish they could experience this formalized grammar in the actual canonical texts they look forward to studying. It's quite a simple parallel with programming students who find syntax drills detached from practical coding applications (Hoyos, 2023).

This comparison of Latin instruction and programming pedagogy brings out a broader challenge in educational methodology. There's a clear disconnect between abstract rules and meaningful application. Many Latin programs follow a strict structure where students master complex grammatical constructions, such as noun declensions and verb conjugations (Figure 1.2), before reading actual Latin literature or historical texts. This means students spend months memorizing rules and parsing stand-alone sentences without developing a deeper understanding of how the language functions in historical, literary, or philosophical contexts. A student may spend an entire semester learning the forms of the ablative absolute or the subjunctive mood without ever translating full passages from Cicero or Ovid. Predictably, this results in the learning experience feeling tedious and disconnected from meaningful application and the student's goals in choosing this difficult course of study to begin with. In the case of programming education, a similar experience threatens student motivation. Programming students are expected to perfect syntax before engaging in more concrete problem-solving or software development (Groton, 2015). Introductory courses in programming begin with syntax drills—such as memorizing data types, loops, and conditionals—before allowing students to build functional applications. For instance, a student in a CS101 course may be required to complete repetitive exercises on sorting algorithms before being introduced to practical applications like data visualization or interactive web design. Students frequently abandon programming when syntax-heavy exercises prevent them from seeing the ultimate rewards—creating games, analyzing data, or building web applications. Without clear connections between technical details

	SINGULAR					PLURAL			
	m. f.	m.	vir	n.		m. f.	m.	vir	n.
Nom.	us	er	ir	um	Nom.	i	i	i	a
Voc.	e	er	ir	um	Voc.	i	i	i	a
Gen.		i			Gen.			orum	
Dat.		o			Dat.			is	
Abl.		o			Abl.			is	
Ac.		um			Ac.	os	os	os	a

FIGURE 1.2
Latin Grammar

and meaningful outcomes, learners lose sight of their broader intellectual and professional aspirations.

Both Latin and programming instruction face similar pedagogical hurdles. Research in these fields points toward interactive, application-first approaches rather than rote memorization. Latin scholars advocate for early exposure to authentic texts instead of isolated grammar drills, while programming experts endorse hands-on projects before intensive syntax training. Yet many programs resist these evidence-based recommendations. Traditional course structures persist, forcing students to master abstract rules—whether Latin grammar forms or programming syntax—before taking on more meaningful content. This delays student contact with authentic texts in Latin and practical applications in coding, often until motivation has already largely run out. The persistence of these outdated approaches suggests that systemic barriers—such as institutional inertia, standardized curricula, and faculty training—continue to delay widespread adoption. Until these changes are realized, students in both disciplines may continue to experience disengagement, struggling to see the relevance of their studies to broader intellectual and professional goals.

As programming education evolves beyond a syntax-first model, a necessary redirection toward software literacy must prioritize computational thinking as a foundational skill. Computational thinking is the ability to break down complex problems into smaller, manageable tasks that a computer can execute. This skill transcends programming languages, allowing learners to work with design strategies that can be adapted to many different detailed implementations (Shute et al., 2017). For example, a student can consider the user interface (UI) of a website to track data and design the workflows for users to follow. In this framework, students first learn to conceptualize problems algorithmically before they encounter the syntax and structure of specific programming languages. This approach has been shown to enhance student engagement and improve problem-solving capabilities across multiple disciplines, including the humanities and social sciences (Subramaniam, Maat, & Mahmud, 2022). Coding assistants extend these benefits by helping students transition smoothly from problem conceptualization to code execution, handling syntax complexities so learners can instead consider logic and design (Silapachote & Srisuphab, 2017). These tools serve not merely as syntax helpers but as collaborative partners in the learning process, allowing students to experiment with algorithmic thinking and conceptual modeling without getting bogged down in implementation details. It is important to continue emphasizing that this recommendation to redirect pedagogy from a long initial study of syntax toward the use of pseudocode or algorithmic planning is not new. The recommendation itself has been made many times before. The difference now is that coding assistants make it possible to put into practice this change in pedagogy.

One of the key aspects of this proposed change is the ability to think algorithmically, which involves breaking down complex tasks into step-by-step instructions. For instance, building upon Mulligan (2021), a humanities student studying Shakespeare might use computational thinking to map the relationships between characters in *Hamlet*, creating an algorithm to track interactions and identify key influencers within the play's social network. In the social sciences, as in Pereira et al. (2024), a researcher studying political polarization might use algorithmic thinking to analyze social media data, such as that on Twitter (now X), developing a step-by-step process to identify key themes, track sentiment changes over time, and model the spread of information (and misinformation) within specific online communities. In business and finance, professionals can develop predictive models for market trends, automate financial reporting, and optimize supply chain logistics through structured, repeatable workflows. In healthcare, medical researchers apply computational thinking to track disease outbreaks, streamline patient data analysis, and enhance diagnostic tools through machine learning models. Even in creative fields such as music and visual arts, artists use algorithmic processes to generate digital compositions, apply generative design techniques, and manipulate large datasets of creative works. This approach helps students across fields structure their analyses more efficiently and develop systematic reasoning skills. Through the framing of computational thinking as a transferable skill, educators can demonstrate its applicability across disciplines, making programming more accessible to students outside of traditional STEM fields (Silapachote & Srisuphab, 2016). Additionally, AI-powered tools are being used to support algorithmic thinking by guiding students through problem decomposition and suggesting potential solutions, which help them refine their logical reasoning (Rich et al., 2022).

Another critical component of software literacy is the ability to design and organize programs effectively. In traditional programming courses, students are often introduced to file management, modular programming, and workflow design only after they have mastered syntax. However, modern curricula are incorporating these skills earlier in the learning process to aim at a holistic understanding of software development (Massaty et al., 2024). So if a student were building a tool to track and analyze all the occurrences of water imagery in James Joyce's *Ulysses*, they might start by creating separate modules for each of the eighteen episodes. The skills learned in designing such a tool not only enhance code readability and maintainability but also mirror organizational techniques used in humanities and social science research. As generative tools become more prevalent, students will be learning to navigate and integrate libraries and APIs. This is a crucial part of extending their repertoire toward building complex projects efficiently (Rim, 2017).

Finally, the ability to specify and plan programs before execution is becoming a central focus in programming education. Writing clear, effective prompts for coding assistants is already becoming as important as crafting a precise search query for a scholarly database (Denny et al., 2024;

Liang et al., 2024). Instead of vaguely asking an AI to "write a function to sort data," students need to learn how to define the problem with appropriate specificity: "Write a Python function that takes a list of dictionaries as input, where each dictionary represents a book with keys for 'title,' 'author,' and 'publication_year.' The function should sort the list in descending order by publication year, then alphabetically by author, and finally by title. The output should be the sorted list of dictionaries." This structured approach enhances logical clarity and improves generated code quality (Bertrand & Namukasa, 2020). Modern curricula are beginning to emphasize testing and debugging earlier, teaching students to validate generated code before deployment. This evolution in programming education, emphasizing computational thinking and clear communication with the tools, has fundamentally reshaped how students approach coding across all disciplines (Rossano et al., 2018).

Coding tools have a clear potential to revolutionize computational methods in the humanities and social sciences. For decades—and in some cases, centuries—historians, linguists, and anthropologists have pored over manual data analyses in building archives, concordances, and other technical documents. These resources are beginning to make possible much more sophisticated and efficient computational power. AI and machine learning systems allow researchers to process large text corpora, create interactive historical maps, and build digital exhibits with unprecedented efficiency (Baiburin et al., 2024). What needs to happen now is a widespread institutional decision to bring these computational capabilities to non-STEM students and scholars throughout higher education. It is possible to interact with complex datasets without requiring advanced programming knowledge, but it requires institutional will. These tools enhance qualitative analysis through intelligent tagging and pattern recognition in large-scale textual data (Gao et al., 2023). Such capabilities make computational literacy increasingly vital for humanities scholars. The advantages are pretty obvious. A new fusion of traditional qualitative methods with modern data-driven approaches is just around the corner for those who decide to experiment seriously with AI (Zhang, 2023).

Social science research is also undergoing major modifications. Researchers studying the impact of redlining policies on present-day wealth disparities like Graetz and Esposito (2023) can now utilize AI-powered tools to analyze historical census data, overlaying maps from different decades to identify long-term patterns of segregation and economic inequality. They might then create interactive visualizations that allow users to explore the data themselves, comparing neighborhoods and tracking changes over time, communicating complex social trends to a wider audience. This expansion of computational techniques is particularly important in the age of big data, where large datasets require advanced analytical methods to uncover meaningful insights. AI tools are also assisting researchers in conducting qualitative coding more efficiently, enhancing collaboration and improving the reproducibility of findings (Gao et al., 2023). AI-assisted methods enable new forms of cross-disciplinary collaboration, as researchers use computational tools to build common analytical frameworks (Aleynikova & Yarotskaya, 2024). These platforms have changed both how social scientists conduct research and how they apply their findings to business and consumer problems.

Another development in higher education pedagogy more generally is a turn toward project-based learning. This trend affects computer science classrooms as well. Project-based learning and computational thinking have a lot to contribute to programming pedagogy. Hands-on experience is simply and quite intuitively highly valued by early and novice learners. Students tend to enter programming courses hoping to create meaningful projects yet find themselves stuck working through syntax drills and mechanical exercises. When learners must complete numerous exercises before building anything functional, their motivation inevitably suffers. Without immediate, tangible results to show for their efforts, many students lose interest entirely (Rosiene, 2008). For many learners, particularly those outside of STEM disciplines, this overemphasis on delayed gratification and what amounts to a demonstration of mere accurate typing is a barrier to meaningful learning. Unlike fields such as mathematics or physics, where foundational concepts build sequentially, programming offers unique opportunities for early engagement through hands-on, project-based learning. Later chapters in this book—Chapter 4 in particular—will lay out a number of examples of hands-on programming work with AI.

Some educators have responded by introducing interactive and visual-based programming environments that allow students to experiment with code from the beginning, learning syntax gradually through application rather than requiring letter-perfect code before achieving any significant results (Alda & Baralt-Torrijos, 2023). This design-first pedagogy puts the focus on understanding systems architecture and algorithmic thinking before implementing detailed code, creating a more engaging and effective learning experience. AI-powered tools such as GitHub Copilot and Replit's Ghostwriter have further accelerated this ability to enable students to generate and refine code through natural language inputs, reducing the initial barriers posed by syntax-heavy instruction. Instead of forcing learners to master syntax before tackling problem-solving, modern approaches encourage them to explore coding through hands-on projects and iterative design processes (Reek, 1995). Current pedagogical models point to a clear conclusion: programming education needs to move away from basic syntax instruction to deepen students' computational thinking, problem-solving abilities, and technological creativity. The future of programming education lies in its application across academic boundaries, where code becomes a universal tool for inquiry and innovation.

1.2 The Role of AI in Transforming Foundational Curricula

This move from rule-based instruction to practical application, if it is implemented, will change how educators design curricula. AI-powered tools have the capacity to alter the entire system of general education through personalized learning paths, interdisciplinary projects, and enhanced computational analysis. These changes extend to the core design and delivery of foundational courses. Where standardized assessments and fixed content once constrained learning options, new approaches respond dynamically to student needs. These instruments now enable personalized learning experiences by analyzing individual student progress and adapting instructional materials accordingly (Fattah et al., 2023). In undergraduate settings, generative platforms can assist in providing targeted feedback in writing courses, allowing students to refine their arguments and research methodologies more effectively. This feedback can come from a hybrid instructor-AI collaboration which is passed on to the student. But this entire process of prompting the AI for feedback can be handed over to students, involving them in more stages of the learning process. Interactive simulations and virtual learning environments will also introduce students in various disciplines to complex concepts in ways that traditional lectures struggle to achieve (Ejjami, 2024). This necessitates a rethinking of how general education courses are structured, ensuring that the tools are used not merely as a supplementary tool but as an integral component of instructional design (Yoon, 2023).

One of the most immediate applications in general education is the role of the tools in composition and humanities courses, where students engage in iterative writing and research processes. These platforms can support these efforts by speeding up elements of the drafting and revision stages, providing feedback on structure, coherence, and argumentation (Mansour, 2024). AI-assisted research tools allow students to run many searches over large research areas, identifying combinations of research topics that might otherwise never be explored. This capability proves especially valuable in interdisciplinary studies, where students must synthesize information from multiple sources. Through the automation of tasks like citation management, literature reviews, and hypothesis generation, these tools free up students' time to instead consider critical analysis rather than technical research mechanics (Storey & Wagner, 2024). AI-based discussion platforms complement these analytical tools by facilitating collaborative learning—generating prompts and guiding structured debates that help students articulate and defend complex ideas (Sytnyk & Podlinyayeva, 2024). Beyond these discipline-agnostic applications, AI-assisted coding tools could now be used to reshape the way students and professionals engage with programming. Initially, applications in education foregrounded adaptive learning and content generation, but recent advancements have expanded their role into software development and computational problem-solving (Zviel-Girshin, 2024).

Tools such as GitHub Copilot, Cursor, and Windsurf leverage large language models to provide concrete, contextualized assistance, allowing developers to generate large sections of a code base quickly, test the results, and then iterate on other ideas. These platforms integrate seamlessly into existing development environments, making programming more intuitive and less dependent on mastery of language-specific syntax. AI-driven paired programming, where humans and AI work collaboratively, has emerged as an innovative approach, allowing students to refine their problem-solving strategies while receiving generated recommendations (Liu & Li, 2024).

Despite their benefits, concerns remain regarding overreliance on tools, the potential loss of foundational programming skills, and the ethical implications of generated code (Johanyák et al., 2023). These concerns highlight the need for a balanced approach that views the technology as a collaborative partner in the learning process rather than a replacement for developing core computational thinking skills. Assisted coding tools have expanded beyond code generation into more comprehensive software literacy. These platforms could, if implemented with sufficient instructor support, nurture problem-solving abilities in students, as well as computational reasoning and organizational skills (Çela et al., 2024). This could allow educators to reimagine their curricula to balance assistance with core competencies—debugging, code structure, and algorithmic design. GitHub Copilot exemplifies this balance by pairing code suggestions with explanatory context. A student can without much difficulty generate a function in a Python file using GitHub Copilot and then ask it follow-up questions about both the details of the code and the purpose of the function within the codebase. This has the potential to teach students the reasoning behind effective coding practices (Jung, 2020). Through this approach, these platforms become a learning catalyst rather than a substitute for essential programming skills (Sheard et al., 2024).

The tools are also reducing the cognitive load for beginner programmers by acting as mentors that help students grasp high-level concepts while backfilling technical details as needed. Novice programmers have typically faced significant challenges in navigating the complexities of programming logic and debugging errors (Liu & Li, 2024). Platforms now enable students to experiment with code by generating and testing snippets in real time. It would likely breathe new life into curricula if students were taught how to harness an iterative learning process like this. Significant enhancements of student comprehension are possible with this sort of AI-human hybrid practice. Just as one example, new debugging tools can automatically detect logical inconsistencies and suggest potential fixes, accelerating the learning process (Takerngsaksiri et al., 2023). This adaptive guidance allows students to focus their learning on experimenting in real time with programming concepts rather than struggling with technical, code-level roadblocks (Valový & Buchalcevova, 2023).

The rise of generative capabilities in programming education has also facilitated the development of personalized learning models that adapt to individual student needs. Platforms analyze student progress and provide targeted exercises that reinforce weak areas, thereby breaking down learning based on the user's expertise level (Johanyák et al., 2023). For example, tutors such as Iris, a virtual assistant for programming students, offer step-by-step guidance without revealing complete solutions, facilitating independent problem-solving skills (Bassner et al., 2024). The adaptation of the curriculum to suit diverse learning paces with these emergent technologies enables students to receive the support they need without falling behind or feeling overwhelmed (Haindl & Weinberger, 2024). Importantly, this also addresses the Blooms 2 Sigma problem whereby students reach mastery of a learning outcome more effectively with one-on-one tutoring, but the limitations of instructor time and resources have prevented the large-scale application since the publishing of these findings in 1984. This is another example of a pattern we note repeatedly. The idea that one-on-one tutoring makes for better educational outcomes is not a new one. Tightening the feedback loop and giving students many cycles of producing work and receiving targeted feedback on that work has been a goal in education for a long time. The problem has been one of resources. There are not enough teachers to give each student that feedback. With the integration into programming education, this new approach is actually possible. Coding can truly be seen not just as a technical skill but as a cognitive discipline that involves problem-solving, logical reasoning, and algorithmic thinking. These tools are quickly changing how students engage with programming by emphasizing practical applications over a long initial period of instruction in syntax. During this whole process, coding assistants can provide personalized guidance, helping learners navigate challenges and reinforcing key programming concepts through interactive feedback. This evolution in AI-assisted learning has the potential to broaden access to coding education, making it more accessible to individuals from diverse backgrounds and disciplines.

1.3 Bridging STEM and Humanities with Interdisciplinary Thinking

The integration of interdisciplinary methodologies is becoming increasingly essential in the age of AI, as technology reshapes diverse fields and challenges traditional disciplinary boundaries. While this book is designed for all disciplines, the discussion will use STEM and humanities as focal examples due to their perceived differences in approach, methodology, and epistemological values. STEM fields, such as mathematics, engineering, or computer science, emphasize quantitative analysis, empirical validation, and structured problem-solving, whereas the humanities, including philosophy, history, and literary studies, highlight methodologies such as textual analysis, historical contextualization, and comparative interpretation. Historians analyze primary and secondary sources to construct narratives about the past, considering multiple perspectives and assessing the reliability of evidence. Literary scholars examine themes, symbolism, and narrative structures to uncover deeper meanings within texts, often applying frameworks such as gender theory, varieties of literary Marxism, or postcolonial analysis. Linguists use corpus analysis to study language patterns and changes over time, while art historians interpret visual composition, stylistic influences, and cultural significance in artistic works. These methodologies emphasize close reading, contextual research, and synthesis of diverse sources, providing insights that complement the structured approaches of STEM disciplines. These distinctions have reinforced disciplinary silos, but the emergence of the latest generation of generative tools and computational methodologies necessitates a more integrated framework.

While STEM fields excel in technical problem-solving and data-driven methodologies, the humanities contribute critical perspectives on culture and societal impact (Kurup et al., 2021). An opportunity exists here to accomplish both in a single classroom. This interdisciplinary collaboration instills a more holistic approach to addressing practical challenges, enabling the development of innovative solutions to complex, multifaceted problems. Institutions have long recognized the importance of interdisciplinary coursework in promoting adaptability and equipping students for an increasingly complex professional landscape (Vance et al., 2022). Recent initiatives have demonstrated that integrating humanities into more quantitative curricula not only broadens student problem-solving abilities but also brings creativity into academic work in ways that purely technical approaches often overlook (Doğru, 2023). For example, computational linguistics programs combine language analysis with machine learning techniques, enabling students to apply literary and linguistic theories to the development of advanced natural language processing models. This interdisciplinary approach has contributed to breakthroughs in translation, sentiment analysis, and automated text generation, illustrating how humanities methodologies enhance quantitative fields. Similarly, digital humanities projects leverage data visualization and geospatial analysis to uncover historical patterns and trends, demonstrating the value of humanistic inquiry in refining computational models. These integrations highlight how blending qualitative and quantitative perspectives leads to more innovative solutions and prepares students for dynamic, technology-driven careers.

Despite the benefits of interdisciplinary education, resistance persists on multiple fronts. STEM disciplines prioritize quantitative precision and empirical validation, which contrasts with humanities' emphasis on interpretive and theoretical frameworks (Chesley et al., 2018). Many humanists view the rise of computational models as a threat to their intellectual traditions and qualitative methodologies. This tension intensifies as academic departments strive to maintain domain expertise amid growing competition for majors and limited institutional funding. Successfully integrating cross-disciplinary approaches while preserving departmental identity requires careful navigation (Hutson, 2023). The path forward lies in designing curricula that respect and leverage disciplinary strengths and at the same time encouraging mutual exchange. This is a difficult balance and will require innovative pedagogical strategies that promote substantive cross-disciplinary dialog (Nie, 2021). Interdisciplinary projects are a promising approach. Any project that puts students in one discipline in a cooperative environment with students they would usually not work with can dismantle traditional silos (Kersánszki et al., 2022). Initiatives like these create opportunities for students to develop systems thinking and integrate multiple perspectives into coherent problem-solving frameworks.

The fact that AI-driven approaches might play a significant role in creating these sorts of interdisciplinary collaborations might seem surprising to some. But especially in the case of large language models, the tools themselves are inherently interdisciplinary as their training data have been pulled from every area of human inquiry. The knowledge contained in these tools can therefore be combined and recombined in functionally infinite ways, and the output of this work will quite naturally support forms typical across disciplinary boundaries: data analysis, visualization, and advanced reasoning (Wu, 2021). In the humanities, resources can facilitate the creation of interactive digital exhibits (Li et al., 2024). For example, a museum could image recognition or computer vision applications to allow visitors to photograph a fragment of pottery, and have the system instantly provide information about the artifact's origin, style, and potential use, pulling data from a vast archaeological database. This would involve coding the interaction between the image recognition software, the database query, and the user interface as with the groundbreaking work of Di Angelo and team (2021). Alternatively, as with the work of Terras (2022) , a digital archive of historical letters could use aids to transcribe handwritten documents, making them searchable and accessible, and then allow users to create personalized learning paths by selecting specific themes or correspondents to follow. Similarly, students in STEM fields can use generative tools to improve the clarity and style of writing, addressing the common challenge of communicating technical concepts effectively to diverse audiences.

As applications become more complex and powerful, proficiency that goes beyond any one discipline will not only become highly sought after. It will simply become a by-product of working in the ways described above. This makes it possible that technological progress remains aligned with ethical considerations and broader societal needs. Emerging research emphasizes that students trained in both technical and humanistic methodologies exhibit stronger analytical reasoning and adaptability, which are expected skills in today's workforce (Nugraha et al., 2024). These interdisciplinary thinkers are better equipped to understand the social and cultural implications of technological advancements. Innovation of this kind serves human needs rather than advancing for its own sake. As interdisciplinary education continues to gain momentum, new pedagogical models are being developed to support its implementation. Collaborative research projects that integrate a variety of methodologies provide students with experiential learning opportunities that bridge theoretical knowledge and practical application (Savelides et al., 2020). For example, courses in digital humanities leverage computational tools to analyze linguistic patterns, while data science programs integrate contextual analysis to improve algorithmic decision-making and interpret complex datasets more effectively. These interdisciplinary models enhance students' ability to navigate complex problems by equipping them with diverse analytical tools and perspectives (Bartholomew & Uzondu, 2024).

Universities are also creating interdisciplinary research centers built from collaborations between faculties, helping to institutionalize the integration of STEM and humanities disciplines. Combining insights from multiple fields—and, more critically, encouraging true multidisciplinary thinking, where each field retains its integrity—is increasingly vital. Technology is reshaping diverse areas of study and practice, requiring a broader perspective. While fields in the sciences excel in technical problem-solving and data-driven methodologies, the humanities provide critical perspectives on culture and societal impact, ensuring that technological advancements are understood within broader social and historical contexts (Kurup et al., 2021). This interdisciplinary approach allows for a deeper examination of how innovations shape and are shaped by human experience, informing more sustainable and context-aware developments across industries. This interdisciplinary collaboration enables creativity, broadens students' problem-solving abilities, and cultivates adaptability, which is essential for navigating the complexities of the modern professional landscape (Doğru, 2023; Vance et al., 2022). As the technology continues to reshape industries and daily life, it is imperative that education systems adapt by pushing for new forms of cross-disciplinary literacy that prepare students for the evolving demands of the workforce and society. Addressing pressing global challenges—such as climate change, artificial intelligence governance, and bioethics—requires interdisciplinary solutions that merge technical expertise with cultural and philosophical insights (Hsieh et al., 2024). Encouraging collaboration between qualitative and quantitative disciplines will go some way to bend technological advancements toward the best interests of humanity while preparing students for the complexities of an interconnected world. The probable result? A generation equipped to critically engage with both innovation and its broader implications (Hawkins et al., 2018).

As noted, smart tools are allowing traditionally qualitative disciplines such as history, literature, and philosophy to engage with computational analysis. In digital humanities, new applications are being used to reconstruct damaged or incomplete historical documents, advancing scholarship like that of Sabharwal (2015) and Lang and Ommer (2021). Through training models on similar, intact texts, researchers can use the tools to fill in gaps, predict missing sections, and even suggest possible interpretations of fragmented sources. Philosophers and ethicists utilize these models to analyze ethical dilemmas by evaluating large datasets on human decision-making, revealing biases and inconsistencies in moral reasoning. Translation and linguistic analysis tools are improving historical research by making ancient and obscure texts more accessible to modern scholars (Yu, 2024). It's important that the use of these tools for projects that have long been quite intractable is not resisted. Those scholars who work to bring varied technologies into the humanities should be encouraged and funded. The gap between qualitative interpretation and quantitative analysis is the smallest it has ever been, expanding the scope of traditional disciplines while preserving their intellectual rigor (Marchuk et al., 2024).

As these technologies evolve, non-STEM fields shape how ethical, cultural, and philosophical considerations guide development processes. Ethics and philosophy scholars assess the impact on privacy, bias, and algorithmic accountability, helping establish guidelines for responsible use (Aleynikova & Yarotskaya, 2024). Legal experts examine regulatory implications, advocating policies that balance innovation with societal protections. Cultural studies researchers track how generative content recasts media, art, and public discourse, revealing patterns in human-technology interaction (Kamukapa et al., 2024). These diverse perspectives in research and development help align technological advances with social priorities, nurturing responsible innovation (Song, 2017). On the other hand, the tools are also enabling STEM fields to engage more deeply with qualitative skills such as technical writing, data storytelling, and advanced reasoning. Engineers and data scientists increasingly rely on generated reports to translate complex data findings into accessible narratives for diverse audiences (Joseph & Uzondu, 2024). In bioinformatics, generated visualizations help researchers convey genetic data trends to policymakers and the public, facilitating informed decision-making. Additionally, simulations in climate science allow experts to present future environmental scenarios through interactive storytelling, making abstract data comprehensible (Des Kamukapa et al., 2024). This fusion of STEM and humanities methodologies underscores the importance of interdisciplinary literacy, where technical fields benefit from qualitative insights to enhance communication and public engagement (Jantassova & Akhmetova, 2021).

While many of the examples highlighted so far focus on applications in the humanities and social sciences, the interdisciplinary reach of coding extends across all fields, including STEM, business, healthcare, and environmental science as seen in Table 1.2. In bioinformatics, coding is essential for genomic data analysis and disease diagnostics, reorienting how medical research is conducted. In finance, algorithmic trading and risk assessment tools are reshaping investment strategies and fraud detection. Similarly, engineering

TABLE 1.2

Interdisciplinary Applications of Coding

Discipline	Coding Application
Digital Humanities	Text analysis and data visualization for historical documents and literary texts
Linguistics	Corpus analysis and machine learning for language pattern recognition
History	Data-driven historical research and interactive mapping of events
Political Science	AI-driven sentiment analysis and computational modeling of political trends
Journalism	Automated fact-checking, AI-assisted data journalism, and multimedia storytelling
Business Analytics	Predictive modeling, AI-powered market analysis, and decision-support systems
Education	Adaptive learning platforms, intelligent tutoring systems, and curriculum design automation
Environmental Science	Climate modeling, remote sensing analysis, and AI-driven sustainability planning
Bioinformatics	Genomic data analysis, AI-assisted disease diagnostics, and medical image processing
Art and Design	Algorithmic generative art, AI-powered visual design, and computational aesthetics
Music and Audio Processing	AI-assisted music composition, sound synthesis, and algorithmic mixing techniques
Psychology	Computational modeling of behavior, AI-assisted cognitive research, and big data analysis
Sociology	Social network analysis, computational sociology, and AI-powered survey analysis
Legal Studies	AI-assisted legal document review, predictive legal analytics, and automation in case law research
Philosophy and Ethics	Algorithmic ethical decision-making, AI bias detection, and computational philosophy
Healthcare and Medicine	AI-supported patient care prediction, medical robotics, and precision medicine
Marketing and Advertising	AI-powered consumer behavior modeling, targeted advertising, and social media analytics
Finance	Algorithmic trading, AI-powered risk assessment, and fraud detection
Urban Planning	Smart city simulations, GIS-based planning, and AI-powered infrastructure optimization
Architecture	Generative architectural design, AI-supported structural modeling, and simulation-based planning

and environmental science leverage computational modeling for climate simulations, remote sensing, and sustainability planning, demonstrating how coding supports data-driven decision-making in global challenges. The integration into programming also plays a crucial role in architecture and urban planning, where computational design tools assist in smart city development and structural modeling. Even within music, art, and design, algorithmic creativity is redefining how digital content is generated, bridging technical and artistic methodologies. These diverse applications underscore the broad and evolving impact of coding, positioning it as a foundational literacy applicable across all disciplines rather than a skill confined to computer science alone.

1.4 Democratizing Programming Skills across Disciplines

The rise of assisted coding tools is lowering the barriers between qualitative and quantitative fields. Programming and computational thinking are right on the edge of becoming more accessible across disciplines. Formerly, programming required mastery of syntax, logic, and debugging, creating a steep learning curve for individuals outside technical domains. But AI-driven tools such as GitHub Copilot and ChatGPT are now bridging this divide by enabling learners to code with natural language, much like how generative writing tools assist STEM students in articulating complex ideas with greater clarity (Jung, 2020). The word is overused, but a true demonstration of STEM methodologies and practical power currently exists in the same space as the writing and thinking done by students in the humanities, social sciences, and education. The technical barriers are coming down between these latter students and the results made possible by programming and the larger infrastructure programming tools make possible. It is also true that generative writing tools are making scholarly communication more accessible for STEM students, who may struggle with structuring and articulating their research effectively. By reducing the emphasis on drilling syntax and grammar, these tools free learners to spend time on higher-order organization, iterative drafting, and conceptual thinking (Sum et al., 2024).

This iterative learning process is native to AI. This cannot be stressed too much. The speed with which a student can generate essay drafts, for example, creates a new way to write that we ought to start thinking about as the most natural form of work within an algorithmic ecosystem. The same applies to generating code. Students and professionals both are entering a world in which rapid generation of full codebases or full academic articles can be completed in succession until the writer or coder has achieved the desired result. This has never been possible before. It might also escape attention how deeply interdisciplinary this style of work will become. The same underlying method of work will inform practices in currently varied disciplines, teaching students something like a conceptually universal approach to practical thought. This inevitably promotes an interdisciplinary fluency that aligns with the evolving demands of academia and the workforce (Zhuang & Lin, 2024). Beyond syntax assistance, this partnership between machine and human learners encourages design thinking and conceptual modeling, prioritizing what to build before getting into the details of how to build it—a principal move from traditional approaches to programming education.

As assistive tools permeate our digital landscape, coding has evolved from a specialized skill into a basic competency, vital for meaningful participation and innovation throughout diverse fields. Educational institutions now recognize software literacy as a curricular cornerstone—comparable to reading and mathematical proficiency (Schieferdecker, 2024). The emergence of AI-assisted coding environments offers contextual, immediate guidance that invites learners without technical backgrounds to explore programming principles through intuitive interaction. This phenomenon is evident in humanities research, where these applications now support scholars conducting digital text analysis by handling complex data processing tasks that previously demanded extensive programming knowledge (Valový & Buchalcevova, 2023). This evolution expands access to computational thinking and simultaneously creates conduits for interdisciplinary collaboration, with coding aptitude serving as a connective thread rather than an obstacle between academic domains (Zhuang & Lin, 2024). As these tools become more sophisticated, they increasingly support systems design and software architecture principles, allowing students to engage with higher-level concepts from the outset of their learning journey.

The impact of enhanced coding literacy extends well beyond university settings into diverse professional spheres. Consider supply chain operations, where intelligent systems now enhance logistics coordination, anticipate market fluctuations, and streamline inventory protocols—yielding substantial operational efficiencies and cost reductions (Shobhana, 2024). In journalism, computational platforms equip investigative reporters with tools to extract insights from complex datasets and create compelling visual narratives (Liu & Li, 2024). Such developments underscore how programming knowledge has outgrown its conventional boundaries within computer science departments and emerged as a universal competency that warrants integration throughout educational curricula, reflecting its status as an essential form of modern literacy (Kotsiantis, Verykios, & Tzagarakis, 2024). This has been a talking point for quite some time, resulting in the cliched pronouncements that everyone ought to "learn to code." How exactly everyone might set aside the time to learn technical skills in the middle of all the other work a student or professional (or professor) has to accomplish has been glossed over in these utopian-sounding recommendations. But if it turns out quite surprisingly to be true very suddenly that everyone can learn to code without actually learning the syntax of code—then it becomes a different story. The real benefits of knowing what it means to design a technical solution for any problem begin to come into view, and it is exciting to think about the variety of classrooms in which this exact kind of design thinking might be taught.

As this kind of teaching begins to be explored and practiced, the role of AI in coding education will need to be theorized. It will be best understood as work with a collaborative partner rather than a substitute for human programmers. While tools streamline repetitive tasks and provide code suggestions, they also require learners to critically engage with the underlying logic and structure of their programs (Gao et al., 2023). This approach means active learning. It creates a classroom in which students analyze generated recommendations and make informed decisions on their implementation. Debugging systems also contribute to this process by identifying errors and providing explanations, enabling students to build a deeper understanding of coding logic (Tan & Lim, 2023). The iterative interaction between tools and human learners facilitates the situation where coding remains an active, rather than passive, skill development process (Mutanga, Lecheko, & Revesai, 2024). At the same time, enhanced collaboration is expanding opportunities for peer learning and team-based programming. Coding platforms facilitate cooperative workflows by providing real-time coding assistance and improving efficiency in group projects (Bakharia & Abdi, 2024). In professional settings, these solutions are being used to support software engineers by streamlining development cycles and reducing the time needed to debug and optimize code (Gulwani, 2022). As technologies continue to evolve, their role in coding education and practice will increasingly emphasize collaborative problem-solving, ensuring that machine learning remains an enabler rather than a replacement for human creativity and innovation.

1.5 Challenges and Opportunities for Inclusivity in AI Integration

The growing adoption of assistive educational tools demands attention to equitable access. While platforms increasingly offer personalized education and adaptive support, disparities in financial and technological resources limit their reach, especially in underfunded schools and rural areas (Eden et al., 2024). Meeting this challenge calls for practical solutions: cloud-based systems that run on low-bandwidth networks, mobile applications that minimize hardware requirements, and government-backed initiatives that expand access to marginalized communities (Sytnyk & Podlinyayeva, 2024). These platforms can extend their reach by incorporating multilingual capabilities, allowing students beyond major technology hubs to engage fully with educational content (Yadav, 2024).

New accessibility features also provide direct support for students with disabilities, expanding learning opportunities through speech-to-text capabilities, adaptive interfaces, and language translation. Tools can offer customized learning experiences based on individual needs, such as generating text-based explanations for visually impaired students or adjusting pacing for learners with cognitive differences. These advancements look to reduce barriers to education with the use of this technology instead of reinforcing them (Lampou, 2023). However, widespread adoption depends on making these technologies affordable and embedding universal design principles into smart systems. Collaboration between educators, technology developers, and policymakers will be key in scaling accessibility features across different learning environments. Open-source tools and subsidized educational technology programs can further facilitate inclusivity rather than becoming another obstacle to equitable education (Alali & Wardat, 2024).

As tools reshape education, they present an opportunity to augment problem-solving skills. The fear that problem-solving will become a lost art replaced by robots misses the whole point of our argument. Problem-solving will become a more directly emphasized part of an education in programming, whether this happens to be in a full course devoted to programming or in non-STEM classes exploring an embedded use of code. Regardless, the thinking process most required will be analyzing a problem, working with an algorithmic assistant to develop code that can address the problem, and iterating over bugs and deployment issues to bring the code to production, whatever production means in an academic context. To facilitate this entire vision, tutoring systems will be able to offer real-time assistance and personalized learning experiences, helping students build confidence in coding, writing, and analytical thinking (Farahani & Ghasemi, 2024). Platforms like GitHub Copilot and writing tools like Claude already provide contextual support, allowing students to engage with complex concepts at their own pace while reinforcing foundational skills, and the next generation of tools to assist with coding will only improve students' ability to "think like coders" using natural language. Rather than assuming these machines threaten cognitive development, structured integration allows students to actively engage with concepts while using them as a supportive learning aid.

Educators can design AI-enhanced curricula that encourage critical thinking and active problem-solving, balancing automation with hands-on learning. Intelligent platforms can be programmed to prompt students to justify their choices, verify generated solutions, and explore multiple approaches to a problem (Jose & Jose, 2024). AI literacy courses can further empower students to understand model limitations, recognize biases, and develop computational reasoning skills. Additionally, incorporating structured debugging exercises, where students troubleshoot errors before consulting generated suggestions, reinforces core competencies and reinforces that tools support rather than supplant deep learning (Rashmi, 2023).

To facilitate a situation where integration expands access to learning rather than reinforcing existing disparities, educational institutions must adopt strategies that promote equitable smart learning environments. Establishing clear guidelines for use in education helps safeguard adaptive technologies that prioritize accessibility, accountability, and transparency (Jianzheng & Xuwei, 2023). As such, personalized learning platforms should cater to a diverse range of learners. For instance, machine learning could be used to generate customized coding challenges based on a student's past performance and learning style, providing targeted practice in areas where they need improvement, while also offering more open-ended, creative projects for those who thrive on exploration. Research by Rekha et al. (2024) has already demonstrated the viability of this in other areas. Additionally, developing AI literacy as a core component of education enables students, regardless of background, to actively engage with and benefit from the technologies. Equipping teachers with training in AI pedagogy and integrating AI fluency into curricula prepares the ground for critical engagement, helping students interpret generated outputs, assess information reliability, and apply augmented insights to problem-solving (Elam, 2024). As these tools continue to reshape education, expanding equitable access and responsible implementation will allow these tools to empower diverse learners, bridge digital divides, and create more dynamic, inclusive learning environments (Agarwal & Vij, 2024).

The integration into programming education presents an opportunity to expand access, enhance inclusivity, and lower traditional barriers that have limited participation in coding. Rather than viewing these machines as a threat to fairness and accessibility, their implementation can serve as a tool for bridging educational gaps. Enhanced learning environments provide adaptive assistance, allowing students with diverse backgrounds and learning styles to engage with coding concepts in ways previously unavailable. Learners in underfunded schools and non-STEM fields, as well as those with disabilities, can use these tools to develop computational literacy without the traditional constraints of syntax-first instruction. Practical solutions—such as open-source tools, mobile-first learning platforms, and government-backed digital education initiatives—are already working to close the digital divide. Expanding these efforts can facilitate a solution where the technology serves as a catalyst for inclusivity, rather than reinforcing existing inequities. While the latest solutions continue to streamline learning and lowering entry barriers, they must complement rather than replace foundational problem-solving skills. Coding tools allow students to experiment with programming logic before mastering syntax, but curriculum design must still emphasize critical engagement with the generated solutions. Strategies such as structured debugging exercises, assistive code reviews, and iterative project-based learning enable students to actively engage with the outputs and develop reasoning and troubleshooting skills alongside such support. AI literacy in coding education equips students to critically evaluate the assistant's recommendations, recognize biases, and refine automated solutions. Success depends on thoughtful course design that treats the technology as a catalyst for problem-solving rather than a shortcut around it.

Programming education, reimagined through these new platforms, has become more approachable and versatile. Where syntax-first instruction once created barriers, automated computational thinking invites participation from creative professionals and researchers across fields. Students now tackle meaningful projects immediately, building confidence while developing deeper conceptual understanding. The future of programming education lies in integrative curricula that reward exploration and critical reasoning, creating learning spaces where students from every discipline can thrive in developing software literacy and systems thinking capabilities that will serve them throughout their careers.

References

Agarwal, P., & Vij, A. (2024). Assessing the challenges and opportunities of artificial intelligence in Indian education. *International Journal for Global Academic & Scientific Research, 3*(1), 36–44.

AlAli, R., & Wardat, Y. (2024). Opportunities and challenges of integrating generative artificial intelligence in education. *International Journal of Religion, 5*(7), 784–793.

Alda, E., & Baralt-Torrijos, J. (2023, March). An expression-oriented approach to programming education. In *2023 IEEE Integrated STEM Education Conference (ISEC)* (pp. 282–285). IEEE.

Aleynikova, D., & Yarotskaya, L. (2024). AI implications for vocational foreign language teaching and learning: New meaning. *Tambov University Review. Series: Humanities.* https://doi.org/10.20310/1810-0201-2024-29-1-46-56.

Baiburin, A., Berezkin, Y., Boitsova, O., Gromov, A., Kovalenko, K., Kovalyova, N., & Utekhin, I. (2024). Forum 60: Ai in the social sciences and humanities. In *Antropologicheskij Forum* (Vol. 2024, No. 60, pp. 11–68). Russian Academy of Science.

Bakharia, A., & Abdi, S. (2024). Shaping programming and data science education: Insights from GenAI technical book trends. *2024 IEEE International Conference on Advanced Learning Technologies (ICALT)*, 116–120.

Bassner, P., Frankford, E., & Krusche, S. (2024). Iris: An ai-driven virtual tutor for computer science education. In *Proceedings of the 2024 on Innovation and Technology in Computer Science Education V. 1* (pp. 394–400).

Bertrand, M., & Namukasa, I. (2020). Integrating computational thinking and mathematics. *Advances in Educational Technologies and Instructional Design.* https://doi.org/10.4018/978-1-7998-1479-5.ch005

Çela, E., Fonkam, M. M., & Potluri, R. M. (2024). Risks of AI-assisted learning on student critical thinking: a case study of Albania. *International Journal of Risk and Contingency Management (IJRCM)*, 12(1), 1–19.

Chesley, A., Parupudi, T., Holtan, A., Farrington, S., Eden, C., Baniya, S., & Laux, D. (2018). Interdisciplinary pedagogy, integrated curriculum, and professional development. https://docs.lib.purdue.edu/cgi/viewcontent.cgi?article=1014 &context=aseeil-insectionconference

Denny, P., Leinonen, J., Prather, J., Luxton-Reilly, A., Amarouche, T., Becker, B. A., & Reeves, B. N. (2024, March). Prompt Problems: A new programming exercise for the generative AI era. In *Proceedings of the 55th ACM Technical Symposium on Computer Science Education V. 1* (pp. 296–302).

Denny, P., Luxton-Reilly, A., Tempero, E., & Hendrickx, J. (2011). Understanding the syntax barrier for novices. *Proceedings of the 16th Annual Conference on Innovation and Technology in Computer Science Education*, 208–212.

Di Angelo, L., Di Stefano, P., Guardiani, E., & Morabito, A. E. (2021). A 3D informational database for automatic archiving of archaeological pottery finds. *Sensors*, 21(3), 978.

Doğru, S. (2023). Integration of STEM education to humanities: Examining interdisciplinary links in basic chemistry course according to student views. *Research on Education and Psychology*, 7(Special Issue 2), 128–139.

Eden, C. A., Chisom, O. N., & Adeniyi, I. S. (2024). Integrating AI in education: Opportunities, challenges, and ethical considerations. *Magna Scientia Advanced Research and Reviews*, 10(2), 006–013.

Edwards, J., Ditton, J., Trninic, D., Swanson, H., Sullivan, S., & Mano, C. (2020, August). Syntax exercises in CS1. In *Proceedings of the 2020 ACM Conference on International Computing Education Research* (pp. 216–226).

Elam, K. M. (2024). Exploring the challenges and future directions of big data and AI in education. *Journal of Artificial Intelligence General science (JAIGS) ISSN: 3006-4023*, 5(1), 81–93.

Ejjami, R. (2024). The future of learning: AI-based curriculum development. *International Journal For Multidisciplinary Research*, 6(4). https://doi.org/10.36948 /ijfmr.2024.v06i04.24441

Farahani, M., & Ghasemi, G. (2024). Artificial intelligence and inequality: Challenges and opportunities. *International Journal of Innovation in Education*, 9, 78–99.

Fattah, H. A., Vadivel, B., Shaban, A. A., & Shanmugam, K. (2023). Enhancing English language education: The impact of AI integration in the classroom. *International Journal of Humanities and Education Development (IJHED)*, 5(6), 116–123.

Gao, J., Cao, J., Yeo, S., Choo, K. T. W., Zhang, Z., Li, T. J. J., Zhao, S., & Perrault, S. T. (2023). Impact of human-AI interaction on user trust and reliance in AI-assisted qualitative coding. *ArXiv, abs/2309.13858*.

Gao, J., Choo, K. T. W., Cao, J., Lee, R., & Perrault, S. T. (2023). CoAIcoder: Examining the effectiveness of AI-assisted human-to-human collaboration in qualitative analysis. *ACM Transactions on Computer-Human Interaction*, 31(1), 1–38.

Graetz, N., & Esposito, M. (2023). Historical redlining and contemporary racial disparities in neighborhood life expectancy. *Social Forces*, 102(1), 1–22.

Groton, A. H. (2015). Facing the facts about teaching Latin. *Syllecta Classica*, 15, 179–192.

Gulwani, S. (2022). AI-assisted programming: applications, user experiences, and neuro-symbolic techniques (keynote). *Proceedings of the 30th ACM Joint European Software Engineering Conference and Symposium on the Foundations of Software Engineering.* https://doi.org/10.1145/3540250.3569444.

Haindl, P., & Weinberger, G. (2024). Does ChatGPT help novice programmers write better code? Results from static code analysis. *IEEE Access, 12*, 114146–114156.

Hawkins, J. N., Yamada, A., Yamada, R., & Jacob, W. J. (Eds.). (2018). *New directions of STEM research and learning in the world ranking movement: A comparative perspective.* Springer International Publishing.

Hill, G. (2016). Review of a problems-first approach to first-year undergraduate programming. *Lecture Notes in Computer Science, 9973*, 73–80.

Hsieh, Y. C., Wang, Y. M., Cao, J., & Shen, C. C. (2024, June). STEM education model in new media courses research: AIGC graphic application and impact. In *Proceedings of the 3rd International Conference on Educational Innovation and Multimedia Technology, EIMT 2024, March 29–31, 2024, Wuhan, China.*

Hutson, J. (2023). The role of collaborative authorship in decentered research innovation: An interdisciplinary, interdepartmental, and interinstitutional model to accelerate research culture in teaching institutions. *Information, Medium & Society: Journal of Publishing Studies, 21*(1), 7–24.

Jantassova, D., & Akhmetova, D. (2021). *Innovative training of engineers through the integration of the art component into the STEM University.* Bulletin of the Karaganda University. Pedagogy series.

Jianzheng, S., & Xuwei, Z. (2023). Integration of AI with higher education innovation: Reforming future educational directions. *International Journal of Science and Research (IJSR), 12*(10), 1727–1731.

Jose, J., & Jose, B. J. (2024). Educators' academic insights on artificial intelligence: Challenges and opportunities. *Electronic Journal of e-Learning, 22*(2), 59–77.

Joseph, O. B., & Uzondu, N. C. (2024). Curriculums development for interdisciplinary STEM education: A review of models and approaches. *International Journal of Applied Research in Social Sciences, 6*(8), 1575–1592.

Johanyák, Z., Cserkó, J., & Pásztor, A. (2023). AI-assisted university programming education in practice. *2023 IEEE 35th International Conference on Software Engineering Education and Training (CSEE&T)*, 185–186.

Jung, H. (2020). A study on the current state of artificial intelligence-based coding technologies and the direction of future coding education. *The International Journal of Advanced Culture Technology, 8*(3), 186–191.

Kamukapa, T. D., Lubinga, S., Masiya, T., & Sono, L. (2024). Assessing the integration of AI competencies in undergraduate public administration curricula in selected South African higher education institutions. *Teaching Public Administration,* 01447394241266443.

Kersánszki, T., de Meester, J., Spikic, S., & Takács, J. M. (2022). Opportunities for integrated education in STEM. *Opus et Educatio, 9*(2). https://doi.org/10.3311/ope.502

Kotsiantis, S., Verykios, V., & Tzagarakis, M. (2024). Ai-assisted programming tasks using code embeddings and transformers. *Electronics, 13*(4), 767.

Kurup, P. M., Yang, Y., Li, X., & Dong, Y. (2021). Interdisciplinary and integrated STEM. *Encyclopedia, 1*(4), 1192–1199.

Lampou, R. (2023). The integration of artificial intelligence in education: Opportunities and challenges. *Review of Artificial Intelligence in Education, 4*, e15–e15.

Lang, S., & Ommer, B. (2021). Transforming information into knowledge: How computational methods reshape art history. *DHQ: Digital Humanities Quarterly, 15*(3). http://digitalhumanities.org/dhq/vol/15/3/000560/000560.html

Li, J., Zheng, X., Watanabe, I., & Ochiai, Y. (2024). A systematic review of digital transformation technologies in museum exhibition. *Computers in Human Behavior,* 108407.

Liang, J. T., Yang, C., & Myers, B. A. (2024, February). A large-scale survey on the usability of ai programming assistants: Successes and challenges. In *Proceedings of the 46th IEEE/ACM International Conference on Software Engineering* (pp. 1–13).

Lister, R. (2011). Computing education research: Programming, syntax, and cognitive load. *ACM Inroads, 2*(2), 21–22.

Liu, J., & Li, S. (2024). Toward artificial intelligence-human paired programming: A review of the educational applications and research on artificial intelligence code-generation tools. *Journal of Educational Computing Research,* 07356331241240460.

Mansour, N. (2024). Redefining architectural pedagogy: Navigating the integration of midjourney AI in design education. *112th ACSA Annual Meeting Proceedings, Disruptors on the Edge.* https://doi.org/10.35483/acsa.am.112.25

Marchuk, I., Nagorna, N., & Ivanova, N. (2024). Interdisciplinary integration in the process of teaching humanities in higher education institutions. *Collection of Scientific Papers of Uman State Pedagogical University.* https://doi.org/10.31499/2307-4906.1.2024.302202

Massaty, M. H., Fahrurozi, S. K., & Budiyanto, C. W. (2024). The role of AI in fostering computational thinking and self-efficacy in educational settings: A systematic review. *IJIE (Indonesian Journal of Informatics Education), 8*(1), 49–61.

Mulligan, J. (2021). Computation and interpretation in literary studies. *Critical Inquiry, 48*(1), 126–143.

Mutanga, B. M., Lecheko, M., & Revesai, Z. (2024). Navigating the grey area: Students' ethical dilemmas in using AI tools for coding assignments. *IJIE (Indonesian Journal of Informatics Education), 8*(1), 15–24.

Nelson, G. L. (2017, August). Comprehension-first pedagogy and adaptive, intrinsically motivated tutorials. In *Proceedings of the 2017 ACM Conference on International Computing Education Research* (pp. 287–288).

Nie, J. (2021). Research on STEM curriculum integration technology. *2021 3rd International Conference on Computer Science and Technologies in Education (CSTE),* 37–42.

Nugraha, M. G., Kidman, G., & Tan, H. (2024). Interdisciplinary STEM education foundational concepts: Implementation for knowledge creation. *Eurasia Journal of Mathematics, Science and Technology Education, 20*(10), em2523.

Pereira, C., da Silva, R., & Rosa, C. (2024). How to measure political polarization in text-as-data? A scoping review of computational social science approaches. *Journal of Information Technology & Politics,* 1–14. https://doi.org/10.1145/3132698

Rashmi, D. (2023). Unlocking the potential of AI in education: Challenges and opportunities. *International Journal for Multidisciplinary Research (IJFMR), 5*(4), 1–11.

Reek, M. M. (1995, March). A top-down approach to teaching programming. In *Proceedings of the Twenty-sixth SIGCSE Technical Symposium on Computer Science Education* (pp. 6–9).

Rekha, K., Gopal, K., Satheeskumar, D., Anand, U. A., Doss, D. S. S., & Elayaperumal, S. (2024, May). Ai-powered personalized learning system design: Student engagement and performance tracking system. In *2024 4th International Conference on Advance Computing and Innovative Technologies in Engineering (ICACITE)* (pp. 1125–1130). IEEE.

Rich, P., Bartholomew, S., Daniel, D., Dinsmoor, K., Nielsen, M., Reynolds, C., Swanson, M., & Winward, E. (2022). Trends in tools used to teach computational thinking through elementary coding. *Journal of Research on Technology in Education, 56*(3), 269–290.

Rim, H. (2017). A study on teaching using website 'Code.org' in programming education based on computational thinking. *Journal of Korea Multimedia Society, 20*(2), 382–395.

Rosiene, C. P. (2008, October). Instructing non-majors programming: Knowledge organization by illustration. In *2008 38th Annual Frontiers in Education Conference* (pp. F1C–23). IEEE.

Rossano, V., Roselli, T., & Quercia, G. (2018). Coding and computational thinking with Arduino. *Proceedings of the International Conference on Computer Science Education* (pp. 451–459).

Sabharwal, A. (2015). *Digital curation in the digital humanities: Preserving and promoting archival and special collections.* Chandos Publishing.

Savelides, S. C., Fasouraki, R., Georgousis, E., Kolokotroni, K., & Savelidi, M. S. (2020). Interdisciplinary educational approach STEM and HASS knowledge fields using ICTs support. Case of an application for a pilot experiment. *European Journal of Engineering and Technology Research,* 33–42. https://doi.org/10.24018/ejeng.2020.0.CIE.1797

Sheard, J., Denny, P., Hellas, A., Leinonen, J., Malmi, L., & Simon. (2024, March). Instructor perceptions of AI code generation tools-a multi-institutional interview study. In *Proceedings of the 55th ACM Technical Symposium on Computer Science Education V. 1* (pp. 1223–1229).

Shobhana, N. (2024). AI-powered supply chains towards greater efficiency. In *Complex AI dynamics and interactions in management* (pp. 229–249). IGI Global.

Shute, V. J., Sun, C., & Asbell-Clarke, J. (2017). Demystifying computational thinking. *Educational Research Review, 22,* 142–158.

Silapachote, P., & Srisuphab, A. (2016). Teaching and learning computational thinking through solving problems in artificial intelligence: On designing introductory engineering and computing courses. *IEEE International Conference on Teaching, Assessment, and Learning for Engineering (TALE),* 50–54.

Silapachote, P., & Srisuphab, A. (2017). Engineering courses on computational thinking through solving problems in artificial intelligence. *International Journal of Engineering Pedagogy, 7*(3), 34–49.

Song, D. (2017). Artificial mind: Interdisciplinary learning. *NeuroQuantology, 15*(3), 107–113.

Storey, V. A., & Wagner, A. (2024). Integrating Artificial Intelligence (AI) Into adult education: Opportunities, challenges, and future directions. *International Journal of Adult Education and Technology (IJAET), 15*(1), 1–15.

Sytnyk, L., & Podlinyayeva, O. (2024). AI in education: Main possibilities and challenges. *Scientific Collection «InterConf+», 45*(201), 569–579.

Subramaniam, S., Maat, S., & Mahmud, M. S. (2022). Computational thinking in mathematics education: A systematic review. *Cypriot Journal of Educational Sciences.* https://orcid.org/0000-0001-9297-1995

Sum, K. C., Ng, K.-H., Siu, S.-T., Chui, H.-Y., Au, C.-L., & Li, C. F. (2024). AI-assisted microcontroller-based kits for STEM education. *2024 IEEE Integrated STEM Education Conference (ISEC)*, 1–4.

Takerngsaksiri, W., Warusavitarne, C., Yaacoub, C., Hou, M. H. K., & Tantithamthavorn, C. (2023). Students' perspectives on AI code completion: Benefits and challenges. *ArXiv, abs/2311.00177.*

Tan, C. W., & Lim, K. Y. (2023). Revolutionizing formative assessment in STEM fields: Leveraging AI and NLP techniques. *2023 Asia Pacific Signal and Information Processing Association Annual Summit and Conference (APSIPA ASC)* (pp. 1357–1364).

Terras, M. (2022). Inviting ai into the archives: The reception of handwritten recognition technology into historical manuscript transcription. *Digital Humanities Research, 2,* 179.

Valový, M., & Buchalcevova, A. (2023). The psychological effects of AI-assisted programming on students and professionals. *2023 IEEE International Conference on Software Maintenance and Evolution (ICSME)* (pp. 385–390).

Vance, E., Glimp, D., Pieplow, N., Garrity, J., & Melbourne, B. (2022). Integrating the humanities into data science eduation. *Statistics Education Research Journal.* https://doi.org/10.52041/serj.v21i2.42

Yadav, D. S. (2024). Navigating the landscape of AI integration in education: Opportunities, challenges, and ethical considerations for harnessing the potential of artificial intelligence (AI) for teaching and learning. *BSSS Journal of Computer, 15*(1), 38–48.

Yoon, J. (2023). Integrating AI tools and linguistic content in college education. *Convergence English Language & Literature Association.* https://doi.org/10.55986/cell.2023.8.3.349

Yu, K. (2024). Utilizing AI in liberal arts education. *Barun Academy of History.* https://doi.org/10.55793/jkhc.2024.20.221.

Zhang, Y. (2023). Generative AI has lowered the barriers to computational social sciences. *ArXiv, abs/2311.10833.*

Zhou, S., Livingston, I. J., Schiefsky, M., Shieber, S. M., & Gajos, K. Z. (2016, May). Ingenium: Engaging novice students with Latin grammar. In *Proceedings of the 2016 CHI Conference on Human Factors in Computing Systems* (pp. 944–956).

Zhuang, T., & Lin, Z. (2024). The why, what, and how of AI-based coding in scientific research. *arXiv preprint arXiv:2410.02156.*

Zviel-Girshin, R. (2024). The good and bad of AI tools in novice programming education. *Education Sciences, 14*(10), 1089.

2

The Limitations of Traditional Syntax-Focused Coding Education in Non-STEM

Syntax-first coding instruction creates significant cognitive barriers for non-STEM learners. Many introductory courses center on memorization and debugging exercises early in the learning process, overwhelming students unfamiliar with computational logic and undermining their intrinsic motivation. AI-assisted tools allow students to offload syntax burdens by breaking them down into authentic learning experiences. Shifting the emphasis to HTML and JavaScript as accessible entry points enhances this approach. Interactive, visually engaging outcomes provide immediate reinforcement, making programming more intuitive and managing productive failure in low-stakes environments. New platforms guide learners through real-time feedback, automated syntax corrections, and contextualized code explanations, reducing frustration and promoting experimentation. Delaying complex debugging and logic-heavy exercises allows students to develop confidence before tackling technical problem-solving. Project-based learning, supported through generated insights and interactive assistance, encourages exploration across disciplines. Greater accessibility strengthens retention, countering attrition rates common in traditional coding education. Generative instruction supports a conceptual foundation, reframing programming as a flexible skill applicable across humanities, social sciences, and creative fields. Structured engagement with practical applications replaces reliance on rote syntax, making programming an essential digital literacy rather than an isolated technical domain.

2.1 Why Traditional Approaches Fail to Engage Non-STEM Students

Traditional programming curricula tend to rely on syntax-first teaching frameworks, yet extensive reliance on the memorization necessary for the learning of syntax continues to alienate many students outside of computer science. As outlined in Chapter 1, syntax-first strategies demand an early focus on language-specific rules and structures, prompting learners to drill grammar-like details in isolation. Whether this happens through literal

DOI: 10.1201/9781003637738-2

drills or through problem sets, memorization becomes the practical target aimed at during the early stages of coding instruction. As stated already, this is understandable. In order for a person to code prior to coding assistants, the only option is to type coding syntax into a code editor or a REPL environment until the code runs without errors. Without these solutions, even a theoretical alternative has been difficult to imagine. Pair programming might be suggested as a creative solution, with the more experienced coder typing in the correct syntax while the novice thinks through the problem. But this has not been the practice, mostly because introductory programming courses do not have any experienced coders outside of the professor. Something like rote memorization therefore becomes the necessary goal. This approach creates an exceptionally high cognitive load for beginners, particularly those unfamiliar with computational thinking models. Cognitive load theory, which examines how working memory limitations affect learning, helps explain why syntax-first instruction is problematic: novices must simultaneously process unfamiliar syntax rules, computational concepts, and problem-solving strategies, quickly overwhelming their working memory capacity and diminishing intrinsic motivation to continue learning.

Researchers have noted that this approach, while suitable for technically inclined individuals, tends to overshadow the broader conceptual and problem-solving dimensions that motivate non-STEM learners (Alda & Baralt-Torrijos, 2023). The emphasis on error avoidance, rather than creative exploration, leads many students to perceive programming as an exercise in careful editing and line-by-line scanning for correctness. This perception is reinforced by experienced instructors suffering from the "curse of knowledge"—a cognitive bias where experts find it difficult to remember or understand the perspective of novices. Instructors who have internalized programming syntax over years of practice frequently underestimate how challenging these abstract rules appear to beginners, creating a substantial gap between instruction and student comprehension. According to Mbiada et al. (2024), such instructional models can impede engagement among those who prioritize practical application and interdisciplinary connections. Many non-STEM learners view programming through the lens of professional goals—journalism students seeking data visualization skills or business majors hoping to develop market analytics—and rarely encounter meaningful examples within syntax-bound lessons. These learners are seeking authentic learning experiences that connect directly to their disciplinary contexts, but traditional approaches separate classroom exercises from real-world applications. The disconnect between decontextualized syntax drills and authentic programming tasks creates significant barriers to skill transfer, as students struggle to apply classroom knowledge to practical scenarios.

Early struggles with syntax errors can solidify the view that programming lacks connection to practical applications. Instead of experiencing coding as a resource for creative problem-solving, students become trapped in cycles of frustration with compiler errors and syntax minutiae before experiencing any meaningful success. This failure to provide early wins undermines student confidence and prevents the development of productive failure—the valuable learning that occurs when students struggle with challenging problems in supportive environments. These trends underscore a need for pedagogical reform that foregrounds critical thinking, conceptual understanding, and tailored contextualization over syntax acquisition (Table 2.1).

Non-STEM students frequently struggle to integrate coding tasks with professional or scholarly pursuits because existing course design fails to bring out the relevance of loops, variables, or basic algorithms to industry-specific scenarios (Fojcik et al., 2022). Courses in business, communications, or the humanities commonly position programming as an elective skill rather than a tool that naturally emerges from language-centered work. This limits opportunities for students to collaborate on projects that demonstrate the value of coding across disciplines. Teachers who rely mostly or entirely on syntax-first instruction perpetuate—usually without meaning to—exclusionary barriers. It is simply the case that professors assume a foundational level of computational thinking that many undergraduates from diverse backgrounds do not share. When instructors cannot provide personalized guidance, many students fall behind in syntax drills and abandon programming courses entirely.

Coding platforms present an alternative: functioning as cognitive experiments that involve students in deciding how to expand their own capabilities. What will work best for them in teaching an assistant to handle routine syntax concerns? And how do they want to design the more complex conceptual aspects of their work? Because these environments provide automated error detection and immediate feedback, students become intermediaries between the projects assigned to them by their courses and the assistants they choose to rely on for mechanical accuracy. This is a new method for teaching conceptual understanding. By offloading the cognitive burden of syntax memorization, these tools create mental space for higher-order thinking about program design and problem-solving strategies. These environments encourage experimentation and connect coding principles to real-world applications in each student's field. The interactive nature of these systems introduces new layers to the educational process and initiates students into task management and planning—underappreciated aspects of software development. For students outside of STEM, the idea of building one-off applications for humanities or business projects takes shape and builds student confidence regardless of prior experience. For students within STEM curricula, stages of software development that are more often introduced in later coursework become a natural part of deciding how to instruct a kind of employee or intern who can help with the syntactic side of coding. When thoughtfully implemented, these tools help students master core principles through active engagement rather than rote memorization, making programming accessible to learners from every academic discipline.

TABLE 2.1

Why Traditional Programming Approaches Fail for Non-STEM Students

Issue with Traditional Programming Approach	Why This Is a Problem	Proposed Solution
Syntax-First Focus Creates High Cognitive Load	Many students struggle with syntax-heavy instruction before grasping coding logic, leading to frustration and disengagement.	Introduce AI-powered tools that handle syntax concerns, allowing students to look at planning and application.
Lack of Immediate, Tangible Results	Early coursework built on repetitive drills rather than functional applications, making programming feel irrelevant.	Incorporate project-based learning that allows students to see immediate, meaningful outcomes from their work.
Disconnect between Programming and Real-World Applications	Students do not see how programming skills apply to their own academic or professional interests, leading to low retention.	Provide real-world coding scenarios relevant to journalism, business, and the humanities to increase engagement.
Exclusionary Barriers for Non-STEM Students	Programming is often introduced with technical prerequisites that discourage students from humanities, business, and other disciplines.	Reduce technical prerequisites through assistance, making programming more accessible to all academic backgrounds.
Overemphasis on Debugging Before Conceptual Understanding	Introductory courses emphasize error correction over logic building, making coding feel like a series of frustrating technical exercises.	Use debugging to provide contextual explanations rather than penalizing minor syntax errors early on.
Rigid Assessment Models Discourage Experimentation	Assessments prioritize strict correctness over problem-solving strategies, discouraging students from experimenting with code.	Implement assessments that evaluate logic building, creativity, and conceptual understanding instead of rote correctness.
Failure to Scaffold Learning for Beginners	Traditional approaches assume computational fluency before introducing programming concepts, leaving beginners without adequate structuring.	Use reinforcement and adaptive learning platforms to help beginners gradually develop coding fluency.
Delayed Exposure to Creative and Applied Problem-Solving	Courses introduce syntax drills before problem-solving applications, leading to disengagement among non-technical learners.	Encourage early-stage projects using code generation, reinforcing problem-solving over syntax drills.

(Continued)

TABLE 2.1   (CONTINUED)

Why Traditional Programming Approaches Fail for Non-STEM Students

Issue with Traditional Programming Approach	Why This Is a Problem	Proposed Solution
Pedagogical Models Prioritize Rote Memorization	Memorization of syntax rules does not develop computational thinking skills or promote deeper learning.	Change from syntax memorization to computational thinking and logical problem decomposition.
Limited Interdisciplinary Relevance	Few examples of how programming is useful in journalism, business, education, or the humanities, leaving non-STEM students uninterested.	Demonstrate interdisciplinary applications of programming by integrating coding projects into humanities, business, and education curricula.

Most programming courses begin with intensive syntax training and debugging exercises. Non-STEM students, if they enroll in programming classes, typically start out expecting to develop logical reasoning through hands-on projects. Instead, they encounter syntax exercises and debugging routines that feel disconnected from their goals. This emphasis places significant cognitive demands on learners, as mastering syntax before understanding its functional purpose can increase frustration and disengagement (Alda & Baralt-Torrijos, 2023). For instance, Edwards et al. (2018) argued that separating syntax practice from problem-solving in introductory programming courses will build foundational coding proficiency before engaging in computational thinking. Their Phanon curriculum introduces web-based exercises that progress incrementally, requiring students to complete simpler syntax drills before advancing to more complex structures. For example, an early exercise on iteration prompts students to replace a placeholder with a correct range() function call to print numbers from 0 to 3, while later exercises ask them to construct loops printing even numbers up to 20. These exercises rely on repetition, with progressively fewer hints, reinforcing language mechanics without requiring deep problem-solving. While this model aims to reduce early frustration and cognitive overload, it remains grounded in syntax-first instructional design, reinforcing the assumption that programming should be taught as a sequence of exercises before applying concepts to scenarios students can imagine themselves facing. Research supporting syntax-first models continues to emphasize repetition and memorization as the primary means of reducing errors, with students completing hundreds of syntax exercises per semester before engaging in projects (Edwards et al., 2020).

It is possible this is among the best methods for teaching students to internalize syntax rules. Structured reinforcement works for learning syntax for natural languages, and a patient and disciplined student will likely benefit from the method in a course teaching a progression from basic control structures to functions and beyond. In the absence of coding assistants, students have no choice but to learn syntax first and postpone computational problem-solving or interdisciplinary experiments until later. Still, even though precise code structure may be necessary for technical accuracy, its prioritization in early coursework threatens to overshadow opportunities for experimentation and ideation, both of which are critical for developing computational thinking. Traditional pedagogical frameworks offer limited flexibility for students to explore programming in ways that align with their interests, further reinforcing the perception that perfect code is a gateway guarding an inaccessible discipline. Addressing these barriers requires a restructuring of programming instruction, one that emphasizes conceptual problem-solving and applied computational literacy over strict adherence to syntax rules in the initial stages of learning.

A primary limitation of syntax-first programming education is the lack of immediate, tangible results, which can deter students who are unfamiliar with computational logic. Many introductory courses foreground extensive syntax-teaching problem sets and isolated coding exercises, postponing opportunities for students to apply their knowledge in meaningful ways (Fojcik et al., 2022). This delay contradicts established principles of cognitive load theory and intrinsic motivation: when students cannot see the practical outcomes of their learning efforts, their motivation diminishes as cognitive resources are consumed by seemingly disconnected tasks. This delay contrasts sharply with pedagogical approaches in other disciplines, where students regularly engage in discussion-based learning, creative exploration, or hands-on experimentation from the outset. Without an early demonstration of how programming can be used to solve relevant problems, non-STEM learners often struggle to recognize its value, leading to high attrition rates. This issue is particularly pronounced in courses where assessments focus mostly on syntactic correctness and debugging. The structure of many programming courses reinforces a rule-based learning model that fails to connect coding with practical, discipline-specific applications. Instruction might value abstract discussions on algorithmic efficiency, data structures, and computational logic, despite the fact that non-STEM learners may have little prior exposure to these concepts or their relevance to everyday problem-solving (Alda & Baralt-Torrijos, 2023).

This approach reflects a broader tendency in programming pedagogy to prioritize theoretical knowledge at the expense of hands-on engagement, which can alienate students who struggle to see how these principles apply to their academic or professional pursuits. Disciplines such as journalism, business, and the social sciences increasingly incorporate computational tools, yet introductory coding courses rarely tailor instruction to these fields.

Instead, they maintain a one-size-fits-all curriculum that emphasizes technical precision over contextualized learning, missing an opportunity to integrate coding as a valuable interdisciplinary skill. To enhance engagement, programming education must move toward more contextually relevant instruction that aligns with students' fields of study, ensuring that coding is framed as an adaptable skill rather than an isolated technical discipline.

Recent developments in introductory computer science assignments, such as those at Rutgers University, reflect a decision to integrate practical applications earlier in the learning process while still adhering to a syntax-first instructional model. Assignments like Fruit Costs and Character Counter (https://introcs.cs.rutgers.edu/assignment-5/) maintain traditional programming fundamentals—working with arrays, reading files, and processing textual data—but introduce more scenario-based activities that provide a more engaging context for students. For example, Fruit Costs requires students to read data from a file, manipulate arrays, and apply sorting logic to determine the lowest-cost fruits, reinforcing computational thinking through tangible applications. Likewise, Character Counter has students analyze character frequency in a text file, exposing them to underlying concepts in data processing and compression techniques commonly used in fields like linguistics and cybersecurity. These assignments provide a possible model of bridging theoretical learning with applied problem-solving, offering students a structured introduction to core programming constructs without requiring immediate deep engagement in complex problem-solving. At the same time, these assignments still assume syntax mastery as a prerequisite for meaningful engagement with computational logic. Students must first navigate constraints such as strict file handling procedures, careful attention to output formatting, and automated assessment parameters, which reinforce syntax precision before exploring broader problem-solving strategies. While these exercises provide valuable exposure to industry-relevant workflows, they remain within the syntax-first approaches, prioritizing low-level technical accuracy as a simple necessity if any actual programs are to be written.

Another challenge lies in the assessment models that dominate traditional programming courses. Many introductory courses rely on high-stakes, syntax-driven assessments where minor errors can result in significant penalties, discouraging students from experimenting with creative solutions (Sullivan et al., 2021). This approach is particularly discouraging for non-STEM learners, who may be unfamiliar with the correctness-based grading common in computing disciplines. Unlike assessments in the humanities or social sciences, where argumentation and conceptual reasoning are often prioritized, programming assessments typically emphasize error-free execution and strict syntactic adherence. These assessment models make it difficult to create space for productive failure—the valuable learning that occurs when students make mistakes in safe, supportive environments and learn from those mistakes. As a result, students become risk-averse, more concerned with avoiding mistakes rather than exploring different ways to solve problems. More flexible assessment models, which evaluate students based on their approach to problem-solving rather than on syntactic precision alone, could provide a more supportive framework for learning programming in interdisciplinary contexts. Recognizing that coding is as much about logical structuring and creative problem-solving as it is about syntax mastery is crucial in making programming education more inclusive and accessible to a wider range of students.

Until very recently, with the release of coding assistants, recommending "problem-solving" or "program design" over syntax mastery would be like recommending that students in English composition courses be taught how to write at the "paragraph level" instead of using individual sentences. It might be useful as a thought experiment to imagine writing an essay a paragraph at a time or even a full section at a time instead of laboring over subjects and predicates. But writing, like coding, still has to be typed in one character at a time. This sort of objection would be decisive without a tool that can write paragraphs at a time for the student. But now that such a tool exists, it is possible to experiment with conceptual design over word-by-word composition. Smart tools offer a compelling avenue for innovating programming education by dismantling many of the barriers imposed by syntax-heavy instruction. These next-generation learning platforms—exemplified by tools such as GitHub Copilot, GPT models within Cursor, or Replit Ghostwriter—introduce real-time error detection, adaptive guidance, and immediate feedback, opening opportunities for non-STEM learners who might otherwise be deterred by technical intricacies. Unlike pedagogies that demand memorization of syntax from the outset, automated systems emphasize interactive, project-based experiences, allowing instructors to reframe assignments away from the frustration of early debugging tasks toward gaining confidence by engaging with tangible projects rather than spending hours honing syntax precision (Johanyák et al., 2023). Such a transition is particularly valuable for learners with limited exposure to programming, as it empowers them to explore essential computational concepts without the cognitive burden of constant syntax correction. Through these platforms, students can generate functional code snippets or test rudimentary prototypes almost immediately, which cultivates a sense of mastery and encourages further exploration. This model of instruction, by foregrounding curiosity and creativity, appeals to a wider pool of learners who may not be drawn to abstract exercises or isolated technical drills. Ultimately, the move from rule-bound instruction to facilitated experimentation bolsters accessibility, thereby cultivating a more inclusive culture around coding education that benefits students across a range of disciplines.

Enhanced writing serves as a useful guide for redesigning programming instruction involving smart tools for a number of reasons. Even though GitHub Copilot preceded the broader introduction of chat applications into writing-intensive university courses, in certain ways, the use of AI for writing is a simpler test case that can help theorize new pedagogies for coding. In writing classrooms, the tools help insecure writers engage with logical reasoning and high-level problem-solving before focusing on sentence-level revisions. Proofreading is a simpler kind of debugging in that it involves fewer tools. The comparison is not exact or one-to-one, but it is useful to keep remembering the parallels between coding and writing and the challenges each will encounter in making productive and ethical use of the technology. Making these comparisons frequently also encourages an interdisciplinary habit of mind, which will be valuable if the thesis of this book reflects future practice.

Begin by imagining a student with poor writing skills entering a college English composition course and being confronted immediately with grammar-heavy worksheets. Now compare this with computer science curricula mandating early exposure to languages such as C, Java, or Python. Though C is more notorious for this, each of these languages necessitates scrupulous attention to punctuation, typing, and error handling. This requirement can be daunting for students who do not anticipate the level of technical rigor involved, sometimes leading to early attrition or a pervasive sense of inadequacy. Coding assistants mitigate these pitfalls by helping learners in structuring algorithms and organizing code logic using clear, conversational prompts rather than abstract syntax commands (Zviel-Girshin, 2024). In doing so, students develop foundational computational thinking skills through a more intuitive process, with algorithms guiding them toward effective code organization and solution generation. Smart systems serve as facilitative tools in this context, providing temporary support that can gradually fade as students develop their expertise. This structured approach has the added benefit of addressing diverse learning curves, as novices can move to syntax-intensive languages at a pace that reflects their growing understanding of logic and design principles. Educators who integrate machine learning platforms within their classrooms can thereby create graduated levels of complexity, lessening the likelihood that students will feel overwhelmed early in the term. Over time, this careful escalation in difficulty enhances learner engagement by ensuring mastery of each conceptual milestone before introducing new technical layers.

If supplemented with simple projects, this process of using assistive technologies that help with the syntax will create an interesting new fusion of the practical with the conceptual. Students outside STEM will be equally equipped to learn through this method. Tools like GitHub Copilot streamline coding by automating complex completions, eliminating the need to memorize intricate methods or library functions. ChatGPT complements this automation by translating dense programming concepts into language that resonates with humanities and business students. Replit Ghostwriter adds real-time debugging suggestions and refinement options, offering feedback that adapts to learner progress. Together, these tools transform the classroom into a space for iterative experimentation, where students refine their work through continuous cycles of validation. Researchers emphasize that this form of dynamic support not only enriches the cognitive experience but also heightens motivational levels, as learners observe direct connections between their exploratory actions and concrete results (Valový & Buchalcevova, 2023). By moving the balance of effort away from error correction and toward planning and creative thinking, AI-driven pedagogy reinvigorates the act of learning to code, engaging students who might otherwise become discouraged. Most significantly, this reorientation supports non-STEM learners to build tangible skills and create robust, discipline-relevant projects before becoming lost in the technical and quite unforgiving details of syntax. This makes it more likely that more students will complete such courses, seeing the value of programming as an adaptable toolset rather than a narrow technical specialty.

To fully realize the benefits of augmented instruction, academic institutions will need to carry out deliberate redesigns of programming curricula. It will be important to do more than just rewrite syllabi or rethink the choice of languages. Advances in infrastructure move so quickly now that ongoing experiments with AI-assisted projects should be used in each course to guide class redesign in between semesters for the foreseeable future. In practice, this might involve orchestrating early, AI-supported project work that aligns with students' fields of study—such as analyzing social media trends for communications majors or automating financial calculations for business students (Liu & Li, 2024). Such targeted projects can illustrate how coding is now able to move outside of conventional STEM applications and will broaden the appeal of programming modules within non-STEM courses as well as existing computer science offerings. Structured curricula should also incorporate regular milestones for collaborative assignments where learners can exchange creative solutions and develop a sense of shared expertise. Through the embedding of these experiences within a supportive framework, students build computational fluency while appreciating the practical relevance of programming in their chosen domains. AI-driven education is clearly on the edge of a future where coding is no longer relegated to a specialized class of technical experts. Programming is poised to become a universally accessible instrument for interdisciplinary problem-solving and innovation.

2.2 The Need for Immediate Wins: Hooking Students with Practical Applications

In the same spirit as this critique of syntax-heavy instruction, educators in introductory programming courses must acknowledge the value of

immediate wins—tangible achievements that boost motivation and clarify the applicability of coding skills. Cognitive load theory reinforces this
need, as early successes create intrinsic motivation that helps students persist when facing more complex challenges. The problematic scenario is one
in which students are constrained to lower-level tasks, such as memorizing
syntax and performing debugging drills, before being introduced to planning applications or at least specifications for applications the students might
dream of taking to market someday. This delayed gratification can erode
student interest, especially for non-STEM individuals who find it more difficult to see clear links between coding principles and their professional or
academic pursuits (Alda & Baralt-Torrijos, 2023).

By contrast, platforms like GitHub Copilot, Replit Ghostwriter, and
ChatGPT, as implemented within editors like Cursor or Windsurf, give
learners near-instant access to the world of proficient coding. Admittedly,
this is a kind of illusion. But much of the early learning process is an illusion
of knowledge that further practice converts to actual understanding. In these
coding environments, students analyze, refine, and critique generated solutions—applying the kind of "editorial thinking" valued across collaborative,
knowledge-oriented professions. This approach reflects broader changes in
professional practice, where the automation of routine tasks creates space for
intellectual creativity. Students can now build working programs and prototypes in their earliest coursework, sparking enthusiasm for increasingly
complex computational challenges. When introduced as interactive problem-
solving exercises rather than syntax drills, these experiences build student
confidence naturally and create opportunities for productive failure—where
students learn from mistakes in low-risk, supportive environments. Early
integration of these solutions connects coding concepts to concrete objectives, showing students immediately how programming serves as a versatile
tool for real-world problems (Marwan et al., 2020).

Introducing these assistants into programming curricula requires conversations about rethinking pedagogical goals. In English courses, it will
become necessary to ask whether sentence-level proficiency is a required
goal for every student or whether some general education writing courses
might serve students better by assuming sentence-level skill via generative tools and teaching students higher levels of organizing arguments and
research. Similar questions about coding at the "sentence level" will be just
as challenging as English professors debating the nature of writing itself.
Even if radical goals are not adopted and syntactic competence is retained as
a goal, it will still be important to reconsider how students develop and demonstrate computational competencies. Some will certainly argue that tools
such as GitHub Copilot may mitigate the mechanical hurdles of introductory
coursework, but these same tools introduce the risk of learners relying on
outputs without understanding the logic behind them (Mbiada et al., 2024).
To counteract this potential superficiality, educators must guide students to

probe, evaluate, and interpret generated code. A plausible revised goal of introductory courses will be to address directly this potential reliance on automated assistance. Rather than allowing code generation to become a simple "whack-a-mole" exercise—where learners fix errors as they appear— curricula should emphasize the reasoning processes that underlie each fix. Students can be taught to collaborate with their tools in a way that engages with algorithmic design and problem decomposition. As students gain confidence, they move beyond simply editing generated code to develop and express their own solutions, treating technology as an active collaborator in the process.

The emphasis on practical, applied learning highlights deployment as a crucial educational component. Modern coding instruction recognizes that students learn best when they can recast abstract concepts into working applications—projects they can share with peers and continuously improve through real-world testing and feedback. Although introductory programming courses have emphasized syntax and algorithmic logic, they often marginalize the process of hosting and maintaining applications in live environments (Korada, 2022). This omission leaves many students ill-prepared for professional contexts, where deploying stable and secure web services constitutes a critical skill. Introducing students early to foundational deployment strategies—such as configuring web servers or integrating continuous delivery pipelines—can bridge the gap between classroom exercises and workplace demands (Nimje, 2024). HTML and JavaScript afford a particularly straightforward introduction, enabling novices to publish interactive projects on the web without complex toolchains. Meanwhile, low-code and no-code platforms open up these capabilities further, allowing students to spend time on design, content, and functionality rather than intricate configuration tasks (Rao et al., 2023). By underscoring deployment from the outset, educators highlight the tangible value of coding expertise and position learners to develop marketable skill sets. In this manner, centering attention on deployment not only nurtures technical proficiency but also instills confidence by demonstrating how learners' efforts manifest in public-facing, accessible applications.

Building on the importance of deployment, the next step in evolving coding education involves leveraging smart platforms to sustain student engagement through interactive tasks. Traditional assignments, which rely on relatively pre-scripted problems, often limit learners' ability to explore novel or personalized project pathways (Kazemitabaar et al., 2024). Intelligent environments, in contrast, tailor challenges to each student's development, providing real-time feedback and presenting adaptive exercises that align with individual goals. This immediacy of response mitigates common frustrations—such as waiting for instructor review or repeatedly debugging the same error—thus cultivating a more positive learning atmosphere (Marwan et al., 2020). The iterative success model offered by new platforms encourages students to experiment and refine solutions, reinforcing a growth mindset integral to persistent intellectual engagement. This approach creates perfect conditions for productive failure, where students can take risks, make mistakes, and learn from those errors in an environment that provides immediate guidance without judgment. Educators can also embed deployment tasks into these interactive exercises, ensuring that the coding process culminates in tangible, web-accessible outputs. When combined, these elements redesign programming from a series of isolated steps into an ongoing, dynamic conversation between learners, automated feedback mechanisms, and practical applications. As students witness the immediate impact of their code, they become active participants in a feedback loop that deepens conceptual understanding and supports long-term retention.

Moving from a focus on individualized feedback, it is also crucial to align introductory coding lessons with the diverse academic or professional interests of students through supported, domain-specific tasks. Traditionally, course outlines present programming challenges pulled from mathematics, physics, or the history of theoretical computation. These problem sets can be particularly apt to drain motivation for non-STEM learners who struggle to perceive how low-level syntax drills apply to their fields. This disconnect directly contradicts the principles of authentic learning, which emphasize the importance of situating education in contexts relevant to students' goals and interests. New resources counter this limitation by automatically customizing tutorials and problem sets to resonate with varied disciplines—such as text analysis for journalism students or automated financial reporting for business majors (Fenu et al., 2024). By tying coding basics to recognizable projects, educators offer a clearer trajectory for applying programming skills outside the computer science realm. This strategy not only sparks higher motivation but also streamlines the transition from conceptual understanding to tangible outcomes, thanks to rapcode generation and debugging. Studies reveal that learners who tackle contextualized projects display heightened problem-solving abilities and deeper knowledge retention (Dann et al., 2022). In essence, weaving domain-specific tasks into early coursework nurtures a sense of immediate utility, thereby making programming an inclusive and interdisciplinary skill rather than a narrowly specialized tool.

Expanding on the role of contextualized projects, educators can further support learners by using platforms to break down programming concepts into small, structured milestones. Conventional teaching approaches often inundate students with a broad array of variables, loops, and syntax rules in rapid succession, contributing to cognitive overload (Shaka et al., 2023). In contrast, a step-by-step framework enables students to focus on individual elements of programming—such as understanding a single data type or perfecting a basic loop—before adding complexity. Assistants like ChatGPT and GitHub Copilot excel at generating incremental prompts and supplying immediate feedback, allowing learners to correct misunderstand-ings and reinforce newly acquired skills (Marwan et al., 2020). This iterative process engenders frequent "wins," where students successfully implement mini-features or small code segments, encouraging satisfaction and further engagement. Over time, these achievements accumulate into a robust skill set, enabling novices to tackle larger, more sophisticated tasks with confi-dence. When deployment is integrated into these micro-tasks, learners also gain experience in updating and testing live applications, bridging the gap between textbook practice and real-world application in a manageable, moti-vating format.

Another significant dimension involves adaptive coding environments that permit natural language interaction, effectively inverting the traditional sequence of learning. Rather than first mastering syntax intricacies, stu-dents can articulate program goals and logic in human-readable text, with the machine translating these descriptions into functioning code (Rao et al., 2023). This approach lowers initial barriers to entry, enabling learners to refine their problem-solving strategies before contending with the syntactic nuances of a chosen language. Research suggests that students exposed to this method develop superior debugging and algorithmic reasoning skills because they gain a conceptual grasp of what the program should achieve, independent of technical jargon (Pope et al., 2024). By allowing novices to navigate code creation at a more intuitive level, natural language systems reduce early-stage failures and enhance the sense of control and agency. Additionally, these adaptive environments can incorporate real-time deploy-ment previews, thus reinforcing the connection between logical ideas and live, interactive outputs. Through such an approach, we transcend mere cod-ing assistance and the system becomes a catalyst for student-led discovery and iterative improvement.

Natural language interactions with such tools have reimagined introduc-tory programming as a realm of creative exploration and design. When novices can delegate syntax polishing and typographical troubleshooting to automated assistants, the classroom dynamic reorients (Korada, 2022). This liberation creates room for projects where visual aesthetics, user experi-ence design, and narrative development take center stage—elements often neglected in traditional beginner curricula despite their power to broaden coding's appeal. Consider how platforms like Replit Ghostwriter offer real-time debugging guidance and optimization suggestions, inviting students to venture into sophisticated territory such as game mechanics or multimedia integration (Fenu et al., 2024). The consequence extends beyond efficiency: learners develop genuine ownership of their programming journey as they channel their energy toward conceptualizing distinctive features and craft-ing responsive user interactions. When interfaces break down the techni-cal aspects, programming evolves from an exercise in memorizing bracket placements and function declarations into a genuine creative endeavor.

This approach particularly resonates with students from non-STEM backgrounds, who discover meaningful connections when coding becomes a vehicle for expression and problem-solving within their existing passions and disciplinary interests.

Continuing the emphasis on creativity and user-centered design, front-end programming stands out as an especially effective entry point for augmented curricula. Languages like HTML, CSS, and JavaScript yield immediate visual results, allowing students to see the impact of their efforts as they modify a web page or implement interactive elements (Nimje, 2024). This rapid feedback loop, augmented by generative suggestions, not only enriches the learning process but also boosts learner confidence by showcasing tangible outcomes early on (Kazemitabaar et al., 2024). For instance, platforms like CodeAid and Webflow can generate layout options or recommend CSS modifications, reducing the initial technical overhead. As beginners develop competencies in these front-end technologies, they become better positioned to transition into more complex realms of programming, including back-end frameworks and data-intensive applications. Studies indicate that learners who begin with front-end tasks in enabled environments tend to advance more quickly to full-stack projects, likely because they have already established a comfortable familiarity with deploying and iterating on live web applications (Shaka et al., 2023).

Incorporating assistants at this stage thus provides a robust framework for integrating creativity, frequent concrete feedback, and structured skill progression. A compelling illustration of this assisted, project-based learning can be seen in assignments that guide students toward implementing a functional web browser. Exercises of this sort blend graphical user interface (GUI) development, event-driven programming, and deployment in a manner immediately applicable to both academic and professional contexts. Students learn to handle features like page rendering, browser navigation history, and user-driven events, exposing them to core principles of software engineering without overwhelming them with technical minutiae. Debugging and code-generation tools facilitate this process, offering real-time suggestions that help students navigate potential pitfalls while still requiring them to reason about application structure (Marwan et al., 2020). Research highlights that such interactive, real-world assignments can significantly improve engagement and problem-solving acumen, especially when learners can preview their work in a live environment. Educators who leverage applications in these projects enable newcomers to acquire deployment-ready programming skills—ranging from front-end design to back-end architecture—within a single, unifying assignment. As a result, students not only leave introductory courses with a robust portfolio piece but also gain confidence in their capacity to translate conceptual lessons into tangible, user-facing software.

2.3 Addressing Attrition and Retention in STEM and Non-STEM Classrooms

Retention in programming courses remains a formidable challenge, particularly among learners who fail to perceive the immediate relevance of early exercises. Traditional curricula frequently defer hands-on engagement, centering initial lessons on syntax mastery and debugging rather than applications built for believable business or consumer use cases. This delayed immersion leads many non-STEM students to disengage, as they approach coding primarily to enhance research, creative initiatives, or career-related skill sets rather than to master technical minutiae. The problem is exacerbated by the cognitive load created by syntax-heavy instruction, where students must devote significant mental resources to memorizing rules before experiencing any meaningful success. Scholars have noted that early exposure to purposeful, goal-directed assignments aligned with student interests can markedly bolster retention, given that it underscores the practical utility of programming (Fenu et al., 2024). Through enabling learners to create discipline-specific projects from the outset, platforms provide a structured yet flexible avenue for immediate, meaningful participation, thereby reinforcing motivation and conceptual understanding prior to tackling more intricate syntax. Educators who introduce such deployable, interactive applications early in the curriculum cultivate an environment in which coding is perceived not as an abstract technical hurdle, but as a potent means for innovation and problem-solving (Table 2.2).

One promising strategy for mitigating attrition entails integrating guided feedback and support into initial coursework, thereby allowing students to circumvent early syntax frustration and concentrate on designing functional applications. Tools such as GitHub Copilot, ChatGPT, and Replit Ghostwriter function as cognitive prosthetics, offering real-time code generation, error correction, and contextual clarifications, reducing cognitive load and instilling confidence in novice programmers (Kazemitabaar et al., 2024). Instructors who tailor these resources to domain-specific projects—ranging from automated text analytics for journalism to financial modeling for business—demonstrate coding's direct relevance to diverse professional pathways. Studies indicate that students who engage with interactive, career-focused assignments consistently exhibit elevated persistence levels and stronger conceptual retention (Marwan et al., 2020). Through such tailored, supported instruction, learners gain a sense of autonomy over their progress, as the platforms dynamically adjust to individual needs and skill gaps. This personalized structure not only enhances the early coding experience but also diminishes the likelihood of students abandoning the course before reaching advanced, syntax-intensive topics. These adaptive methods strengthen academic continuity and facilitate engagement among a broader population

TABLE 2.2

Reasons for Attrition in Programming Education and Solutions

Reason for Attrition	Why This Is a Problem	Proposed Solution
Early Syntax Frustration	Syntax-heavy instruction overwhelms students before they understand programming logic, leading to disengagement.	Use debugging tools to reduce syntax frustration and allow students to focus on logic and structure.
Delayed Exposure to Practical Applications	Students do not see the immediate relevance of coding, making it feel abstract and disconnected from their interests.	Incorporate project-based learning early, using real-world applications to demonstrate coding's value.
Disconnect between Student Expectations and Instruction	Many students expect to build applications or analyze data but encounter syntax drills and debugging exercises instead.	Align coursework with student goals by integrating coding projects relevant to their academic disciplines.
Lack of Personalized Support	Without adaptive learning tools, students struggle to keep pace, leading to frustration and attrition.	Implement tutoring and foundational tools that adjust difficulty based on individual learning progress.
Rigid Assessment Models	Assessments center on syntactic correctness rather than conceptual problem-solving, discouraging experimentation.	Revise assessments to evaluate logical reasoning, creativity, and applied problem-solving rather than rote syntax accuracy.
Limited Interdisciplinary Integration	Courses rarely tailor programming instruction to fields like journalism, business, or humanities, limiting its perceived value.	Exp interdisciplinary coding applications to show programming's relevance across all fields.
Perceived Complexity and Intimidation	Many non-STEM students view programming as highly technical and inaccessible, discouraging them from persisting.	Introduce learning models that guide students through coding gradually, reducing perceived complexity.
One-Size-Fits-All Curriculum Design	Traditional curricula assume prior computational thinking skills, disadvantaging students without programming backgrounds.	Develop adaptive curricula that provide multiple learning pathways based on students' backgrounds and interests.
Insufficient Hands-On Learning	Courses emphasize theoretical syntax over project-based learning, reducing engagement and motivation.	Use generated templates and real-time feedback to reinforce learning through hands-on coding exercises.
High Cognitive Load in Early Stages	Students are expected to handle syntax, debugging, and problem-solving simultaneously, increasing cognitive overload.	Break down coding instruction into manageable stages, allowing students to build confidence progressively.

of learners, both within and beyond fields like computer science, successfully transitioning from novice to proficient programmer.

One of the primary reasons students disengage from programming education is early frustration with syntax-heavy instruction, which can act as a
barrier to developing computational thinking. Traditional curricula emphasize mastery of syntax and debugging before students engage with practical
problem-solving, creating an environment that feels detached from real-
world applications. Research suggests that students who struggle with early
syntax errors and debugging challenges experience higher cognitive load,
which leads to increased frustration and decreased motivation to continue
learning programming (Chipchase et al., 2017). Many non-STEM learners approach coding with an expectation of applying computational skills
to their respective disciplines, yet they encounter pedagogical models that
prioritize technical correctness over conceptual engagement. This disconnect creates an environment antithetical to productive failure—instead of
learning from mistakes in a supportive environment, students experience
failure as discouraging and demotivating. Early syntax instruction leads
to increased attrition rates, particularly among students who do not see
immediate connections between programming and their academic interests
(Greener, 2018). Learning platforms can mitigate these issues by automating
syntax correction and offering real-time feedback, allowing students to concentrate on conceptual understanding and application-based learning rather
than rote memorization.

Delayed exposure to practical applications of coding is another significant
factor contributing to disengagement, particularly for non-STEM students.
Many introductory courses fail to introduce students to real-world coding
scenarios until they have mastered syntax and debugging, delaying the
gratification of applying their knowledge in meaningful ways. Research has
shown that students who do not experience early, tangible applications of
programming concepts are more likely to drop out of coding courses, particularly when compared to those who engage with interactive, project-based
learning from the start (Saito & Smith, 2017). This gap between theoretical
instruction and practical application is especially evident in non-computer
science disciplines, where students expect coding to be a tool for analysis,
visualization, or creative expression rather than an isolated technical skill.
A lack of hands-on projects in the early stages of programming education
erodes student interest, making it more difficult to retain non-STEM learners
who may otherwise benefit from computational literacy (Azmi et al., 2016). To
bridge this divide, curricula must incorporate both assistance and domain-
specific applications that allow students to see the immediate relevance of
programming within their fields of study.

A principal disconnect exists between student expectations of coding as
a creative, applied skill and the reality of syntax-focused, abstract instruction, further exacerbating disengagement. Students often arrive in programming courses eager to create applications, analyze data, and build automated

systems. Instead, they encounter abstract syntax rules and debugging drills that seem divorced from their aspirations (Nicholson & Putwain, 2014). This disconnect particularly affects non-STEM learners in journalism, business, and the arts, who view programming as a tool to advance their existing work. Traditional instruction insists on technical mastery before any practical application, implying that only those with specialized expertise can succeed at coding. McKay and Dunn (2020) found that students demonstrate greater persistence when coursework directly connects to their academic and career objectives. Intelligent platforms address this challenge by tailoring instruction to individual interests, allowing learners to tackle relevant projects from the start. When educators prioritize hands-on applications early in the curriculum, they help students bridge the divide between their expectations and classroom experiences, strengthening sustained engagement with programming concepts.

One way to do this is to introduce students to HTML and JavaScript early in programming courses to provide a gateway to creating web applications that they can immediately see and share, reinforcing motivation and engagement. Unlike back-end languages requiring complex setup and abstract computational logic, front-end programming enables immediate visual feedback, which has been shown to increase retention in beginner learners (Meehan, 2019). When students can deploy functional projects within the first few weeks of coursework, they gain a tangible sense of accomplishment, making programming feel relevant rather than mechanical. Research suggests that students engaging with interactive, web-based coding exercises develop greater persistence in learning programming concepts than those exposed solely to syntax drills (Tewes, 2019). The ability to see results in real time nurtures curiosity, prompting students to explore more advanced concepts with confidence rather than apprehension. The integration of assisted guidance enables students to experiment with modifying and troubleshooting code in a low-risk, high-reward environment, ensuring that they remain actively engaged. These early successes lay the foundation for deeper computational thinking, encouraging students to approach coding as a problem-solving tool rather than an isolated technical skill.

A hands-on, results-driven approach makes programming feel more relevant and rewarding, significantly increasing student retention and engagement. Studies have shown that learners are more likely to persist in programming coursework when early assignments center on practical applications rather than rote syntax exercises (Umar & Ko, 2022). Incorporating assisted, project-based learning models allows students to create small but meaningful digital projects, reinforcing their learning through immediate visual and interactive feedback. For instance, students designing a basic interactive website or a simple data visualization tool experience direct, real-world applications of their work, which strengthens their understanding of coding principles. Research indicates that providing interactive, exploratory programming exercises leads to higher knowledge retention and conceptual understanding (Inan & Inan, 2015). By allowing students to iterate on their code with automated recommendations, instructors can create an engaging learning environment that mirrors real-world software development. This methodology bridges the gap between theoretical learning and practical problem-solving, ensuring students remain invested beyond introductory coursework.

Demonstrating practical applications of coding early on can support student motivation to learn the technical and theoretical underpinnings as they progress. Many non-STEM learners initially struggle to see the relevance of programming, particularly when early coursework focuses on abstract syntax and debugging rather than applied problem-solving. Research has found that students are more likely to persist in coding courses when introduced to contextualized programming tasks that align with their academic interests (Umar & Ko, 2022). Domain-specific exercises, powered by platforms, allow journalism, business, and humanities students to explore programming applications directly relevant to their fields (Tewes, 2019). Rather than presenting coding as a rigid technical discipline, these customized learning paths demonstrate its versatility as a problem-solving framework with broad applications. Through carefully structured challenges in integrative environments, initial student enthusiasm develops into sustained engagement and deeper mastery of programming concepts.

After identifying reasons for attrition and providing early engagement, assisted learning platforms can then provide adaptive guidance, ensuring students receive personalized support at critical learning stages. Traditional programming education often assumes a one-size-fits-all model, requiring students to master syntax and debugging before engaging with practical applications. However, these platforms offer adaptive learning environments that adjust to individual learning speeds and needs (Johanyák et al., 2023). These systems utilize machine learning algorithms to track student progress, offering real-time feedback and personalized lesson plans that emphasize areas needing improvement (Murthy et al., 2024). Research suggests that students who receive adaptive, machine guidance exhibit greater retention and engagement, as they are less likely to become discouraged by early programming challenges (Wu et al., 2023). The implementation of smart tutoring systems in coding education has proven particularly beneficial for students with no prior programming experience, as these tools provide a low-stress, high-reward environment where learners can experiment with coding in a structured yet flexible manner. By tailoring instruction to individual strengths and weaknesses, learning platforms provide a mechanism to engage students in progress at a sustainable pace.

Lowering entry barriers through generative instruction simplifies early learning curves without sacrificing conceptual depth. Traditional coding education frequently overwhelms beginners with syntax-heavy, error-prone exercises, creating frustration and disengagement (Niu et al., 2022). Augmented instruction mitigates these issues by providing natural language explanations, contextual suggestions, and automated code corrections, allowing students to understand programming concepts before delving into technical complexities (Thuan et al., 2024). These tools facilitate low-stakes experimentation, enabling students to explore computational logic without fear of failure. A study on generated learning content found that interactive, context-aware feedback significantly improves student confidence and ability to apply programming concepts (Johanyák et al., 2023). Through integrating generative instruction, educators can gradually introduce students to more complex coding structures, ensuring that foundational computational thinking skills precede syntax mastery rather than being hindered by it. This approach not only improves student comprehension but also encourages a more inclusive and accessible coding education model.

Debugging tools also minimize early frustration, allowing students to focus on creative problem-solving before tackling complex error resolution. One of the primary challenges in learning to program is navigating syntax errors, logic bugs, and runtime issues, which can often overwhelm beginners and lead to high dropout rates (Johanyák et al., 2023). These debugging tools, such as intelligent code reviewers and automated error detection systems, help students identify and correct mistakes in real time, reducing the cognitive burden of manual debugging (Murthy et al., 2024). These systems do not merely provide answers but instead offer guided explanations, helping students understand the logic behind corrections and develop self-sufficiency in troubleshooting. Research shows that students who use debugging tools demonstrate greater persistence and a higher likelihood of successfully completing coding assignments (Wu et al., 2023). Through debugging assistance, educators can enhance the process of error correction with a taste of conceptual mastery, letting students tackle computational problems without getting derailed by minor syntax issues. This approach builds student confidence while presenting programming as a dynamic, iterative process.

Coding tools have also broadened programming from a computer science specialty into a versatile skill spanning academic disciplines. Where coding was once seen as the exclusive domain of technical majors, it now reaches students in journalism, business, and digital humanities through applications that adapt to diverse contexts (Bolger & Caballero, 2024). Journalists apply natural language processing to analyze text datasets, uncover trends, and automate reporting workflows. Business students harness predictive modeling for market analysis, making data-driven decisions without needing deep coding expertise. These applications demonstrate that coding is no longer confined to software development; instead, learning platforms facilitate computational literacy as a valuable tool for any field requiring data analysis, automation, or digital content creation. Expanding coding pathways beyond computer science to journalism, business analytics, education, and digital humanities requires rethinking how instruction is structured and delivered. Educational platforms that offer customized learning experiences tailored to the needs of each discipline provide domain-specific coding exercises that align with students' professional goals (Jung, 2020). For instance, digital humanities scholars can utilize data visualization tools to map historical narratives, while educators can develop interactive learning platforms that automate grading and adapt content delivery based on student performance. Research suggests that students who engage with programming in a discipline-specific context show higher retention and improved problem-solving skills compared to those following a traditional, generalized coding curriculum (Takerngsaksiri et al., 2023). By integrating interdisciplinary applications, programming education becomes more accessible and relevant to a broader range of students, ensuring that computational skills are embraced across multiple fields.

Adapting curricula to generative workflows allows students to engage with logic and problem-solving first, before tackling debugging and syntax-heavy programming. Many smart learning systems consider intuitive, natural language-based coding environments, where students describe desired outcomes, and the system generates code that they can then refine and troubleshoot (Zhuang & Lin, 2024). This approach enables students to understand programming logic before grappling with syntax constraints, making learning more intuitive and engaging. Platforms such as ChatGPT and GitHub Copilot offer step-by-step explanations and auto-suggestions, allowing students to develop confidence in problem-solving before becoming overwhelmed by syntax errors (Israilidis et al., 2024). By structuring programming courses around progressive problem-solving, educators can create a more inclusive and scalable model that aligns with student learning needs across disciplines.

Algorithmic retention strategies play a crucial role in ensuring that students progress at their own pace, making programming an accessible and scalable literacy rather than an exclusive technical discipline. Traditional programming courses often impose uniform pacing, leading to frustration for students who struggle with syntax-heavy instruction or who lack prior exposure to computational thinking (Seery et al., 2021). Smart learning platforms personalize instruction by tracking student progress and adjusting content dynamically, ensuring that learners receive the necessary support without falling behind. Research suggests that students who receive assisted guidance show greater persistence and long-term engagement in programming coursework (Mozer et al., 2019). This adaptive learning approach is particularly valuable for non-traditional students, allowing them to develop programming fluency through iterative, feedback-driven experiences.

Allowing students to focus on conceptual understanding before syntax mastery enables greater flexibility in learning pathways, reducing the intimidation factor associated with coding. Many introductory programming courses still require syntax-heavy proficiency before students can apply computational skills, which can discourage engagement early on. Enhanced educational tools provide interactive learning environments that emphasize logical problem-solving, allowing students to experiment with coding concepts without being immediately penalized for syntax errors. Research by Yeni et al. (2024) demonstrates that students who begin with conceptual exercises outperform those starting with syntax drills, showing stronger retention of computational thinking skills that transfer across disciplines. This reorientation toward higher-order reasoning makes programming more accessible to learners with diverse approaches to problem-solving.

Such automated assistance creates an environment where students can explore and experiment as they develop computational mastery aligned with their academic interests. Traditional instruction often prioritizes technical correctness, but intelligent interfaces encourage students to test ideas and refine solutions through immediate feedback (Mozer et al., 2019). This experimental approach reflects contemporary software development practices, where creative problem-solving emerges through cycles of testing and refinement. Students who participate in guided exploratory projects demonstrate greater persistence in their programming studies and maintain these skills throughout their careers (Adenubi & Samuel, 2024). The integration of these tools changes programming education from rigid syntax instruction into a dynamic discipline centered on practical applications, equipping students with the creative and analytical capabilities needed in professional environments.

2.4 Early Deployment for Early Wins

Critics of the practical-first approach frequently posit that students may lack robust debugging and troubleshooting abilities when generated outputs prove erroneous or incomplete. However, recent evidence indicates that postponing intricate troubleshooting tasks until learners have gained confidence through initial successes creates deeper engagement and stronger problem-solving competencies in students (Jung, 2020). A flipped pedagogical framework, in which beginners spend the most time on rapidly deploying functional prototypes with assistance, underscores coding as a creative, goal-oriented activity rather than an unrelenting experience of finding and correcting syntax errors (Table 2.3) (Israilidis et al., 2024). By allowing learners to construct small, deployable projects early in the curriculum, educators reinforce the immediacy and utility of programming in real-world contexts. Tools like GitHub Copilot, ChatGPT, and Replit Ghostwriter accelerate learning through immediate, context-aware feedback, removing many obstacles that traditionally discourage newcomers to programming. Interactive coding tasks provide constant reinforcement, creating early victories that sustain student interest—especially valuable for those incorporating programming into interdisciplinary research and creative projects (Bolger & Caballero, 2024). When instruction begins with practical applications rather

TABLE 2.3

Recommendations for Early Deployment in Programming Education

Recommendation	Rationale
Prioritize Functional Deployments Early	Allow students to create small, deployable projects early on, reinforcing motivation and showing immediate utility.
Leverage Real-Time Feedback	Use tools like GitHub Copilot, ChatGPT, and Replit Ghostwriter to provide instant, interactive coding feedback.
Introduce Visually Oriented Web Development	Start with HTML, CSS, and JavaScript to offer tangible, visual outputs that reinforce coding logic before syntax mastery.
Incorporate Assisted Design and Digital Literacy	Link coding education to familiar digital practices, such as content creation tools and social media platforms, to increase relevance.
Scaffold Learning with Adaptive Tutors	Personalize learning pathways with tutors that adjust difficulty levels dynamically, ensuring optimal engagement and progression.

than abstract concepts, students discover meaningful connections to their work, leading to stronger retention and continued enthusiasm for programming. This reorganization of foundational coursework prioritizes functional deployment over syntax memorization, creating an environment where students build confidence through practical successes before tackling advanced debugging and algorithmic concepts.

As novices advance in their studies, a focus on generated outputs transitions naturally into an exploration of their inherent limitations, prompting students to refine or replace imprecise code. Upon revisiting these early projects, learners can apply a stronger understanding of programming logic to debug and optimize their applications, having already experienced the satisfaction of producing workable prototypes at the onset of their studies (Mozer et al., 2019). This contrast stands in marked relief to conventional models, where beginners are swamped by syntax errors before they ever perceive coding's capacity for practical problem-solving. Preliminary research further suggests that structured assisted instruction—especially when paired with low-stakes project-based learning—cultivates an intuitive sense of computational thinking, helping students detect patterns in automated errors and devise methodical solutions (Seery et al., 2021). At the time of the conclusion of such a course, learners can undertake comprehensive debugging and troubleshooting with a sense of purpose, equipped with both hands-on familiarity and a foundational comprehension of coding principles. This strategic, graduated integration thus broadens the appeal of programming for students in humanities, business, and other disciplines, reinforcing the notion that computational thinking constitutes a dynamic, interdisciplinary skill rather than a niche technical specialty. In so doing, early wins and iterative feedback alter initial learning hurdles into catalysts for sustained exploration, ultimately empowering a diverse population of learners to thrive within an evolving coding landscape.

Smart web technologies present an opportunity to reimagine beginner-level programming courses by delivering instant, adaptive feedback that enhances student engagement. Unlike traditional models that rely on delayed instructor grading, platforms such as ChatGPT, GitHub Copilot, and Replit Ghostwriter allow learners to correct mistakes in real time, facilitating a more dynamic and iterative coding experience (Murthy et al., 2024). This immediate reinforcement greatly diminishes frustration, enabling students to refine their logic through trial and error without fixating on rote memorization of syntax (Wu et al., 2023). Additionally, natural language input options encourage learners to articulate desired outcomes in plain language, which the interface translates into functional code—a process that foregrounds computational thinking before delving into syntax details (Johanyák et al., 2023). Studies have shown that this method bolsters student confidence and reduces attrition rates, as novices can work at a pace that matches their comprehension, gradually ascending to more complex coding tasks (Thuan et al., 2024). Adaptive tutors further customize the learning trajectory by monitoring each student's performance, thereby adjusting the difficulty of subsequent challenges to maintain optimal engagement (Niu et al., 2022). In effect, this level of personalization not only supports students who may struggle with initial concepts but also keeps advanced learners motivated by introducing more complex problems in a timely manner. Thus, supportive systems reframe early coding exercises as interactive, low-stakes explorations rather than daunting technical hurdles, setting the stage for higher retention and stronger problem-solving skills among diverse learners.

Another key strategy for ensuring early wins involves capitalizing on web-based, visually oriented programming languages such as HTML and CSS, which allow students to create tangible, appealing projects without the intricate setup often associated with back-end development. HTML and CSS provide near-instant visual feedback, an approach shown to boost student motivation and a sense of accomplishment (Tew et al., 2017). Design tools, including CodePen and Webflow, go a step further by automating repetitive styling tasks and suggesting optimizations, thereby enabling learners to devote energy to creative exploration and conceptual understanding (Johanyák et al., 2023). JavaScript expands these possibilities by infusing interactivity, showcasing to newcomers how coding can directly influence real-world user experiences (Bolger & Caballero, 2024). When integrated into AI-powered platforms, JavaScript projects become a gateway for dynamic exercises—such as building quizzes, simple games, or interactive dashboards—that reinforce iterative problem-solving while minimizing frustrations from syntax errors (Zhuang & Lin, 2024). This low-friction, highly visual approach resonates strongly with non-STEM audiences, who may not initially identify as "coders" yet find immediate value in bringing creative ideas to life. By starting with front-end web development in a supportive environment, educators effectively introduce a pathway where students can refine foundational skills—like logic, layout, and basic event handling—before transitioning into more advanced programming domains. Such an emphasis on early, visually gratifying successes cultivates the resilience and confidence necessary for students to progress beyond surface-level familiarity and engage in deeper computational problem-solving.

This process of linking coding education to students' existing digital literacy further cements the role of programming as a relevant, accessible discipline. Many learners already possess experience with content creation platforms and social media tools, so weaving design and web development into these familiar digital practices eases the transition into formal coding principles (Bolger & Caballero, 2024). Researchers have noted that aligning new technical skills with existing digital competencies increases both engagement and comprehension, as students readily perceive how programming complements their day-to-day digital interactions (Niu et al., 2022). Platforms such as Wix ADI and Webflow leverage this familiarity by providing visually oriented interfaces, supplemented with generated code suggestions that teach underlying logic in manageable increments. Through project-based exercises—like personal portfolio sites or interactive multimedia galleries—students quickly discover how coding augments their capacity to share, analyze, and present information creatively (Murthy et al., 2024). Autocompletion and code-generation features guide them through step-by-step refinements, ensuring that each revision adds to conceptual clarity rather than devolving into rote syntax practice (Wu et al., 2023). This experiential model broadens the appeal of programming beyond computer science majors, as it underscores how coding can enhance research projects, creative endeavors, and professional skill sets in virtually any field. Ultimately, framing programming as a natural extension of digital literacy, rather than an isolated technical hurdle, promotes an inclusive educational environment where learners from all disciplines can acquire foundational coding skills, gain confidence through early accomplishments, and maintain sustained interest in pursuing more advanced computational tasks.

2.5 Shifting Troubleshooting and Debugging to Later Stages

A pivotal change in programming pedagogy involves postponing the rigorous emphasis on debugging until students have internalized core coding principles. Conventional courses prioritize syntax correctness from the outset, compelling novices to fix errors before they fully grasp the underlying logic of their code. This mismatch frequently leads to discouragement, especially for non-STEM learners who find themselves juggling syntax complexities alongside broader conceptual challenges. This approach directly contradicts cognitive load theory principles, as students must simultaneously master unfamiliar syntax while troubleshooting errors, overwhelming their working memory and creating significant barriers to learning. Instead, orienting curricula around immediate, hands-on projects in HTML and JavaScript allows learners to cultivate confidence and familiarity before delving into the intricacies of troubleshooting (Johanyák et al., 2023). Through foregrounding creativity and exploration early on, instructors reinforce the notion that programming is a versatile tool for crafting solutions, rather than an arcane set of rules. Learning platforms strengthen this approach by supplying real-time feedback, mitigating syntax-related frustrations, and enabling novices to explore coding's possibilities without becoming mired in early-stage debugging (Wu et al., 2023).

Incorporating debugging at a later point in the curriculum empowers learners to develop robust problem-solving strategies once they possess a solid conceptual foundation. Studies reveal that students operating within assisted environments identify error patterns more effectively and refine their coding processes, rather than relying on trial and error (Murthy et al., 2024). Tools like GitHub Copilot and ChatGPT facilitate this growth by offering context-aware suggestions that learners can evaluate, interpret, and refine, thus foregrounding continuous improvement rather than repetitive error resolution (Thuan et al., 2024). By treating debugging as an integral step in the broader problem-solving continuum—rather than an initial barrier—educators guide students toward thoughtful engagement with both generated outputs and code logic. This progression creates ideal conditions for productive failure—where students can take risks and learn from mistakes within a supportive environment that encourages experimentation and growth. This progression aligns with professional software development practices, where iterative testing and refinement evolve alongside project goals rather than impeding early creative exploration. As a result, learners develop confidence in their capacity to diagnose and correct errors, reinforcing the significance of structured experimentation and supporting a more intuitive entry into programming education.

In fact, delaying rigorous debugging tasks until students have established a foundational understanding of coding logic can markedly lower frustration and attrition rates in introductory programming courses. Traditional curricula often introduce syntax correction and error resolution prematurely, burdening novices with both conceptual and technical hurdles (Wei et al., 2024). This steep learning curve proves especially daunting for non-STEM learners unfamiliar with computing basics, who may become discouraged when forced to tackle complex bugs before grasping essential problem-solving strategies (Shang & Sen, 2024). A more effective approach emphasizes conceptual mastery, allowing students to focus on building small, deployable projects using languages such as HTML and JavaScript before immersion in debugging challenges (Barros, Pinheiro, & Delgado, 2015). In these initial phases, tools provide real-time feedback and reduce syntax-related road-blocks, enabling students to experiment with coding constructs, enhance logical thinking, and gain confidence in their abilities (Wu et al., 2023). When debugging is finally introduced, learners approach it as a natural extension of their existing competencies rather than an overwhelming barrier. Studies show that this staged approach results in improved retention and stronger overall outcomes, as students have already formed meaningful connections between code structure, logic, and application (Johanyák et al., 2023). By balancing conceptual exploration and hands-on deployment before directing attention to error-correction skills, educators cultivate a more sustainable, motivating learning environment.

The development of coding proficiency flourishes when students encounter success through carefully structured project work, creating a foundation for sophisticated debugging practices. This approach replaces traditional sink-or-swim error resolution with a series of creative challenges that cultivate both technical skill and intellectual curiosity (Wei et al., 2024). Within this framework, intelligent learning environments reshape the development cycle, offering students immediate insight into how their code modifications affect program behavior. When students encounter coding obstacles, assistants like ChatGPT and GitHub Copilot contextualize these challenges, elevating the discussion beyond syntactical corrections to explore underlying programming principles and architectural decisions (Thuan et al., 2024). This collaborative dynamic reframes problem-solving as an interactive dialog between programmer and technology, replacing isolated troubleshooting with guided discovery (Murthy et al., 2024). As students document their progression through increasingly complex challenges, they develop a concrete record of their growing capabilities. This evolutionary approach reorients debugging from a potential source of discouragement into a catalyst for deeper code comprehension and refinement. Studies demonstrate that students who engage with these enhanced learning environments display markedly improved problem-solving capabilities and resilience, citing the structured guidance and contextual support as key factors in their development (Renzella et al., 2024).

Debugging can also illuminate broader coding principles by explaining why errors arise, rather than merely suggesting mechanical fixes. Many new programmers fixate on resolving individual mistakes, overlooking the logical underpinnings that caused them (Renzella et al., 2024). Modern systems—such as HypoCompass and Compiler-Integrated Conversational AI—offer context-rich explanations, connecting syntax flaws to deeper structural or algorithmic issues (Ma et al., 2023). This helps students see how small details can affect the integrity of the entire program, strengthening the link between debugging and conceptual clarity (Wei et al., 2024). In addition, such tools underscore metacognitive strategies by prompting users to reflect on the thought process behind each correction, thus equipping them for more complex tasks in later coursework. With repeated exposure to explanations from their automated assistants, learners gradually internalize debugging heuristics, enhancing their capacity to tackle a range of coding challenges independently (Shang & Sen, 2024). Through cultivating this iterative skill set, educators create a climate of continuous learning where missteps become opportunities for insight and improvement, rather than sources of anxiety or discouragement.

Debugging tools help students master code organization, styling, and maintainability—essential skills often overlooked in introductory programming courses. Modern code review systems and optimization tools encourage learners to consider clarity and efficiency rather than simple error patching (Barros, Pinheiro, & Delgado, 2015). Instead of overwhelming beginners with complex debugging tasks, this approach lets them improve their technique gradually through guided recommendations (Wei et al., 2024). As students implement incremental structural improvements, they learn to prevent cascading design flaws and resolve errors more efficiently in complex projects. The process reveals how subtle architectural changes can dramatically enhance code readability and performance, helping students understand programming as a craft that evolves through practice (Shang & Sen, 2024). When students embrace supported code refinement early in their learning, they produce more elegant solutions and develop sophisticated debugging techniques that serve them well as challenges mount (Renzella et al., 2024). This combination of rapid deployment, staged debugging practice, and continuous improvement creates a learning environment that values innovation and thoughtful code development over mere error prevention.

As this chapter has argued, delaying rigorous debugging tasks until students establish foundational coding proficiency can significantly enhance both confidence and retention across STEM and non-STEM audiences. Through an emphasis on early deployment, project-based exploration, and generative feedback, educators create an environment where newcomers learn to approach coding as an adaptable tool rather than an imposing technical barrier. Structured, iterative exposure to debugging—guided by algorithmic explanations—allows learners to develop robust problem-solving and metacognitive skills, ultimately transforming potential stumbling blocks into opportunities for deeper understanding. In parallel, assisted refactoring promotes better coding habits and conceptual clarity, ensuring that students acquire the discipline of writing maintainable, efficient code. Together, these strategies champion a more inclusive, goal-oriented approach to programming education—one that prioritizes meaningful creativity and innovation over rote syntax drills. As the curriculum progresses, learners are better equipped to tackle advanced technical challenges with confidence, harnessing the instrument not as a crutch but as a collaborative partner in the ongoing process of computational discovery.

References

Adenubi, A., & Samuel, N. (2024). Revolutionizing education with artificial intelligence and machine learning: Personalization, retention, and resource optimization. *Kasu Journal of Computer Science.* https://doi.org/10.47514/kjcs/2024.1.2 .0015

Alda, E., & Baralt-Torrijos, J. (2023). An expression-oriented approach to programming education. *2023 IEEE Integrated STEM Education Conference (ISEC)*, 282–285.

Azmi, S., Iahad, N. A., & Ahmad, N. (2016). Attracting students' engagement in programming courses with gamification. *2016 IEEE Conference on e-Learning, e-Management and e-Services (IC3e)*, 112–115.

Barros, L. N., Pinheiro, W. R., & Delgado, K. V. (2015). Learning to program using hierarchical model-based debugging. *Applied Intelligence, 43*, 544–563.

Bolger, E., & Caballero, M. (2024, March). Using natural language processing to explore instructional change strategies in undergraduate science education literature. In *Proceedings of the 55th ACM Technical Symposium on Computer Science Education V. 2* (pp. 1930–1930).

Chipchase, L., Davidson, M., Blackstock, F., Bye, R., Colthier, P., Krupp, N., Dickson, W., Turner, D. E., & Williams, M. T. (2017). Conceptualising and measuring student disengagement in higher education: A synthesis of the literature. *The International Journal of Higher Education, 6*(2), 31–42.

Dann, C., Redmond, P., Fanshawe, M., Brown, A., Getenet, S., Shaik, T., & Li, Y. (2022). Making sense of student feedback and engagement using artificial intelligence. *Australasian Journal of Educational Technology.* https://doi.org/10.14742/ajet.8903

Edwards, J. M., Ditton, J., Trninic, D., Swanson, H., Sullivan, S., & Mano, C. (2020, August). Syntax exercises in CS1. In *Proceedings of the 2020 ACM Conference on International Computing Education Research* (pp. 216–226).

Edwards, J. M., Fulton, E. K., Holmes, J. D., Valentin, J. L., Beard, D. V., & Parker, K. R. (2018, October). Separation of syntax and problem solving in introductory computer programming. In *2018 IEEE Frontiers in Education Conference (FIE)* (pp. 1–5). IEEE.

Fenu, G., Galici, R., Marras, M., & Reforgiato, D. (2024, June). Exploring student interactions with AI in programming training. In *Adjunct Proceedings of the 32nd ACM Conference on User Modeling, Adaptation and Personalization* (pp. 555–560).

Fojcik, M., Fojcik, M. K., Høyland, S. O., & Hoem, J. (2022). Challenges in teaching programming. *Education and New Developments, 1.* https://doi.org/10.36315 /2022v1end034

Greener, S. (2018). Student disengagement: Is technology the problem or the solution?. *Interactive Learning Environments, 26*(6), 716–717.

Inan, H., & Inan, T. (2015). 3Hs education: Examining hands-on, heads-on and hearts-on early childhood science education. *International Journal of Science Education, 37*(12), 1974–1991

Israilidis, J., Chen, W.-Y., & Tsakalerou, M. (2024). Software development and education: Transitioning towards AI-enhanced teaching. *2024 IEEE Global Engineering Education Conference (EDUCON)* (pp. 1–6).

Johanyák, Z., Cserkó, J., & Pásztor, A. (2023). AI-assisted university programming education in practice. *2023 IEEE 35th International Conference on Software Engineering Education and Training (CSEE&T)* (pp. 185–186).

Jung, H.-W. (2020). A study on the current state of artificial intelligence-based coding technologies and the direction of future coding education. *The International Journal of Advanced Culture Technology, 8*(3), 186–191.

Kazemitabaar, M., Ye, R., Wang, X., Henley, A. Z., Denny, P., Craig, M., & Grossman, T. (2024, May). Codeaid: Evaluating a classroom deployment of an llm-based programming assistant that balances student and educator needs. In *Proceedings of the CHI Conference on Human Factors in Computing Systems* (pp. 1–20).

Korada, L. (2022). Low code/no code application development-opportunity and challenges for enterprises. *International Journal On Recent And Innovation Trends In Computing And Communication, 10*(11), 209–218.

Liu, J., & Li, S. (2024). Toward artificial intelligence-human paired programming: A review of the educational applications and research on artificial intelligence code-generation tools. *Journal of Educational Computing Research*, 07356331241240460.

Ma, B., Chen, L., & Konomi, S. (2024). Enhancing programming education with ChatGPT: A case study on student perceptions and interactions in a python course. *Communications in Computer and Information Science*, 113–126. https://doi.org/10.48550/arXiv.2403.15472

Marwan, S., Gao, G., Fisk, S., Price, T., & Barnes, T. (2020). Adaptive immediate feedback can improve novice programming engagement and intention to persist in computer science. *Proceedings of the 2020 ACM Conference on International Computing Education Research*. https://doi.org/10.1145/3372782.3406264

Mbiada, A. K., Isong, B., & Lugayizi, F. (2024). PyLe: An interactive tool for improving python syntax mastery in non-computing students. *Journal of Information Systems and Informatics, 6*(2), 1008–1034.

McKay, L., & Dunn, J. (2020). Critical consciousness as a response to student disengagement: An initial teacher education case study. *Teaching Education, 31*(2), 162–176.

Meehan, S. (2019). *The effects of coding integration on student engagement and academic achievement in a 5th grade mathematics class* [Unpublished master's thesis]. Saint Catherine University.

Mozer, M., Wiseheart, M., & Novikoff, T. (2019). Artificial intelligence to support human instruction. *Proceedings of the National Academy of Sciences, 116*(9), 3953–3955.

Murthy, N., Kavya, S., Hemalatha, M. R., Kousalya, M. D., & Kavyashree, M. (2024). AI enabled personalized learning platform. *International Journal For Multidisciplinary Research*. https://doi.org/10.36948/ijfmr.2024.v06i03.23253

Nicholson, L., & Putwain, D. (2015). Facilitating re-engagement in learning: A disengaged student perspective. *The Psychology of Education Review, 39*(2), 37–41.

Nimje, P. (2024). The rise of low-code/no-code development platforms. *International Journal of Advanced Research in Science, Communication and Technology*. https://doi.org/10.48175/ijarsct-18974

Niu, S. J., Luo, J., Niemi, H., Li, X., & Lu, Y. (2022). Teachers' and students' views of using an AI-aided educational platform for supporting teaching and learning at Chinese schools. *Education Sciences, 12*(12), 858.

Pope, N., Vartiainen, H., Kahila, J., Laru, J., & Tedre, M. (2024, July). A no-code AI education tool for learning AI in K-12 by making machine learning-driven apps. In *2024 IEEE International Conference on Advanced Learning Technologies (ICALT)* (pp. 105–109). IEEE.

Rao, N., Tsay, J., Kate, K., Hellendoorn, V., & Hirzel, M. (2023). AI for low-code for AI. *ArXiv*.

Renzella, J., Vassar, A., Solano, L. L., & Taylor, A. (2024). Scaling CS1 support with compiler-integrated conversational AI. *ArXiv, abs/2408.02378*.

Saito, A., & Smith, M. (2017). Measurement and analysis of student disengagement in higher education: A preliminary study. *The International Journal of Higher Education, 5*(2), 29–46.

Seery, K., Barreda, A. A., Hein, S. G., & Hiller, J. L. (2021). Retention strategies for online students: A systematic literature review. *Journal of Global Education and Research, 5*(1), 72–84.

Shaka, M., Carraro, D., & Brown, K. (2023). Personalised programming education with knowledge tracing. *Proceedings of the 2023 Conference on Human Centered Artificial Intelligence: Education and Practice.* https://doi.org/10.1145/3633083.3633220

Shang, S., & Sen, G. (2024). Empowering learners with AI-generated content for programming learning and computational thinking: The lens of extended effective use theory. *Journal of Computer Assisted Learning, 40*, 1941–1958.

Sullivan, S., Swanson, H., & Edwards, J. (2021, March). Student attitudes toward syntax exercises in CS1. In *Proceedings of the 52nd ACM Technical Symposium on Computer Science Education* (pp. 782–788).

Takerngsaksiri, W., Warusavitarne, C., Yaacoub, C., Hou, M. H. K., & Tantithamthavorn, C. (2023). Students' perspectives on AI code completion: Benefits and challenges. *ArXiv, abs/2311.00177*.

Tew, Y., Tang, T. Y., & Lee, Y. (2017). A study on enhanced educational platform with adaptive sensing devices using IoT features. *2017 Asia-Pacific Signal and Information Processing Association Annual Summit and Conference (APSIPA ASC)* (pp. 375–379).

Tewes, A. (2019). The effects of incorporating coding on student experience and understanding of middle school mathematical concepts. Retrieved from Sophia, the St. Catherine University repository website: https://sophia.stkate.edu/maed/312

Thuan, T., De, N., & Văn Toai, N. (2024). Developing an adaptive learning platform based on artificial intelligence (AI) to personalize the learning experience. *International Journal of Management and Organizational Research, 3*(3), 34–38.

Umar, M., & Ko, I. (2022). E-learning: Direct effect of student learning effectiveness and engagement through project-based learning, team cohesion, and flipped learning. *Sustainability, 14*(3), 1724.

Valový, M., & Buchalcevova, A. (2023). The psychological effects of AI-assisted programming on students and professionals. *2023 IEEE International Conference on Software Maintenance and Evolution (ICSME)* (pp. 385–390).

Wei, Z., Lee, A. T. L., Lee, V. C. S., & Chan, W. (2024). Toward AI-facilitated learning cycle in integration course through pair programming with AI agents. *2024 36th International Conference on Software Engineering Education and Training (CSEE&T)* (pp. 1–5).

Wu, H., Fa, D., Wu, X., Tan, W., Chang, X., Gao, Y., & Weng, J. (2023). Research on the construction of intelligent programming platform based on AI-generated content. *Proceedings of the 15th International Conference on Education Technology and Computers.*

Yeni, S., Nijenhuis-Voogt, J., Saeli, M., Barendsen, E., & Hermans, F. (2024). Computational thinking integrated in school subjects–A cross-case analysis of students' experiences. *International Journal of Child-Computer Interaction*, 42, 100696.

Zhuang, T., & Lin, Z. (2024). The why, what, and how of AI-based coding in scientific research. *arXiv preprint arXiv:2410.02156.*

Zviel-Girshin, R. (2024). The good and bad of AI tools in novice programming education. *Education Sciences.* https://doi.org/10.3390/educsci14101089

3

The Power of AI Coding Assistants: Unlocking Computational Potential for All

Generative tools, including GitHub Copilot, Cursor, and Replit's Ghostwriter, are changing the coding education landscape by lowering cognitive barriers and broadening access to programming. This chapter examines the strengths of these smart platforms, illustrating how they reduce syntax-related hurdles through natural language inputs and, in so doing, broaden access to code generation for learners with varied backgrounds. Although these assistants expedite development by streamlining repetitive or error-prone tasks, they also raise concerns regarding overreliance on automated outputs and diminished critical thinking in problem-solving. The emphasis on their role in alleviating cognitive overload in this discussion highlights how these assistants allow students to concentrate on conceptual design, creativity, and computational thinking rather than rote syntax memorization. The chapter also explores the collaborative potential of generative coding environments, detailing how multidisciplinary teams can engage productively in software projects without extensive technical training. Through real-world illustrations, readers will witness how the tools augment workflows, spur innovative solutions, and encourage deeper engagement with computational concepts. Ultimately, the chapter argues that, when integrated judiciously, coding assistants promote a more inclusive, interactive, and innovation-driven approach to programming instruction, positioning computational literacy as an attainable skill for diverse learning communities.

3.1 Overview of AI Tools and Their Strengths

The widespread adoption of coding assistants has initiated a significant transformation in the way learners engage with programming. Rather than forcing students to memorize syntax, troubleshoot errors manually, and refine basic sequential code repeatedly, modern tools such as GitHub Copilot, Vercel, and Replit enable users to focus on problem-solving and conceptual understanding (Johanyák et al., 2023). These systems draw upon extensive machine learning datasets, supplying real-time suggestions and automated debugging support that streamlines the developmental process. Students

DOI: 10.1201/9781003637738-3

gain immediate insights into potential pitfalls, ranging from syntax issues to inefficient coding patterns, thus minimizing frustration while cultivating confidence and fluency. Researchers highlight that these platforms are especially beneficial for non-traditional learners, as they mitigate the steep learning curve associated with traditional programming curricula (Ma et al., 2024). By bridging skill gaps and facilitating interactive feedback, coding tools contribute to a more inclusive learning environment, where technical hurdles are less likely to deter students from diverse academic and professional backgrounds.

What is particularly noteworthy about this technological evolution is the ongoing pivot from passive assistants to more autonomous learning agents. These emerging systems do more than just correct syntax or suggest code snippets—they have the potential to participate actively in the educational process by generating personalized exercises, providing adaptive challenges based on student performance, and offering conceptual explanations that address foundational programming principles (Kazemitabaar et al., 2024). This will require conscious planning on the part of instructors to adapt coding tools to pedagogical purposes rather than the commercial ones they have grown out of. But as these technologies mature, we are witnessing the emergence of assistants that can analyze student coding patterns, identify conceptual misunderstandings, and tailor subsequent challenges to address specific learning gaps. This agentic approach represents a profound pivot from tools that merely assist with coding mechanics to intelligent partners that contribute meaningfully to pedagogical strategies. As they continue to evolve, the capacity of these solutions to personalize instruction and anticipate user needs will further enhance their educational impact, turning initial code drafts into opportunities for iterative improvement. These systems will be able to function as collaborative partners rather than mere utilities, capable of not only implementing code but also suggesting architectural improvements and even participating in higher-level design conversations. Consequently, programming education no longer hinges on rote memorization of syntax or manual debugging; instead, it opens a dynamic space for creative engagement and purposeful exploration where students and their increasingly bespoke assistants collaboratively solve complex computational problems.

Beyond their role in code generation, these assistants can also function as real-time mentors, delivering context-sensitive guidance that supports problem-solving and experimentation. As mentioned already, this depends on instructors and curriculum designers consciously adapting existing functionality to a more hand-holding pedagogical environment. But this is certainly possible if effort and resources are committed to it. This ability to detect errors before execution reduces the trial-and-error cycle that can overwhelm new programmers, thereby encouraging students to adapt their logic swiftly and learn from constructive feedback (Wei et al., 2024). Tools like Replit Ghostwriter exemplify this approach by integrating seamlessly into project-based learning contexts, nudging learners to look beyond syntax drills and consider broader algorithmic strategies. Students benefit from individualized pacing, as these platforms can scale difficulty and complexity in alignment with user progress, building up to more advanced assignments as confidence grows (Shang & Sen, 2024).

The evolution toward more agentic systems is particularly evident in how these tools actively redirect attention toward deeper computational thinking skills—such as problem decomposition and efficient code structure—rather than emphasizing repetitive syntax drills. Through natural language processing capabilities, these systems can interpret a student's intent, guiding them toward optimal solutions while explaining the underlying logic and principles. This represents a significant advancement beyond simple autocompletion, as the tools begin to function as collaborators in the learning process, engaging with students in a dialog about design choices and implementation strategies. Educators who incorporate code assistance into coursework will create an environment where programming becomes a creative, collaborative endeavor, appealing to a range of disciplinary interests. Over time, this fusion of guided instruction, real-time error detection, and context-aware recommendations will likely reshape the norms of coding education. Students will develop robust problem-solving competencies while feeling supported by automated, intelligent feedback that increasingly resembles personalized human mentorship.

Over the years, a wide range of coding assistants have emerged, each offering different capabilities tailored to various aspects of the software development lifecycle (Table 3.1). Some tools specialize in code completion and autocompletion, while others on code generation, security, debugging, and compliance. Among some of the well-known coding assistants are Tabnine, Codeium, and Microsoft IntelliCode, which enhance coding efficiency through real-time suggestions and autocompletion (Hliš et al., 2023). Tabnine (https://www.tabnine.com/) provides context-aware code completions, integrating with multiple IDEs and over 80 programming languages, making it a flexible tool for developers working across different stacks. Similarly, Codeium (the creator of Windsurf) (https://codeium.com/) offers real-time autocompletion features and supports numerous programming languages, helping developers reduce keystrokes and improve coding speed. Microsoft's IntelliCode (https://visualstudio.microsoft.com/services/intellicode/), integrated into Visual Studio and Visual Studio Code, uses models based on best practices from open-source projects to provide intelligent coding recommendations that align with industry standards (Vaithilingam et al., 2023). These assistants automate significant parts of coding workflows, allowing developers to focus on problem-solving rather than syntax memorization.

Beyond autocompletion, some tools specialize in intelligent code generation, testing, and codebase management. OpenAI Codex and Qodo Gen are designed to understand and generate code across multiple languages, making them invaluable for both learning and production-level development

TABLE 3.1

AI-Powered Coding Assistants and Their Capabilities

AI Tool	URL	Description
Tabnine	Tabnine	A code assistant providing context-aware completions, integrating with multiple IDEs and supporting over 80 programming languages.
Codeium	Codeium	Offers real-time autocompletion features, supporting multiple programming languages to reduce keystrokes and improve coding speed.
Microsoft IntelliCode	IntelliCode	Integrated into Visual Studio and Visual Studio Code, using models to provide intelligent coding recommendations.
OpenAI Codex	OpenAI Codex	The model behind GitHub Copilot, capable of understanding natural language queries and reshaping them into functional code.
Qodo Gen	Qodo Gen	Provides integrated tools for writing, testing, and reviewing code, useful for individual developers and team-based workflows.
GitLab Duo	GitLab Duo	An AI-powered DevSecOps platform that specializes in security, compliance, and automation within software development workflows.
Sourcegraph Cody	Sourcegraph Cody	A code intelligence platform that enhances large-scale codebase navigation, refactoring, and maintenance.
Codiga	Codiga	Automated code analysis tool that helps developers adhere to best practices while improving code maintainability.
AskCodi	AskCodi	Assists with code generation and documentation, enabling structured, well-documented code with minimal effort.
Cursor	Cursor	A code assistant focusing on code generation, code completion, and infrastructure deployment, improving workflow automation.
Windsurf	Windsurf	A coding assistant that supports code generation and workflow automation, particularly for deployment tasks.

(Chang et al., 2024). OpenAI Codex (https://openai.com/index/openai -codex/), the model behind GitHub Copilot, excels at understanding natural language queries and reconfiguring them into functional code snippets. Qodo Gen (https://www.qodo.ai/) takes this further by offering integrated tools for writing, testing, and reviewing code, making it useful for both individual developers and team-based workflows (Trummer, 2025). Meanwhile, tools like GitLab Duo and Sourcegraph Cody extend beyond traditional code assistance by enhancing DevSecOps workflows and enabling large-scale code maintenance. GitLab Duo (https://about.gitlab.com/gitlab-duo/) looks at security, compliance, and automation, ensuring that generated code aligns with best DevOps practices, while Sourcegraph Cody (https://sourcegraph

.com/cody) helps developers navigate and refactor massive codebases, making it an essential tool for enterprise-level development (Ng et al., 2024).

These advanced assistants not only enhance productivity but also introduce smarter, security-conscious workflows in software engineering. As these tools become increasingly sophisticated, they are evolving from mere assistants that respond to specific queries toward autonomous agents capable of proactively identifying opportunities for optimization, suggesting architectural improvements, and even participating in high-level design decisions. This evolution represents a pivotal change in how we conceptualize the generative role in software development and education—from tools that simply augment human capabilities to collaborative partners that contribute meaningful insights to the development process. For developers seeking debugging, documentation, and security, tools like Codiga and AskCodi provide real-time analysis and intelligent recommendations (Berabi et al., 2024). Codiga (https://www.codiga.io/) offers automated coding analysis, helping developers adhere to best coding practices while improving maintainability. AskCodi (https://www.askcodi.com/), on the other hand, is designed to assist with code generation and documentation, enabling developers to quickly generate structured, well-documented code with minimal effort. These tools complement traditional coding assistants by ensuring that code is not only generated efficiently but also optimized for performance, readability, and security (Shanuka et al., 2024).

Most recently at the time of writing, Cursor (https://www.cursor.com/) and Windsurf (https://codeium.com/windsurf) have gained significant traction in the coding assistant space, particularly due to their code generation, code completion, and infrastructure deployment capabilities. Unlike traditional tools that primarily center on syntax assistance, Cursor and Windsurf play a crucial role in planning, workflow automation, and deployment, highlighting the broader functions in programming beyond just writing lines of code (Terragni et al., 2025). Their integration into end-to-end development processes reinforces the idea that coding assistants should not only help generate code but also facilitate infrastructure management and operational efficiency (Kotsiantis et al., 2024). However, this book will primarily focus on GitHub Copilot, Vercel, and Replit Ghostwriter, as these tools offer accessible entry points for educators looking to integrate generative coding into coursework for the first time. These platforms provide intuitive, user-friendly assistance, making them ideal for instructors and students seeking to explore automated programming while maintaining a balance between automation and conceptual learning (Liu & Li, 2024). Through the use of these recommended tools, educators can effectively lay out enhanced coding exercises, ensuring that students engage with programming as a creative and problem-solving discipline rather than just a technical exercise (Pan et al., 2024).

The remainder of this book will focus on GitHub Copilot (https://github .com/features/copilot), Vercel (https://vercel.com/templates/next.js/ai -code-translator), and Replit Ghostwriter (https://replit.com/learn/intro-to

-ghostwriter), three of the most influential coding tools or platforms as of early 2025 (Table 3.2). These tools not only support code generation and completion but also provide infrastructure, deployment pipelines, and project management solutions, making them ideal for educators integrating smart coding into coursework. They recognize that writing syntax is only a fraction of software development—real-world coding requires planning, collaboration, version control, and deployment. Using these platforms enables educators to offer students a more holistic, hands-on experience, bridging the gap between learning to code and actually building and deploying applications (Porter & Zingaro, 2024).

GitHub Copilot was the first coding assistant to demonstrate the power of generative AI in software development, setting the stage for the role in programming education and industry adoption (Wermelinger, 2023). Built on OpenAI Codex, Copilot provides real-time code suggestions, automates repetitive tasks, and assists with debugging, significantly increasing developer productivity. Its tight integration with Visual Studio Code makes it accessible to beginners while also being an industry-standard tool for professional developers. GitHub itself is the leading platform in the world for version control and collaborative coding, meaning students who learn GitHub workflows gain immediately transferable skills for professional software

TABLE 3.2

GitHub Copilot, Vercel, and Replit Ghostwriter for Educators

AI Tool	URL	Capabilities	Use Cases for Educators
GitHub Copilot	GitHub Copilot	Code completion, real-time syntax suggestions, debugging assistance, integrates with Visual Studio Code and JetBrains IDEs.	Ideal for teaching version control, collaborative coding, and industry-standard workflows. Helps students transition from syntax exercises to real-world project collaboration.
Vercel	Vercel	Simplified app deployment for React and Next.js, coding assistant (v0), integrated chat-based development, automates cloud deployment.	Great for teaching web development and deployment, allowing students to build and deploy full applications with minimal friction. Suitable for courses covering modern web frameworks like React and Next.js.
Replit Ghostwriter	Replit Ghostwriter	Cloud-based coding environment, code generation and completion, debugging assistance, seamless project building and deployment.	Best suited for beginner-friendly programming courses, allowing students to write, test, and deploy code in a controlled, accessible environment. Reduces infrastructure barriers and reinforces iterative learning.

development (Kinsman et al., 2021; Mastropaolo et al., 2024). Nearly every modern software developer must learn GitHub, making it an essential component of coding education.

The integration of GitHub Copilot into introductory programming courses allows educators to help students transition seamlessly from learning syntax to contributing to real-world projects, reinforcing the importance of documentation, collaboration, and iterative development (Patani et al., 2024). What distinguishes Copilot from simpler code-completion tools is its capacity to understand context and intent, functioning more as an intelligent coding partner than a mere suggestion engine. This reflects the evolution toward more agentic systems that can participate meaningfully in the development process, suggesting architectural patterns, identifying potential edge cases, and even explaining the rationale behind coding decisions. As students become comfortable working with Copilot, they learn to communicate their intentions more clearly, a skill that translates directly to professional development environments where precise specification is essential for successful project outcomes.

Next, Vercel is one of the most important players in modern web development and deployment, particularly for React and Next.js applications. Unlike traditional platforms that require complex DevOps configurations, Vercel revolutionized the process by simplifying app deployment, allowing developers to go from code to production with minimal friction (Fenner, 2025). With the rise of automation in software development, Vercel introduced v0, a coding assistant that allows developers to build, refine, and deploy applications within an integrated chat-based development environment. This means that students can write code, get generated recommendations, and deploy applications—all within a single workflow (Udoidiok et al., 2024).

What makes Vercel particularly valuable in educational contexts is how it modifies the traditional development pipeline into a conversational process. Students can describe what they want to build in natural language, and the interface not only generates code but also explains its implementation decisions. This conversational interface represents a significant step toward intelligent systems that function as collaborative agents rather than passive tools, actively engaging with students about architectural choices, performance considerations, and best practices. The assistant adapts to student level of expertise, providing more detailed explanations for beginners while offering more sophisticated recommendations to advanced users. Educators introducing web development into their courses can use Vercel to teach not just syntax, but also modern deployment practices, ensuring that students build fully functional, scalable applications. The emphasis of the platform on assisted coding, automation, and frictionless deployment positions it as a powerful tool for teaching real-world development skills that extend beyond programming logic alone (Alabbas & Alomar, 2024). This aligns perfectly with the evolution from assistants to agents, as Vercel's capabilities help students understand the entire software development lifecycle, from conception to deployment, cultivating a more comprehensive understanding of how code functions in production environments.

Finally, Replit started as a cloud-based coding environment designed to remove infrastructure barriers for beginners, allowing students to write, run, and test code within a simple, browser-based interface. As coding assistance became more prevalent, Replit introduced Ghostwriter, an integrated coding assistant that enables real-time code completion, debugging, and contextual guidance (Lakshman & Abhinav, 2024). Unlike GitHub and Vercel, which cater primarily to professional developers, Replit is designed for beginners and educators, making it an ideal entry point for students learning programming for the first time. What makes Ghostwriter particularly innovative is its adaptive learning capabilities that go beyond simple code suggestions. The system observes how students approach problems, identifies patterns in their coding style and common mistakes, and tailors its guidance accordingly. This represents a significant advancement toward autonomous learning agents that can personalize the educational experience based on individual learning trajectories. For instance, if a student consistently struggles with certain concepts, Ghostwriter might provide more detailed explanations or suggest simpler implementations before introducing more complex solutions. The platform provides a seamless coding pipeline where students can build, refine, and deploy applications without leaving the Replit ecosystem. The integration of such assisted learning and project deployment into a single workflow enables Replit to reduce cognitive overload and provides students with instant feedback, reinforcing coding concepts through practice and iteration (Plate & Hutson, 2024). As this technology continues to evolve, we're likely to see even more sophisticated capabilities, such as automatically generating customized exercises based on a student's skill level or suggesting project ideas that build upon concepts they've recently mastered.

Coding assistants such as those that will be highlighted as recommended tools moving forward—GitHub Copilot, Vercel, and Replit Ghostwriter—have reshaped software development by automating repetitive coding tasks, minimizing developer fatigue, and improving overall efficiency for both students and professionals. These platforms reduce the burden of manually generating boilerplate code and repeatedly correcting minor syntax errors, thereby enabling learners to focus on core concepts and logical structures rather than rote syntax (Liu et al., 2024). GitHub Copilot, for example, can autocomplete function definitions (Figure 3.1), produce common code blocks, and even generate entire modules based on natural language prompts, diminishing the need for manual repetition (Thakkar, 2023). Likewise, Vercel v0 streamlines React and Next.js development, automating project design so that learners can concentrate on application logic rather than intricate configuration details (Alabbas & Alomar, 2024). Replit Ghostwriter specifically caters to beginners by handling infrastructure setup, syntax error correction, and code formatting, allowing novice programmers to spend more time

```
 sentiments         gatk_cql.py       pose_experiment.py       testreviews.m

1  #!/usr/bin/env ts-node
2
3  import { fetch } from "fetch-h2";
4
5  // Determine whether the sentiment of text is positive
6  // Use a web service
7  async function isPositive(text: string): Promise<boolean> {
8      const response = await fetch("http://text-processing.com/api/sentiment/", {
9          method: "POST",
10         body: `text=${text}`,
11         headers: {
12             "Content-Type": "application/x-www-form-urlencoded",
13         },
14     });
15     const json = await response.json();
16     return json.label === "pos";
17 }
```

FIGURE 3.1
Github Code Completion

mastering computational thinking skills than troubleshooting trivial mistakes (Figure 3.2) (Lakshman & Abhinav, 2024).

These automated processes lower the cognitive load associated with coding, ensuring that learners develop higher-order skills rather than becoming mired in mechanical syntax memorization. As these tools evolve, they're increasingly capable of not just generating code but also providing conceptual explanations that help students understand why certain approaches are preferred over others. This educational component reframes these tools from simple productivity enhancers into active participants in the learning process, providing insights that would traditionally come from human instructors. Beyond this capacity to automate syntax, coding platforms excel at delivering contextual feedback and intelligent suggestions, thereby narrowing skill gaps in programming education. Many newcomers struggle to grasp the hierarchical relationships within code, as well as the logic that underpins each function or data structure. Tools such as GitHub Copilot and Replit Ghostwriter address these challenges by providing not only auto-completion but also inline explanations that clarify why a particular snippet or approach is appropriate (Head et al., 2020). For instance, GitHub Copilot might suggest a Python function while simultaneously highlighting common pitfalls, guiding students to handle edge cases effectively (Figure 3.3) (Porter & Zingaro, 2024). This explanatory approach reflects the evolution toward systems that do not just produce code but actively teach programming concepts, functioning as pedagogical agents that sequentially unfold, allowing understanding through contextualized explanations. When a student encounters a difficult concept, these systems can provide multiple examples with varying complexity, helping to build a more nuanced understanding of abstract programming principles.

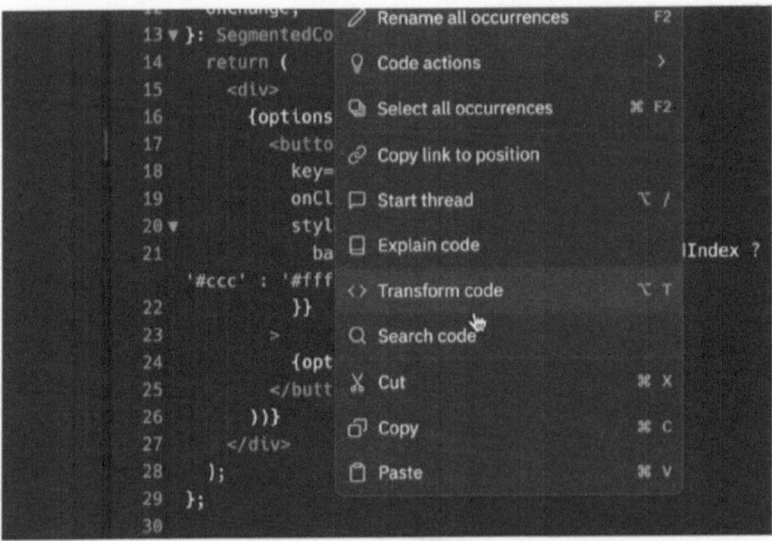

FIGURE 3.2
Replit Ghostwriter Interface

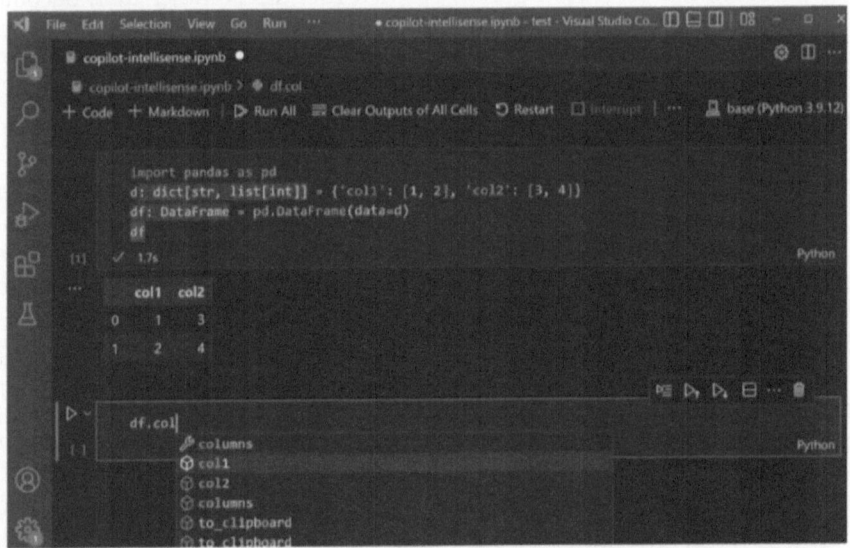

FIGURE 3.3
GitHub Copilot Suggestions

Vercel v0 similarly adapts these principles for web-driven tasks, recommending best practices and code organization tips specific to React and Next .js frameworks (Figure 3.4) (Constança, 2023). This form of context-sensitive support encourages learners to internalize coding logic, equipping them

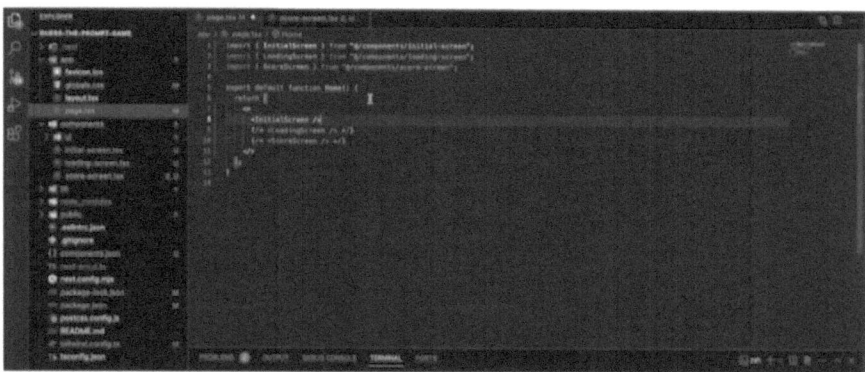

FIGURE 3.4
Vercel v0 Interface

with a deeper understanding of how various components interact and why certain design decisions are made. Through the emphasis on explanations over mere completion, these platforms encourage a self-directed learning environment that supports students from diverse academic backgrounds. Therefore, this emphasis on contextual learning increases access to programming education, showing novices that coding is not solely about syntax acquisition but about developing robust problem-solving competencies.

Moreover, the real-time feedback loop provided by coding assistants such as Replit Ghostwriter, GitHub Copilot, and Vercel v0 catalyzes an interactive learning experience that moves beyond static tutorials. Replit Ghostwriter stands out for its browser-based environment, allowing students to write, test, and deploy code on one platform without the complexities of local installation or version control (Ruff & Giacobe, 2022; Yanagisawa, 2012). This frictionless environment encourages experimentation and iterative development—key practices in professional coding workflows that are traditionally difficult to teach in academic settings. GitHub Copilot extends this interactivity through integration with Visual Studio Code, offering on-the-spot suggestions, corrections, and refinements that guide students in iterative coding practices (Karkalas, 2022). As the technology advances, Copilot is becoming increasingly adept at understanding a developer's intentions, functioning less as a tool and more as a collaborative partner that can anticipate needs and suggest solutions before problems are fully articulated. This proactive assistance represents a significant step toward autonomous coding agents that can participate meaningfully in the development process.

Vercel v0 enhances these workflows by handling deployment details for web development projects, encouraging students to experiment with live applications while avoiding excessive infrastructure setup. This immersive, hands-on approach invites learners to quickly test new ideas, observe immediate outcomes, and refine their understanding of programming concepts through concrete practice. The enablement of on-demand experimentation allows students to cultivate critical thinking skills and facilitate deeper engagement with computational principles, thus changing coding from a passive exercise into a dynamic, discovery-oriented discipline. Through these interactive platforms, students transition from memorizing syntax to applying analytical reasoning, ultimately establishing a stronger, more enduring foundation in programming.

3.2 Navigating the Limitations of AI Coding Assistants

Coding assistants have dramatically sped up software development by offering real-time code suggestions, debugging assistance, and contextual recommendations. However, as these tools become more prevalent, it is crucial to recognize that they are assistive technologies rather than replacements for human problem-solving. While tools such as GitHub Copilot, Replit Ghostwriter, and Vercel v0 can streamline coding tasks, they should complement, not override, the problem-solving processes that define strong programming skills (Kazemitabaar et al., 2023). As such, smart code generation may provide solutions, but critical thinking, logical structuring, and debugging skills remain relevant skills for writing efficient and secure code. This distinction between tools and agents is particularly important as systems become more sophisticated. Even as these technologies evolve toward more autonomous operation, they function best when augmenting human creativity and problem-solving rather than replacing it. The most effective educational approaches recognize these tools as collaborative partners in the learning process—one that can reduce cognitive load on mechanical tasks while freeing students to engage more deeply with conceptual challenges. This collaborative framework emphasizes the synergy between human insight and machine efficiency.

Without human oversight, generated outputs can perpetuate inefficiencies, introduce security vulnerabilities, or fail to align with project-specific requirements (Bukhari et al., 2023). Even the most advanced systems sometimes produce code that works technically but misses nuanced requirements or makes assumptions that don't align with the broader project context. Therefore, rather than allowing these assistants to dictate coding decisions, students and professionals must learn to engage critically with their suggestions, refining and improving them based on a deeper understanding of computational principles—they are after all "assistants."

This critical engagement represents an essential skill for the future of programming education. Students must learn to evaluate generated code for correctness, efficiency, and security—skills that require a deeper understanding of programming principles than simply accepting whatever is suggested via the algorithm. This evaluation process itself becomes an important learning opportunity, as students must apply their knowledge to assess whether the suggestions align with best practices and project requirements. Through this collaborative dialog between human and machine, students develop a more nuanced understanding of programming concepts while benefiting from the ability to handle repetitive or mechanical coding tasks.

Concerns about overreliance on generated code remain prevalent, particularly when students and developers accept outputs without probing their underlying logic (Zviel-Girshin, 2024). Research suggests that learners who rely heavily on automated assistance lose opportunities to engage deeply with central problem-solving processes, jeopardizing their capacity to debug and reason about computational tasks (Takerngsaksiri et al., 2024). The risk is that students might develop a superficial understanding of programming concepts, knowing how to prompt systems but lacking the deeper knowledge needed to evaluate or modify the resulting code. This could create a generation of developers who can produce code quickly but struggle when faced with novel problems that require foundational understanding.

Similar criticisms have been made regarding the use of large language models (LLMs) such as ChatGPT, where insufficient critical engagement with textual output can erode student analytical skills (Lo et al., 2024). In programming contexts, the failure to question generated solutions can entrench errors and diminish algorithmic thinking—vital competencies in software development (Kazemitabaar et al., 2024). When students accept code without understanding its underlying logic, they miss opportunities to develop the analytical reasoning and debugging skills essential for addressing novel problems. Counteracting this dynamic calls for course designs that prompt students to refine outputs, justify their modifications, and assume responsibility for quality control. Rather than simply accepting generated code, students should be encouraged to propose alterations, explain their reasoning, and develop a critical eye for optimization opportunities. This approach means the tools change from potential shortcuts into powerful learning aids that break down understanding to different steps while still requiring students to apply and demonstrate their knowledge. The process reflects industry practice whereby examples can be seen with Google where 25% of new code is generated then subsequently reviewed by their engineers (Edwards, 2024).

As these systems evolve toward more agentic capabilities, educators must develop new pedagogical approaches that encourage students to view this helpful machine as a collaborative partner rather than an oracle. This might involve structured exercises where students critique and improve generated solutions, or assignments that require students to explain the reasoning behind automated suggestions in their own words. Through positioning use of these tools as that of a participant in an ongoing conversation about code quality and design, educators can help students develop both technical skills and the critical judgment needed to use these powerful tools effectively. While the tools expedite the coding process, foundational logic and problem-solving still demand attention, as no automated system can substitute for an informed understanding of how programming components interact (Liu & Li, 2024). This recognition doesn't diminish the value of generative assistants but rather highlights the need for balanced educational approaches that leverage these tools while ensuring students develop core computational thinking skills. The goal should be symbiotic learning, where the assistant handles routine coding tasks while students spend time on higher-order thinking skills like algorithm design, architectural planning, and identifying edge cases that might not be immediately apparent to automated systems.

In practice, educators should blend automated support with structured, hands-on assignments that reinforce reasoning skills (Renzella et al., 2024). For instance, instructors might present generated templates as a launching point, requiring students to optimize or adapt the code to address performance or security parameters. Such tasks help learners internalize core concepts while making use of these resources. This approach acknowledges the potential while ensuring students develop the foundational skills needed to work effectively with these tools. Rather than viewing assisted coding as a threat to traditional education, it represents an opportunity to refocus classroom time on higher-order thinking skills that remain uniquely human.

In the same vein, incremental coding labs can effectively introduce debugging in a controlled setting. For example, educators can supply intentionally flawed AI-produced code for students to analyze and correct, thus prompting a deeper look at the logic underlying each function call (Shang & Sen, 2024). This approach transforms potential weaknesses of these systems into pedagogical opportunities, using the limitations of automated code generation as a context for developing critical analysis skills. When students must identify and fix problems in generated code, they engage more deeply with programming concepts than they might when simply writing code from scratch. Whether these projects involve poor time complexity or hidden security glitches, the aim is to encourage students to develop systematic diagnostic skills. Peer code reviews can deepen this process, as learners discuss the rationale behind proposed fixes on the part of the tool, collectively drawing conclusions about coding conventions and best practices. These collaborative activities help students understand that programming is not just an individual pursuit but a social process that benefits from diverse perspectives and critical feedback. Through such interactive exercises, students forge a clearer connection between conceptual problem-solving and practical debugging, mirroring real-world development workflows.

As coding assistants become more sophisticated, evolving from simple suggestion engines toward autonomous agents capable of complex reasoning, educators must adapt their teaching strategies accordingly. Rather than treating these systems as fixed tools, instructors should help students understand the underlying mechanisms and limitations of generated code. This might include discussions about how training data influences outputs, or exercises that explore edge cases where systems typically struggle. By demystifying these technologies, educators can help students develop a more nuanced understanding of when to rely on machine assistance and when human intervention is essential. Real-world implementation of assisted code generation also requires an emphasis on responsible use. Although these tools can dramatically accelerate development cycles, they may contain inadvertent bugs or produce incorrect logic, opening the door to security vulnerabilities or flawed output (Bukhari et al., 2023). This risk is particularly acute as systems grow more complex, sometimes generating solutions that work but contain subtle inefficiencies or security flaws that might not be immediately apparent. Courses should integrate discussions on the need for careful scrutiny of automated responses, so that students proactively assess potential risks and refine solutions as necessary. These discussions might include case studies of real-world failures of generated code, or exercises where students evaluate the security implications of different implementation approaches. Through framing generative solutions as collaborative aids rather than infallible directives, educators help learners cultivate a vigilant, analytical perspective that upholds standards of code quality (Kazemitabaar et al., 2023). This approach aligns with industry expectations, where developers must constantly evaluate automated outputs for reliability, performance, and compliance.

Successfully integrating coding assistants into educational practice inevitably invites controversy, but these reservations echo earlier debates in software development history. The transition from assembly to higher-level languages, for instance, sparked apprehension about efficiency and loss of granular control, while the emergence of object-oriented frameworks in the 1990s prompted critiques concerning performance overhead and excessive code complexity (Edwards, 2024). In each case, initial skepticism gradually gave way to recognition of how these advances enhanced developer productivity and enabled more complex applications. The key was ensuring that programmers understood both the benefits and limitations of these new approaches, rather than treating them as magical solutions to all coding challenges. Today's integration of AI into coding practices faces resistance from practitioners concerned about losing control of development processes and inadvertently creating new errors. Yet experience with previous technological advances suggests a solution: well-designed educational approaches that combine hands-on exercises, collaborative review, and ethical discussions help students develop robust analytical and problem-solving abilities (Takerngsaksiri et al., 2024). These approaches acknowledge the potential of assistive coding while ensuring students develop the critical faculties needed to use these tools effectively.

When thoughtfully implemented, tools complement rather than replace human judgment, allowing programming education to embrace modern workflows while nurturing the underlying skills that drive success in computational fields. This balanced approach positions coding assistants as partners in the educational process—tools that can handle routine coding tasks while freeing students and educators to focus on the creative, analytical, and architectural aspects of programming that remain distinctly human domains. As these technologies continue to evolve toward more autonomous operation, this partnership model becomes even more crucial, ensuring that students understand both how to leverage capabilities and when human oversight and judgment remain essential.

3.3 Leveraging AI to Reduce Cognitive Overload

While automated code generation has gained traction in many computer science departments, it is equally important to examine its role in reducing cognitive overload and its associated benefits to provide a balanced perspective. As noted, one of the ways these tools have accomplished this reduction is by moving away from syntax memorization toward conceptual learning. Cognitive overload in education occurs when students are presented with more information than their working memory can effectively process, leading to frustration, disengagement, and diminished learning outcomes (Benko et al., 2019). In programming education, this often happens when learners are required to simultaneously manage syntax rules, debugging, logic structuring, and problem-solving, overwhelming their cognitive capacity (Haindl & Weinberger, 2024). This cognitive burden is particularly challenging in introductory programming courses, where students must navigate unfamiliar syntax while also grasping abstract computational concepts. The mental effort required to remember precise syntax rules often leaves limited cognitive resources for understanding the deeper logic and structure of programming problems. Even small errors like missing semicolons or incorrect indentation can halt progress entirely, creating frustration that detracts from the learning experience. As students struggle with these mechanical aspects, they have less mental capacity to engage with higher-order concepts like algorithm design or data structure selection.

Many learners, particularly those new to coding, struggle with syntax errors before they fully grasp programming logic, which can lead to disengagement. Coding assistants, such as GitHub Copilot, Replit Ghostwriter, and Vercel v0, help mitigate these challenges by offering real-time suggestions, explaining code structures, and auto-correcting minor errors (Kazemitabaar et al., 2024). These features enable students to spend more time on problem-solving strategies and logic building rather than being hindered by syntax complexity.

What makes these tools particularly valuable is their evolution from simple syntax checkers to intelligent learning partners that provide contextualized guidance. When a student encounters a complex programming concept, assistants can generate multiple examples with varying complexity, explain the underlying principles, and even suggest coding exercises tailored to the student's current skill level. Instructors need to teach students about this capability and how the students can best invoke it, but the capacity for explanation and teaching on the part of the tools is already quite strong. This personalized design and framework allows students to progress at their own pace, receiving the right amount of support at each stage of learning. Rather than overwhelming students with all possible syntax variations at once, these systems can introduce complexity gradually as students demonstrate mastery of foundational concepts. Research has shown that students using coding tools exhibit higher retention rates and improved problem-solving capabilities compared to those following syntax-first instruction (Takerngsaksiri et al., 2024). By reducing the cognitive load associated with memorizing syntax rules and debugging trivial errors, these tools free students' mental resources for deeper engagement with programming concepts. This pivot in focus from mechanical details to conceptual understanding promotes more meaningful learning experiences and better prepares students for real-world programming challenges where problem-solving skills are more valuable than memorized syntax.

These tools also make programming more accessible to non-STEM students, allowing a broader range of learners to develop computational thinking skills. Many students, such as those studying business, journalism, or digital humanities, require coding skills but lack the technical background traditionally expected in programming courses. Intelligent platforms help bridge this gap by providing interactive, real-time feedback and personalized recommendations that adjust to the pace of learning for each student. This increasing accessibility of programming education is particularly significant as computational thinking becomes increasingly valuable across disciplines. By lowering the initial barriers to entry, assisted coding enables students from diverse backgrounds to engage with programming concepts without being deterred by syntax complexity. This inclusive approach acknowledges that computational literacy is becoming an essential skill for many professions, not just those traditionally associated with computer science. As these tools evolve into more autonomous learning agents, they become even more effective at bridging disciplinary gaps, translating domain-specific problems into computational frameworks that non-technical students can understand and implement.

For example, students can input a general programming question into Replit Ghostwriter and receive a step-by-step breakdown of the logic behind a particular function (Haindl & Weinberger, 2024). This allows learners to develop a conceptual understanding of programming before diving into syntax-heavy exercises, reducing cognitive load and increasing engagement. Research has found that students who engage with a step-by-step approach to develop a stronger understanding of computational concepts and demonstrate increased confidence in coding tasks (Renzella et al., 2024). The evolution of these tools from passive assistants to active learning agents is changing how students engage with programming concepts. Rather than simply providing answers, advanced systems can identify conceptual misunderstandings, suggest alternative approaches, and even generate customized examples that address specific learning gaps. This interactive guidance helps students build mental models of programming concepts, facilitating deeper understanding and more effective transfer of knowledge to new contexts. As these systems become more sophisticated, they increasingly function as personalized tutors that adapt to individual learning styles and pace, providing just-in-time support when students encounter difficulties.

Also, these assistants provide step-by-step guidance for students working through complex coding challenges, ensuring they build foundational knowledge before tackling advanced concepts. Traditional instruction methods often introduce complex programming concepts without sufficient foundation, which can overwhelm students and lead to higher attrition rates (Dawar, 2021; Stachel et al., 2013). Assistive tools such as GitHub Copilot break down complex problems into manageable steps, providing real-time explanations and debugging assistance. This incremental approach to instruction mimics the guidance of an experienced human tutor, who would recognize when a student is struggling and adapt instruction accordingly. Coding assistants can detect patterns in a student's code that indicate confusion or misunderstanding, offering targeted explanations or simpler examples to clarify difficult concepts. As students gain confidence and proficiency, these systems can gradually be used by the instructor to introduce more complex challenges, maintaining an optimal level of difficulty that stretches students' abilities without overwhelming them. This adaptive approach is particularly valuable in large classes where instructors may not be able to provide personalized attention to every student.

This method of instruction has been shown to enhance student comprehension and retention, as learners receive support precisely when they need it, rather than struggling through concepts in isolation (Sinha et al., 2021). Smart learning pathways facilitate student progress at a pace suited to their understanding, reducing the likelihood of frustration and disengagement. By providing immediate feedback on code quality and suggesting improvements, these systems help students develop good programming habits from the beginning, rather than ingraining inefficient or error-prone practices that might be difficult to correct later. Guidance provided by the tools can also support learning advanced programming concepts without overwhelming beginners, making technical fields more accessible to diverse learners. Traditional programming courses often assume a linear path from syntax mastery to application, which does not reflect the iterative, exploratory nature of real-world software development (Ma & Wang, 2024). Coding tools allow students to engage with advanced topics—such as recursion, data structures, and algorithmic optimization—without requiring them to perfect syntax beforehand (Deroy & Maity, 2024).

This approach represents a realignment in programming pedagogy, moving from a sequential model where basic skills must be mastered before advanced concepts can be introduced, to a more integrated approach where students can explore complex ideas with appropriate support. For instance, an assistant might help a beginner implement a sophisticated sorting algorithm by handling the syntactical details while encouraging the student to deeply consider understanding the algorithm's logic and efficiency characteristics. This means that students can explore programming logic in a low-risk, high-feedback environment, reinforcing their learning through hands-on engagement. As these systems evolve toward more autonomous operation, they can increasingly function as creative partners in the learning process, suggesting novel approaches or interesting variations that might not have occurred to students. This collaborative exploration helps students develop a more nuanced understanding of programming concepts and encourages the kind of creative thinking that characterizes successful developers. By presenting multiple valid solutions to the same problem, assistants demonstrate that programming is not about finding a single "correct" answer but about making informed design choices based on specific requirements and constraints. Studies indicate that students who receive assisted guidance for advanced programming concepts are more likely to persist in coding coursework and apply their knowledge in interdisciplinary contexts (Kazemitabaar et al., 2024). This retention effect is particularly significant for students from underrepresented groups who might otherwise abandon technical courses due to feelings of inadequacy or frustration with initial difficulties. By providing a supportive learning environment that reduces unnecessary cognitive burden, assistants help create more inclusive educational experiences that benefit all students.

One of the most time-consuming aspects of programming for students is debugging errors and refactoring code, which can be frustrating, especially for beginners. Coding assistants such as GitHub Copilot and Replit Ghostwriter help streamline workflows by automatically identifying and correcting common coding mistakes in real time (Haindl & Weinberger, 2024). Rather than requiring students to manually search for and correct syntax errors, these tools highlight problematic areas, suggest alternative solutions, and provide contextual explanations. This real-time support means debugging changes from a frustrating bottleneck to a valuable learning opportunity. Instead of spending hours hunting for a missing bracket or semicolon, students can instead think about why errors occur in the first place and how to prevent them in future code. As assistants evolve toward more autonomous operation, they increasingly function as expert debugging partners, not only identifying errors but also explaining common patterns of mistakes and suggesting best practices to avoid similar issues in the future. This educational component helps students develop the systematic debugging skills that are essential for professional programming practice.

Research suggests that students who use debugging tools spend significantly less time troubleshooting minor issues, allowing them more time on problem-solving and design principles (Kazemitabaar et al., 2023). At the same time, these tools help reduce frustration by allowing students to see their debugging and refactoring progress immediately, reinforcing learning through an iterative approach. When students can instantly visualize the effects of their code changes, they are more likely to experiment with different solutions and deepen their understanding of programming logic (Dwivedi et al., 2024). Part of the adjustment to these tools on the pedagogical side is the willingness of professors to loosen the grip of a common belief among many teachers across disciplines: pain is a necessary part of the process. In English classrooms this can take the form of an insistence on the value of grammar worksheets and grilling in syntax and grammar. In programming classes this can be the deep-seated belief that the frustration of searching for that little bug deep in the heart of a C++ file is a necessary initiation in the work of a software developer. We propose skepticism about this belief. A world in which this frustration can be avoided might not be a world full of lazy coders (and writers). Work for the sake of work might lead to diminishing returns.

These assistants are increasingly capable of identifying not just syntactic errors but also logical flaws and inefficient algorithms. By highlighting potential performance bottlenecks or security vulnerabilities, they help students develop a more comprehensive understanding of code quality that goes beyond mere functional correctness. This broader perspective on software development is essential for preparing students for professional environments where factors like performance, security, and maintainability are as important as basic functionality. These tools also help students develop best practices for refactoring, ensuring that they write cleaner, more efficient code. A study on assisted programming environments found that students who engage with real-time feedback exhibit higher persistence and problem-solving abilities compared to those following traditional debugging methods (Biswas & Bhattacharya, 2024). By guiding students through the process of improving existing code, these tools help instill good habits of continuous improvement and critical evaluation that are central to professional development practices.

In fact, one of the most significant benefits of these coding assistants is their ability to provide immediate, tailored feedback, which helps students stay engaged and progress at an optimal learning pace. Traditional programming courses rely on delayed feedback through instructor grading or peer review, which can leave students feeling lost and uncertain about their mistakes (Denny et al., 2024). Tools like Vercel v0 and GitHub Copilot eliminate this bottleneck by providing real-time feedback on syntax, logic, and debugging, ensuring that students can correct mistakes and understand coding concepts without unnecessary frustration. As these systems evolve from simple assistants to more autonomous learning agents, they become increasingly capable of providing nuanced feedback that addresses not just correctness but also style, efficiency, and best practices. Advanced systems can analyze patterns in a student's code over time, identifying recurring issues or areas for improvement and offering targeted suggestions. This longitudinal perspective helps students develop a more coherent understanding of programming principles and their own growth as developers.

These real-time suggestions prevent students from getting stuck on minor errors, allowing them to focus on larger problem-solving and conceptual learning. Research has shown that students who receive immediate feedback demonstrate higher persistence and self-efficacy in programming coursework compared to those who must wait for external feedback (Estévez-Ayres et al., 2024). When students can resolve errors as they occur, they gain a stronger sense of control over their learning process, leading to higher motivation and reduced frustration. These tools provide distinct advantages to students while realigning programming education's priorities—placing greater value on systematic planning and comprehensive documentation than on rote memorization of syntax. This evolution in teaching approach resonates with professional practices and supports our previous advocacy for integrating broader contextual frameworks in foundational coursework. In traditional educational models, introductory programming courses have demanded mastery of syntax and debugging mechanics as prerequisites to meaningful application development, frequently resulting in mental fatigue and student disengagement. In contrast, tools like GitHub Copilot, Vercel v0, and Replit Ghostwriter exemplify an instructional approach centered on conceptual understanding and methodical problem-solving processes (Kazemitabaar et al., 2023). While these aids expedite code creation, they necessitate precise, well-articulated specifications. Students who provide ambiguous or incomplete prompts often receive generic code that lacks educational value (Wang, 2024)—a challenge that mirrors text generation with large language models (Giray, 2023; Plate et al., 2024).

This relationship between input quality and output utility compels students to develop sophisticated documentation capabilities, encouraging thorough software design conceptualization before initiating code generation. Consequently, this emphasis on detailed planning reflects a broader transformation in programming pedagogy—one that transitions from syntax-centric instruction toward process-oriented learning experiences that better prepare students for complex development environments. As intelligent systems become more autonomous and capable of participating in higher-level design decisions, this move toward conceptual understanding and systematic planning becomes even more important, ensuring that students develop the critical thinking skills needed to effectively collaborate with increasingly sophisticated algorithmic partners. This pivot toward process resonates with broader trends in writing pedagogy, where educators have moved away from purely product-centered evaluation toward iterative drafting, revision, and documentation (Kazemitabaar et al., 2023). Much like a composition professor who urges students to outline and revise their arguments, programming instructors must encourage learners to articulate their logic, refine incomplete outputs, and document decision-making processes (Jung, 2020).

This parallel between programming and composition highlights the increasingly creative and communicative aspects of software development. As systems handle more of the mechanical aspects of coding, the uniquely human abilities to conceptualize problems, communicate design intentions clearly, and evaluate solutions critically become more central to the programming process. By emphasizing these aspects of development, educators help students develop transferable skills that will remain valuable even as capabilities continue to advance. The result is a learning environment in which students are assessed not solely on manually typed syntax but also on how they plan, iterate, and improve their code. Paludo and Montresor (2024) likewise found that requiring students to document programming logic and refine outputs promotes more robust problem-solving skills and deeper conceptual understanding. Educators can help students approach programming as a form of iterative composition, where structured planning takes precedence over simple code production. This change in assessment recognizes that in professional environments, developers are judged more on their ability to solve complex problems and create maintainable, efficient code than on how quickly they can type syntax. By aligning educational practices with these professional realities, assisted programming instruction better prepares students for future careers while simultaneously making the learning process more engaging and accessible to diverse learners.

The rise of coding assistants has revealed how essential comprehensive specification writing has become. While documentation and planning were once reserved for advanced courses, with beginners mainly doing syntax drills (Forden et al., 2024), tools have changed this dynamic. Cambaz and Zhang (2024) demonstrate that generated solutions mirror the precision of their prompts—students must learn to create detailed, logically sound guidelines to obtain useful outputs. This requirement for precise specification mirrors professional software development practices, where clear requirements and thoughtful design are essential for successful projects. By introducing these principles early in the educational process, assisted programming helps bridge the gap between academic exercises and real-world development. Students learn not just how to code but how to communicate about code—an essential skill for collaborative development environments. For instance, a terse request submitted to GitHub Copilot can produce a basic function lacking critical context, whereas a thoughtful, extensively documented prompt outlining expected inputs, outputs, and performance goals yields high-quality, context-aware code. As a result, enhanced pedagogy compels even novice programmers to embrace best practices in documentation and logical structuring early in their education, reinforcing vital software engineering and computational thinking principles (Takerngsaksiri et al., 2024).

As these systems evolve toward more agentic capabilities, this emphasis on clear communication becomes even more important. Advanced coding assistants can engage in increasingly sophisticated dialog about design choices, asking clarifying questions and suggesting alternatives when specifications are ambiguous. This collaborative process helps students develop more precise thinking about their code while simultaneously reducing the cognitive load associated with syntax details. The resulting partnership between human creativity and machine implementation capabilities represents a powerful new framework for programming education. Counterintuitively, the capacity to generate code rapidly presents not merely a shortcut but a gateway to enhanced creativity and analytical thinking. When students must articulate precise requirements for systems, they engage in cognitive processes that demand conceptual clarity and architectural foresight (Hsu Wang, 2024). This intellectual discipline parallels traditional pedagogical approaches such as structured writing assignments where conceptual frameworks precede composition.

This emphasis on conceptual clarity represents a significant evolution in programming education, re-centering from the mechanics of coding to the higher-order thinking skills involved in problem decomposition and algorithm design. By freeing students from the cognitive burden of syntax details, assistants allow them to engage more deeply with the creative and analytical aspects of programming that distinguish expert developers. This pivot aligns with cognitive science research suggesting that meaningful learning occurs when students consider conceptual understanding rather than procedural details. The necessity of crafting detailed prompts compels students to interrogate the purpose and logical architecture of their projects—reorienting code generation into an extension of their intellectual process rather than a substitute for original thinking (Jung, 2020). Research by Mahir et al. (2024) illuminates how this engagement cultivates sophisticated technical judgment; students develop nuanced debugging capabilities and algorithmic reasoning as they systematically evaluate and refine generated outputs, learning to approach these suggestions with critical discernment rather than passive acceptance.

This critical evaluation process itself becomes an important learning opportunity, as students must apply their understanding of programming principles to assess whether generative code meets requirements for correctness, efficiency, and security. Through this collaborative dialog between human and machine, students develop a more nuanced understanding of programming concepts while benefiting from the ability to handle repetitive or mechanical coding tasks. This balanced approach positions coding assistants as partners in the educational process—tools that can handle routine coding tasks while freeing students to focus on the creative, analytical, and architectural aspects of programming. In addition to boosting creativity, machine learning constraints inherently promote iterative, exploratory workflows. Just as composition studies stress revision and multiple drafts, enhanced coding invites students to experiment repeatedly, assess preliminary outcomes, and refine their programs incrementally (Wei et al., 2024). Neither GitHub Copilot nor Replit Ghostwriter is guaranteed to produce flawless results on the first attempt; these tools require learners to diagnose faults, apply corrective measures, and optimize for performance or readability. This iterative approach mirrors professional software development practices, where continuous testing, refinement, and optimization are essential aspects of the development process. By engaging with generated code as a starting point rather than a finished product, students learn to view programming as an ongoing conversation rather than a one-time production task. This perspective helps develop resilience and adaptability—qualities that are essential for success in rapidly evolving technical fields.

Such iterative learning aligns with authentic software development, wherein continuous testing and incremental improvements underlie professional coding practices (Jung, 2020). Consequently, students are encouraged to engage actively with the suggestions, forging a participatory rather than passive approach to programming education. This active engagement helps students develop critical evaluation skills and the confidence to make independent judgments about code quality and design choices—abilities that will serve them well in professional environments where tools are increasingly commonplace but human oversight remains essential. Planning and specification writing can no longer remain an afterthought in curricula. Instructors who once prioritized syntax drills now find it crucial to instill process-driven techniques, guiding students to define project goals, articulate prompts clearly, and organize their programs before generating any code (Renzella et al., 2024). This change in educational direction acknowledges that in professional environments, the ability to conceptualize and communicate about code is often more valuable than the mechanical ability to type syntax. By emphasizing these higher-order skills from the beginning, assisted programming education better prepares students for future careers while simultaneously making the learning process more engaging and accessible.

Recent studies confirm that learners who undertake structured planning prior to coding exhibit stronger adaptability and a more sophisticated grasp of software architecture (Takerngsaksiri et al., 2024). Rather than allowing tools to mask conceptual gaps, a process-centered pedagogy safeguards student learning through each generated snippet which deepens students' understanding of how complex systems interconnect. As a result, the assistant becomes a facilitator of systematic thinking rather than a quick fix to bypass essential problem-solving skills. This emphasis on systematic thinking is particularly important as systems become more capable and autonomous. As these tools evolve from passive assistants to active collaborators in the development process, students must develop the critical thinking skills needed to effectively direct and evaluate the non-human contributions. By centering on conceptual understanding and architectural planning, educators can help students develop the higher-order thinking skills that will remain uniquely human even as capabilities continue to advance. Ultimately, coding assistants go beyond accelerating the process of code generation; they force a rethinking of the pedagogical approach to programming instruction. By necessitating precise prompts, transparent documentation, and continuous refinement, these technologies recast coding from a product-centric activity into a process-oriented discipline (Hsu Wang, 2024). This evolution parallels developments in writing pedagogy, where emphasizing process has demonstrably enhanced student learning outcomes (Kazemitabaar et al., 2023).

It cannot be stressed too much that these strong recommendations do not come from a purely novel position. Composition pedagogy has long understood that process should be taught over product. Freewriting activities and brainstorming techniques as well as systems for revising drafts and peer review have all becomes something like pedagogical cliches in English and composition programs. Similar research highlighted throughout the first three chapters of this book shows that programming courses should allow students to participate in more stages of software development than the painstaking drive toward syntactically correct code. What has changed is the arrival of coding assistants (and writing chatbots) that can free students to write a "level up" from the sentence and create paragraphs and sections of papers as well as word-by-word sentences. Tools prepare the ground for a realistic classroom which cultivates computational literacy through active reasoning, methodical planning, and systematic testing. When instructors integrate these processes organically into curriculum design, students develop foundational capabilities—analytical reasoning, algorithmic thinking, structured problem decomposition—that deemphasize basic syntax acquisition as the end-all goal of beginner courses. Through judicious implementation of augmented tools, programming education advances into a new model where conceptual understanding, inventive thinking, and collaborative design occupy the intellectual foreground.

3.4 How AI Fosters Collaboration and Creativity

A compelling illustration of evolving priorities in software development—with implications extending to broader creative domains—shows up in Amjad Masad's reflections on recent generative AI. As Replit's CEO, Masad challenges the enduring Silicon Valley doctrine that "ideas don't matter, only execution," contending instead that automated platforms, including Replit's framework, substantially reduce barriers to coding and operational tasks. During a February 6, 2025, podcast conversation with Matt Turck, Masad notes that as assistants increasingly automate the mechanical aspects of software creation, innovation's true constraint now resides in ideation quality

(Turck, 2025). This perspective represents a reconsideration in how we conceptualize the relationship between technology and human creativity. As systems evolve from passive assistants to collaborative agents capable of implementing complex technical specifications, the limiting factor in innovation moves from technical implementation to creative conceptualization. This new approach has profound implications for how we look at programming education, suggesting that while technical skills remain important, the ability to identify meaningful problems and envision innovative solutions becomes increasingly valuable. This perspective contradicts the historical reality where constructing software—coding, debugging, and optimizing—typically constituted the most demanding component of any project. This reassessment necessitates that educators and industry practitioners recalibrate their focus: while programming proficiency retains its value, it no longer serves as the principal differentiator when these interfaces can generate dependable code from conceptual directives. Instead, the ability to articulate clear requirements, understand user needs, and identify opportunities for innovation becomes the critical skill set for the assisted programming era. In practice, this change means that identifying meaningful problems, defining project goals, and understanding user needs all rise to the forefront of software development. According to Masad, "finding problems to solve is a skill" (Turck, 2025, 1:13:17), underscoring that the capacity to spot inefficiencies or recognize untapped opportunities now holds unprecedented significance in a world where automated assistants can rapidly execute solutions.

This transition toward problem identification and creative ideation represents an evolution in how we conceptualize computational thinking. Rather than primarily looking at implementation details, the most valuable cognitive skills become those related to abstraction, pattern recognition, and the ability to translate real-world challenges into computational frameworks. This "problem-spotting" approach demands creativity and cross-domain thinking, traits more aligned with collaborative ideation than with rote programming. These cognitive processes represent higher-order thinking skills that systems currently cannot replicate, highlighting the continuing importance of human creativity even as implementation becomes increasingly automated. Indeed, just as new users of large language models grappled with the "blank page" dilemma—learning what prompts to pose and how to refine them—developers embracing coding tools must hone the ability to articulate problems in precise, actionable terms (Turck, 2025, 1:13:01). This skill of translating abstract ideas into clear specifications becomes increasingly valuable as systems become more capable of implementing complex technical requirements. The challenge moves from "how to code" to "what to code" and "how to specify requirements effectively," requiring a different set of cognitive and communication skills than traditional programming education has emphasized.

Equally important, the individual who conceives an idea no longer needs to wait on a separate "technical co-founder" to bring it to life; armed with automative assistance, they can refine, iterate, and test prototypes them-selves. This broadening of access to code production heightens both collaboration and creativity, pushing novices and experts alike to concentrate on big-picture thinking rather than the mechanical details of syntax. By lowering the technical barriers to implementation, assisted coding enables a more diverse range of individuals to participate in software development, potentially leading to more innovative solutions that draw on varied perspectives and domain expertise. This framework, therefore, dovetails with the broader argument advanced throughout this book—that assisted development raises the ceiling on creativity and cooperation by moving attention from code execution to conceptual design. When education aligns with this ethos, novice programmers and interdisciplinary teams can more fully realize the collaborative potential of smart environments. As systems evolve toward more agentic capabilities, they become not just tools but partners in the creative process, enabling new forms of human-machine collaboration that amplify human creativity rather than replacing it.

As will be explored in Chapter 4, acknowledging this turn from "how to code" toward "what to code" bears direct implications for curricular and pedagogical models. By incorporating strategies that reward ideation, critical thinking, and open-ended exploration, educators can harness the capacity to automate low-level tasks while empowering learners to excel in high-level, problem-centered innovation. This realignment requires not just new teaching methods but a pivotal reconsideration of what skills are most valuable in an era of assisted programming, emphasizing creative problem-solving, effective communication, and ethical judgment alongside technical implementation skills. One of the most powerful ways these tools can be used for content creation in general is for brainstorming and, in the case of programming, exploring new coding approaches, enabling students and professionals alike to generate alternate solutions and push beyond conventional strategies. Rather than relying solely on personal expertise, learners can pose targeted questions or prompts to systems such as Replit Ghostwriter, which respond with varied examples of functions, logic structures, and methods.

This process provides valuable stimuli for ideation, as users can compare different problem-solving pathways before settling on an optimal design. Through presenting multiple valid solutions to the same problem, assistants demonstrate the creative possibilities within programming and encourage students to think beyond their first attempt at solving a problem. This exposure to diverse approaches helps students develop a more nuanced understanding of programming concepts and promotes the kind of creative thinking that characterizes successful developers. For instance, a student working on a data visualization project might prompt an assistant for charting libraries in Python, only to discover additional functions they had not considered. Through experimentation with multiple options in real time, learners build a deeper understanding of algorithmic possibilities, thereby cultivating a more innovative mindset. This exploratory approach means programming changes from a linear, solution-centered activity into a creative process where multiple valid approaches can be considered and evaluated based on various criteria like efficiency, readability, or maintainability. In essence, assistive brainstorming reduces the cognitive load associated with guesswork and manual research, directing intellectual energy toward building and refining solutions that align with Masad's emphasis on ideation rather than execution (Turck, 2025). Through offloading the burden of remembering all possible functions or implementation details, these systems free students to think more creatively about problem-solving strategies and architectural decisions. This pivot from memorization to creative application represents a significant evolution in how programming is taught and practiced.

Beyond the individual context, these tools also reform how collaborative coding projects unfold. Assistive code review platforms simplify version control, highlighting syntax differences, logical inconsistencies, and potential performance bottlenecks across a shared repository used by a team. This capability is particularly valuable in educational settings, where students often struggle with the social and technical aspects of collaborative development. Through providing automated feedback on code quality and integration issues, assistants help students learn collaborative development practices in a supportive environment. In a remote or interdisciplinary setting—common in both academic group work and professional software development—tools like Replit or GitHub's integrated review features allow multiple contributors to propose code changes in real time, immediately receiving suggestions for improvements. This workflow significantly enhances the iterative nature of collaboration, preventing stagnation caused by waiting for peer feedback (Kazemitabaar et al., 2024).

As smart systems become more agentic and capable of understanding project context, they increasingly function as active participants in the collaborative process rather than passive tools. Advanced assistants can identify potential conflicts between different team members' contributions, suggest integration strategies, and even moderate technical discussions by providing relevant information or alternative perspectives. This evolving role positions AI not just as a tool but as a collaborative partner that enhances team communication and coordination.

As a result, remote and interdisciplinary teams can engage in fluid back-and-forth exchanges, leveraging algorithmic insights to maintain coherent, high-quality code. Through centralizing the review process, the tools also engender a sense of shared ownership in the final product: each team member gains deeper visibility into the overall logic and problem-solving trajectory, reinforcing Masad's claim that the real value of software development now lies in ideation and collaboration (Turck, 2025). These innovations are particularly advantageous for non-STEM learners who wish to engage in computational problem-solving without substantial background in programming. Low-code and no-code platforms such as Replit's simplified interface or specialized data analytics tools give users from diverse disciplines—business, digital humanities, and education—the ability to prototype and experiment with code-driven solutions.

This broadened access to programming enables individuals with domain expertise but limited technical skills to implement their ideas directly, rather than having to translate them for technical collaborators. Through reducing the implementation barrier, assisted programming allows more diverse voices to participate in software development, potentially leading to more innovative and inclusive solutions that address a wider range of human needs and experiences. For instance, a student of literature might use an assistive environment to perform text analysis on historical documents, employing simple prompts to filter or categorize data (Hsu Wang, 2024). Thanks to the capacity to guide them through syntax, these learners can commit more mental resources to identifying research questions, interpreting results, and shaping broader project objectives (Takerngsaksiri et al., 2024). This accessibility of coding removes barriers related to rote coding execution, allowing all participants to concentrate on conceptual development and innovative problem-spotting, even outside of traditional computer science settings. As intelligent systems evolve toward more autonomous operation, they become increasingly capable of translating domain-specific requests into functional code, further lowering the barrier for non-technical users. This evolution enables new forms of collaborative work where domain experts and technical specialists can communicate more effectively, with smart systems serving as intermediaries that translate domain knowledge into technical implementations. This bridging function helps address a persistent challenge in interdisciplinary work, where different expertise areas often struggle to find common language and understanding.

Equally significant is how these tools expand creative coding horizons, particularly within digital arts and humanities disciplines. Through the integration of generative programming techniques with automated recommendations, artists and content creators can explore unprecedented forms of expression—including algorithmic music composition, interactive narratives, and computational art installations (Kazemitabaar et al., 2023). This creative application of assisted programming illustrates how these tools can expand the boundaries of what's possible, enabling non-traditional programmers to implement complex computational ideas that would previously have required extensive technical expertise. By handling the implementation details, assistants allow creators to focus on the creative and conceptual aspects of their work, potentially leading to innovative forms of expression that combine human creativity with computational power. Consider how Replit Ghostwriter enables users to construct web-based exhibits by automatically implementing complex JavaScript loops and generative algorithms that would otherwise prove prohibitively technical for novices. This capability does more than expedite development; it ignites artistic innovation by allowing creators to concentrate on conceptual iterations rather than wrestling with syntactical minutiae.

The framing of conceptual exploration represents an essential rethinking of how we approach creative programming, emphasizing the imaginative possibilities of code rather than its technical implementation. As systems become more capable of handling complex implementations, creators can work at higher levels of abstraction, describing their intentions in conceptual terms rather than detailed technical specifications. This pivot enables more fluid and experimental creative processes, where ideas can be rapidly prototyped and refined without getting bogged down in implementation details. In this context, enhanced programming reimagines the creative workspace as a collaborative environment where computational precision and artistic vision intersect—exemplifying Masad's observation that conceptual originality now surpasses technical implementation as the decisive creative challenge (Turck, 2025). As these tools evolve toward more agentic capabilities, they become not just implementation assistants but creative collaborators, suggesting variations, combinations, and possibilities that might not have occurred to the human creator. This collaborative creative process has the potential to expand the boundaries of computational art and design in ways we are only beginning to explore.

The inherent limitations of assisted coding also serve as unexpected catalysts for creativity, compelling users to refine their project specifications and logical frameworks instead of resorting to mechanical code corrections. When a tool generates code that only partially addresses the intended functionality, learners must articulate more precise or sophisticated prompts—illustrating the growing emphasis on comprehensive planning and conceptual development (Wei et al., 2024). This iterative refinement process encourages deeper engagement with programming concepts as students learn to communicate their intentions more precisely. Rather than accepting suboptimal implementations, students must reflect on what they actually want to achieve and how to express those goals in ways that the tool can understand. This reflective process helps develop metacognitive skills that are valuable not just for programming but for problem-solving more generally. This recursive process highlights the ability to generate structural foundations while still depending on human insight for contextually appropriate, high-quality outcomes. Rather than passively accepting every suggestion, students learn to evaluate its validity, assess its performance efficiency, and devise improvements that enhance overall code quality. This critical evaluation develops important skills in code review and quality assessment that will remain valuable even as implementation capabilities continue to advance.

Through this collaborative dynamic, assistants can amplify human creative and analytical capacities, reinforcing the centrality of critical evaluation, systematic design approaches, and collective problem-solving—principles that align with the evolving landscape of software development. As these systems become more autonomous and capable, this partnership model becomes even more important, ensuring that they serve as an amplifier of human creativity rather than a replacement for human judgment and innovation. As assisted programming continues to evolve, we can expect to see new forms of human-machine collaboration that further expand the boundaries of what's possible. Advanced systems might function not just as implementation tools but as creative partners that can suggest novel approaches, identify patterns across different projects, and even anticipate future needs based on emerging trends. This evolution will require new educational approaches that prepare students not just to use tools effectively but to engage with them as collaborative partners in the creative process. By embracing the complementary strengths of human creativity and machine implementation capabilities, educators can help students develop the skills they will need to thrive in an increasingly automated development environment. This balanced approach recognizes that while the technology can dramatically enhance productivity and lower technical barriers, the uniquely human capacities for creative ideation, ethical judgment, and contextual understanding remain essential components of effective software development. Through this collaborative framework, assisted programming becomes not a replacement for human creativity but a powerful amplifier that enables more people to bring their ideas to life through code.

References

Alabbas, A., & Alomar, K. (2024). Tayseer: A novel AI-powered Arabic Chatbot framework for technical and vocational student helpdesk services and enhancing student interactions. *Applied Sciences, 14*(6), 2547.

Benko, M. H., Vogelsang, K. M., Johnson, K. C., & Babij, A. R. (2019). Strategies to prevent cognitive overload: A team-based approach to improving student success and persistence in a gateway introductory chemistry course. In S. K. Hartwell & T. Gupta (Eds.), *Enhancing retention in introductory chemistry courses: teaching practices and assessments* (pp. 187–200). American Chemical Society.

Berabi, B., Gronskiy, A., Raychev, V., Sivanrupan, G., Chibotaru, V., & Vechev, M. (2024). Deepcode AI fix: Fixing security vulnerabilities with large language models. *arXiv preprint arXiv:2402.13291.*

Biswas, U., & Bhattacharya, S. (2024). ML-based intelligent real-time feedback system for blended classroom. *Education and Information Technologies, 29*(4), 3923–3951.

Bukhari, S., Tan, B., & De Carli, L. (2023, November). Distinguishing AI-and human-generated code: A case study. In *Proceedings of the 2023 Workshop on Software Supply Chain Offensive Research and Ecosystem Defenses* (pp. 17–25).

Cambaz, D., & Zhang, X. (2024, March). Use of AI-driven code generation models in teaching and learning programming: A systematic literature review. In *Proceedings of the 55th ACM Technical Symposium on Computer Science Education V. 1* (pp. 172–178).

Chang, C. I., Choi, W. C., & Choi, I. C. (2024, September). A systematic literature review of the opportunities and advantages for AIGC (OpenAI ChatGPT, Copilot, Codex) in programming course. In *Proceedings of the 2024 7th International Conference on Big Data and Education* (pp. 29–35).

Constança, P. (2023). *Understanding the complexity of creating a codeless web-technology platform* (Doctoral dissertation).

Dawar, D. (2021). Towards improving student expectations in introductory programming course with incrementally scaffolded approach. *Information Systems Education Journal, 19*(4), 61–76.

Denny, P., MacNeil, S., Savelka, J., Porter, L., & Luxton-Reilly, A. (2024). Desirable characteristics for ai teaching assistants in programming education. In *Proceedings of the 2024 on Innovation and Technology in Computer Science Education V. 1* (pp. 408–414).

Deroy, A., & Maity, S. (2024). Code generation and algorithmic problem solving using llama 3.1 405b. *arXiv preprint arXiv:2409.19027*.

Dwivedi, R. K., Bisen, S., Yadav, M., & Yadav, A. (2024). Coding and computational thinking: Empowering students for the digital age. In M. Bhatia & M. T. Mushtaq (Eds.), *Navigating innovative technologies and intelligent systems in modern education* (pp. 10–24). IGI Global.

Edwards, B. (2024). Google CEO says over 25% of new Google code is generated by AI. *Ars Technica*. https://arstechnica.com/ai/2024/10/google-ceo-says -over-25-of-new-google-code-is-generated-by-ai/#:~:text=Adventures%20in %20Augmentation-,Google%20CEO%20says%20over%2025%25%20of%20new %20Google%20code%20is,AI%20to%20continue%20that%20tradition

Estévez-Ayres, I., Callejo, P., Hombrados-Herrera, M. Á., Alario-Hoyos, C., & Delgado Kloos, C. (2024). Evaluation of LLM tools for feedback generation in a course on concurrent programming. *International Journal of Artificial Intelligence in Education*, 1–17. https://doi.org/10.1007/s40593-024-00406-0

Fenner, M. (2025). The Datacite Technology Stack. *Image, 2025*.

Forden, J., Gebhard, A., Berner, M., & Brylow, D. (2024, October). MiniJava on RISC-V: A game of global compilers domination. In *Proceedings of the Workshop Dedicated to Jens Palsberg on the Occasion of His 60th Birthday* (pp. 21–29).

Giray, L. (2023). Prompt engineering with ChatGPT: a guide for academic writers. *Annals of Biomedical Engineering, 51*(12), 2629–2633.

Haindl, P., & Weinberger, G. (2024). Does ChatGPT help novice programmers write better code? Results from static code analysis. *IEEE Access, 12*, 114146–114156.

Head, A., Jiang, J., Smith, J., Hearst, M. A., & Hartmann, B. (2020, April). Composing flexibly-organized step-by-step tutorials from linked source code, snippets, and outputs. In *Proceedings of the 2020 CHI Conference on Human Factors in Computing Systems* (pp. 1–12).

Hliš, T., Četina, L., Beranič, T., & Pavlič, L. (2023). Evaluating the usability and functionality of intelligent source code completion assistants: a comprehensive review. *Applied Sciences, 13*(24), 13061.

Johanyák, Z., Cserkó, J., & Pásztor, A. (2023). AI-assisted university programming education in practice. *2023 IEEE 35th International Conference on Software Engineering Education and Training (CSEE&T)* (pp. 185–186).

Karkalas, S. (2022). *Simplifying authoring and facilitating component reuse of programming tutors* (Doctoral dissertation). University of London.

Kazemitabaar, M., Ye, R., Wang, X., Henley, A., Denny, P., Craig, M., & Grossman, T. (2024). CodeAid: Evaluating a classroom deployment of an LLM-based programming assistant that balances student and educator needs. *Proceedings of the CHI Conference on Human Factors in Computing Systems.* https://doi.org/10.1145/3613904.3642773

Kazemitabaar, M., Hou, X., Henley, A., Ericson, B., Weintrop, D., & Grossman, T. (2023). How novices use LLM-based code generators to solve CS1 coding tasks in a self-paced learning environment. *ArXiv.*

Kazemitabaar, M., Huang, O., Suh, S., Henley, A. Z., & Grossman, T. (2024). Exploring the design space of cognitive engagement techniques with AI-generated code for enhanced learning. *ArXiv.*

Kinsman, T., Wessel, M., Gerosa, M. A., & Treude, C. (2021, May). How do software developers use github actions to automate their workflows?. In *2021 IEEE/ACM 18th International Conference on Mining Software Repositories (MSR)* (pp. 420–431). IEEE.

Kotsiantis, S., Verykios, V., & Tzagarakis, M. (2024). Ai-assisted programming tasks using code embeddings and transformers. *Electronics, 13*(4), 767.

Lakshman, B., & Abhinav, S. (2024). Impact of AI tools in software engineering–boon or a bane. *Journal of Software Engineering Tools & Technology Trends, 11*(1), 15–25p.

Liu, J., & Li, S. (2024). Toward artificial intelligence-human paired programming: A review of the educational applications and research on artificial intelligence code-generation tools. *Journal of Educational Computing Research,* 07356331241240460.

Liu, Y., Le-Cong, T., Widyasari, R., Tantithamthavorn, C., Li, L., Le, X. B. D., & Lo, D. (2024). Refining chatgpt-generated code: Characterizing and mitigating code quality issues. *ACM Transactions on Software Engineering and Methodology, 33*(5), 1–26.

Lo, C. K., Hew, K. F., & Jong, M. S. Y. (2024). The influence of ChatGPT on student engagement: A systematic review and future research agenda. *Computers & Education,* 105100. https://doi.org/10.1016/j.compedu.2024.105100

Ma, B., Chen, L., & Konomi, S. (2024). Enhancing programming education with ChatGPT: A case study on student perceptions and interactions in a python course. *Communications in Computer and Information Science,* 113–126. https://doi.org/10.48550/arXiv.2403.15472

Ma, Y., & Wang, C. (2024). Granularity and adaptive sequencing in automated feedback: Enhancing novice programmers' understanding, engagement, and self-efficacy in introductory computer science courses. *Education and Technology, 1*(1).

Mahir, A., Shohel, M. M. C., & Sall, W. (2024). The role of AI in programming education: An exploration of the effectiveness of conversational versus structured prompting. In M. Mahruf, C. Shohel, & A. Mortby (Eds.), *Practitioner research in college-based education* (pp. 319–352). IGI Global.

Mastropaolo, A., Zampetti, F., Bavota, G., & Di Penta, M. (2024, February). Toward automatically completing github workflows. In *Proceedings of the 46th IEEE/ACM International Conference on Software Engineering* (pp. 1–12).

Ng, K. K., Fauzi, L., Leow, L., & Ng, J. (2024). Harnessing the potential of Gen-AI coding assistants in public sector software development. *arXiv preprint arXiv:2409.17434.*

Paludo, G., & Montresor, A. (2024). Fostering metacognitive skills in programming: Leveraging ai to reflect on code. In *Proceedings of the Second International Workshop on Artificial Intelligence Systems in Education co-located with 23rd International Conference of the Italian Association for Artificial Intelligence (AIxIA 2024), volume—of CEUR Workshop Proceedings.*

Pan, Z., Xie, Z., Liu, T., & Xia, T. (2024). Exploring the key factors influencing college students' willingness to use AI coding assistant tools: An expanded technology acceptance model. *Systems, 12*(5), 176.

Patani, P., Tiwari, S., & Rathore, S. S. (2024). The impact of GitHub on students' learning and engagement in a software engineering course. *Computer Applications in Engineering Education, 32*(5), e22775.

Plate, D., Melick, E., Hutson, J., & Edele, S. (2024). *Generative AI in the english composition classroom: Practical and adaptable strategies.* Taylor & Francis.

Plate, D., & Hutson, J. (2024). Bridging disciplines with AI-powered coding: Empowering non-STEM students to build advanced APIs in the humanities. *ISAR Journal of Arts, Humanities and Social Sciences, 2*(9).

Porter, L., & Zingaro, D. (2024). *Learn AI-assisted Python programming: With Github Copilot and ChatGPT.* Simon and Schuster.

Renzella, J., Vassar, A., Solano, L. L., & Taylor, A. (2024). Scaling CS1 support with compiler-integrated conversational AI. *ArXiv.*

Ruff, M., & Giacobe, N. A. (2022, March). Leveraging browser-based virtual machines to teach operating system fundamentals. *Journal of The Colloquium for Information Systems Security Education, 9*(1), 7–7.

Shang, S., & Sen, G. (2024). Empowering learners with AI-generated content for programming learning and computational thinking: The lens of extended effective use theory. *Journal of Computer Assisted Learning, 40,* 1941–1958.

Shanuka, K. A. A., Wijayanayake, J., & Vidanage, K. (2024). Systematic literature review on analyzing the impact of prompt engineering on efficiency, code quality, and security in crud application development. *Journal of Desk Research Review and Analysis, 2*(1).

Sinha, T., Kapur, M., West, R., Catasta, M., Hauswirth, M., & Trninic, D. (2021). Differential benefits of explicit failure-driven and success-driven scaffolding in problem-solving prior to instruction. *Journal of Educational Psychology, 113*(3), 530.

Stachel, J., Marghitu, D., Brahim, T. B., Sims, R., Reynolds, L., & Czelusniak, V. (2013). Managing cognitive load in introductory programming courses: A cognitive aware scaffolding tool. *Journal of Integrated Design and Process Science, 17*(1), 37–54.

Takerngsaksiri, W., Warusavitarne, C., Yaacoub, C., Hou, M. H. K., & Tantithamthavorn, C. (2024, July). Students' perspectives on AI code completion: Benefits and challenges. In *2024 IEEE 48th Annual Computers, Software, and Applications Conference (COMPSAC)* (pp. 1606–1611). IEEE.

Terragni, V., Vella, A., Roop, P., & Blincoe, K. (2025). The future of AI-driven software engineering. *ACM Transactions on Software Engineering and Methodology.*

Thakkar, P. (2023). *Exploring the design space of AI based code completion engines* (Doctoral dissertation). University of Illinois at Urbana-Champaign.

Trummer, I. (2025). Generating highly customizable python code for data processing with large language models. *The VLDB Journal, 34*(2), 21.

Turck, M. (2025, February 6) The AI coding agent revolution, the future of software, techno-optimism with Amjad Masad, CEO Replit. *The MAD Podcast.* https://www.youtube.com/watch?v=9xhDL2GbzaU

Udoidiok, I., Reza, H., & Zhang, J. (2024, July). Exploring AI integration in software development: Case studies and insights. In *NAECON 2024-IEEE National Aerospace and Electronics Conference* (pp. 375–380). IEEE.

Vaithilingam, P., Glassman, E. L., Groenwegen, P., Gulwani, S., Henley, A. Z., Malpani, R., & Yim, A. (2023, May). Towards more effective AI-assisted programming: A systematic design exploration to improve Visual Studio IntelliCode's user experience. In *2023 IEEE/ACM 45th International Conference on Software Engineering: Software Engineering in Practice (ICSE-SEIP)* (pp. 185–195). IEEE.

Wei, Z., Lee, A. T. L., Lee, V. C. S., & Chan, W. (2024). Toward AI-facilitated learning cycle in integration course through pair programming with AI agents. *2024 36th International Conference on Software Engineering Education and Training (CSEE&T)* (pp. 1–5).

Wermelinger, M. (2023, March). Using github copilot to solve simple programming problems. In *Proceedings of the 54th ACM Technical Symposium on Computer Science Education V. 1* (pp. 172–178).

Yanagisawa, H. (2012, September). Evaluation of a web-based programming environment. In *2012 15th International Conference on Network-Based Information Systems* (pp. 633–638). IEEE.

Zviel-Girshin, R. (2024). The good and bad of AI tools in novice programming education. *Education Sciences, 14*(10), 1089.

4

Re-Centering Coding Education in the AI Age

This chapter presents an approach to programming education that was not possible before coding assistants. Unlike traditional coding pedagogy, which assumes instructor expertise and syntax mastery before application, this chapter introduces a different model: one where both non-STEM instructors and students can engage with meaningful coding projects without prior programming knowledge. This eliminates the historical barrier requiring at least one party—either teacher or student—to possess coding expertise. By rethinking tools not as shortcuts but as collaborators in the learning process, we create pathways for disciplines previously excluded from computational practices to integrate coding across their curricula. The chapter builds practical ideas for designing learning experiences where conceptual understanding and problem-solving take precedence over syntax memorization, with concrete activities reimagined to show both traditional implementations and their assisted counterparts. Through this approach, we reshape coding from a specialized technical skill into an accessible, domain-specific tool for creative and analytical expression across all disciplines.

4.1 A Brief History of Programming Education

The history of software development is rapid innovation, interspersed with pivotal changes that structurally recast both industry practices and academic curricula (Table 4.1) (Jadhav, Kaur, & Akter, 2022). In the 1940s and 1950s, computing was primarily something highly specialized engineers did working on early machines such as ENIAC, where programming entailed manipulating machine language and assembly instructions with punch cards (Haigh & Ceruzzi, 2021). The introduction of the Von Neumann architecture during this period enabled stored programs and sequential execution, laying the groundwork for more structured teaching methods that would emerge in later decades (Collen & Kulikowski, 2015). But learning to code then was restricted to a small cadre of specialists—often the very scientists and engineers building the hardware—who operated in insular research settings. Syntax mastery was paramount because the machines themselves were

DOI: 10.1201/9781003637738-4

TABLE 4.1

History of Coding Education

Era	Period	Key Developments in Teaching Coding	Key Technologies/Concepts
Early Computing	1940s–1950s	- Emphasis on machine and assembly languages in academic settings. - Programming carried out on mainframes using punch cards and manual input.	ENIAC, Von Neumann architecture, machine language, assembly language
Mainframe Era	1960s–1970s	- Introduction of structured programming principles to manage growing complexity. - Early adoption of control structures in coding curricula.	COBOL, Fortran, structured programming, batch processing
Personal Computing	1970s–1980s	- Transition to accessible programming languages (e.g., BASIC). - Emergence of graphical user interfaces (GUIs), enabling more user-friendly computing.	BASIC, MS-DOS, C, Pascal, C++ graphical user interfaces (GUIs)
Internet & Open Source	1990s–early 2000s	- Integration of web technologies (HTML, JavaScript, PHP) into curricula. - Rise of open-source projects and community-driven development.	HTML, JavaScript, PHP, Java, Python, Linux, Apache HTTP Server
Agile & DevOps	2000s	- Growing attention paid to iterative, feedback-driven methodologies (Agile). - Emphasis on continuous deployment and operational collaboration (DevOps).	Agile, DevOps, CI/CD, Git, Jenkins, Docker
AI Integration	2020s–Present	- Emergence of coding tools across multiple disciplines. - Greater focus on opening up coding through interdisciplinary applications.	GitHub Copilot, GPT-4, ChatGPT, generative AI, AI in education

unforgiving, and any educational focus necessarily revolved around low-level instructions and memory management. This era established a pattern that would persist for decades: programming education required specialized knowledge gatekeepers, making it inaccessible to those outside technical fields—a barrier our assisted approach now dismantles.

During the mainframe era of the 1960s, higher-level languages such as COBOL and Fortran came to the fore, reflecting broader economic and governmental demand for robust business and scientific applications (Bessen, 2022). Colleges began to recognize programming as a distinct discipline, incorporating nascent principles of structured programming—a methodology lauded for its maintainability and disciplined use of loops, conditionals, and modular code (Farley, 2021). Computer science programs consequently broadened their scope, moving past machine-level syntax drills toward teaching best practices for large-scale data processing (Campbell-Kelly & Garcia-Swartz, 2015). Even so, education at this juncture remained closely tied to mainframe environments, which employed batch processing. Students often submitted code in batches, receiving delayed feedback that tended to reinforce meticulous syntax correction over exploratory or interactive learning approaches. While this period represented progress, the pedagogical model still assumed instructor expertise and prioritized technical accuracy over creative problem-solving—precisely the hierarchy our assisted approach inverts by allowing non-technical faculty to focus on domain-specific applications first.

The 1970s and 1980s ushered in personal computing and fueled a reevaluation of how, and to whom, programming skills should be taught (Khan et al., 2021). Languages like BASIC flourished due to their accessibility, and the popularity of operating systems such as MS-DOS demonstrated that computing could serve both hobbyists and everyday office users (Bright et al., 2020). Graphical user interfaces introduced on the Macintosh and Windows platforms made computers easier to navigate (Ceruzzi, 2003), prompting an even wider audience to seek programming knowledge. In response, academic programs pivoted toward more hands-on experiences; instead of exclusively teaching coding for mainframes, faculty increasingly integrated personal computers into coursework (Barlaskar, 2020). This pedagogical decision broadened the scope of programming education, yet syntax-centric instruction still played a major role, especially in lower-division courses. The emergence of object-oriented programming (OOP) in the 1980s further complicated the educational landscape, as colleges attempted to familiarize students with advanced concepts like encapsulation, inheritance, and polymorphism (Koti et al., 2024). Although OOP aimed to streamline large-scale software design, many academic settings still relied heavily on traditional lecture formats, relegating project-based learning and conceptual design to more advanced courses. This era brought programming to more people but maintained a basic assumption our approach challenges: that learning to code requires mastering syntax before application—a sequence the tools now allow us to reverse.

The 1990s and early 2000s launched another revolution, thanks to the rapid expansion of the internet and the surge of open-source software. Web-centric languages like HTML, JavaScript, and PHP became central to curricula centered on dynamic, interactive website creation (Ceri et al., 2003). Concurrently, open-source movements, represented by projects such as Linux and Apache, elevated collaborative learning and communal code review—concepts that trickled down into university programs and group-based assignments (Tabarés, 2021; Bretthauer, 2001). Alongside these developments, Agile practices and DevOps methodologies entered the scene, accentuating iterative, feedback-driven development and continuous delivery pipelines (Ogundipe et al., 2024). Colleges gradually aligned with these industry needs, incorporating courses on team-based workflows, distributed computing, and collaborative software engineering (Mishra & Otaiwi, 2020; Mockus et al., 2002). Although syntax mastery remained necessary, the pedagogical framing began tilting toward hands-on project execution and real-world readiness, taking a step away from purely code-level instruction toward broader, system-level competencies. This move toward real-world application foreshadowed our current approach but still assumed that either instructors or advanced students possessed sufficient technical knowledge to implement complex systems—a requirement assistance now eliminates.

These periodic evolutions sparked considerable debate within the computing community; each evolutionary wave ignited passionate discourse about computational efficiency, diminishing programmer agency, and the potential weakening of pedagogical foundations (Edwards, 2024). When higher-level languages first emerged from assembly's technical landscape, they encountered resistance from practitioners concerned about performance degradation—a pattern that would later echo in the skeptical reception of object-oriented methodologies, which many viewed as unnecessarily intricate. In our current era, augmented development tools represent the latest chapter in this continuing narrative, challenging entrenched notions regarding the centrality of manual coding proficiency. As the software ecosystem undergoes continuous reinvention, programming education necessarily adapts in both purpose and approach. Contemporary requirements have reoriented priorities away from syntactic exactitude toward implementing functional solutions in authentic contexts, incorporating cyclical user feedback, and harnessing automation for routine coding tasks. This evolving landscape compels educators to critically assess how intelligent coding systems—coupled with instruction centered on practical problem-solving—can preserve foundational computational thinking principles while simultaneously preparing students to thrive amid changes in the industry. The approach outlined in this chapter represents the most significant pedagogical evolution yet: for the first time, domains without coding expertise—at either the instructor or student level—can meaningfully engage with programming as a creative and analytical tool.

4.2 AI-Assisted Programming Activities for Non-STEM Contexts

After examining the historical evolution of programming education, we now stand at a pivotal juncture where assistive tools reshape who can teach and learn coding. Traditional programming pedagogy has maintained a necessarily hierarchical structure where at least one party—either the instructor or more advanced students—needed to possess technical expertise. This requirement has excluded countless non-STEM disciplines from meaningfully incorporating computational thinking into their curricula. The "before/after translation" approach we introduce here addresses this barrier directly. For each programming activity, we provide two perspectives: first, how the activity would traditionally be taught in a conventional coding course ("before"), requiring detailed syntax knowledge and technical troubleshooting skills; second, how the same learning objectives can be achieved when both instructors and students leverage assistance in the form of a collaborative partner ("after"). This translation does not simply substitute human expertise—it reimagines the entire instructional approach to emphasize conceptual understanding, problem-solving, and domain application over technical implementation. These translations serve multiple purposes. For non-STEM instructors, they demystify coding instruction by providing clear guidance on when and how to leverage the assistance. For curriculum developers, they model a new instructional design approach that focuses on higher-order thinking rather than syntax mastery. And for educational researchers, they represent a practical framework for studying how the tech changes the acquisition of technical skills across disciplines.

4.2.1 Activity 1: Website Deployment (Beginner Level)

4.2.1.1 BEFORE: Traditional Coding Instruction

In a conventional introduction to web development, students typically begin with HTML and CSS basics, spending several weeks learning tags, attributes, and styling properties through structured lessons and increasingly complex exercises. The deployment process is delayed until later in the course, after students had mastered basic syntax and troubleshooting skills.

The instructor would provide detailed step-by-step instructions (filling in the details of the HTML, CSS, and Git syntax to the extent required by students' knowledge):

1. Create a project folder on your computer
2. Open a text editor and create an index.html file
3. Write the HTML structure using proper syntax
4. Create a styles.css file with CSS rules
5. Test locally using a web browser
6. Sign up for a GitHub account
7. Install Git on your computer
8. Learn Git commands for initialization, adding, committing, and pushing
9. Create a new repository on GitHub
10. Connect your local repository to GitHub using git commands in the terminal
11. Configure GitHub Pages in repository settings
12. Troubleshoot any deployment errors that might occur

This approach requires the instructor to understand HTML, CSS, Git, command-line interfaces, and web hosting concepts in detail. Students would need to master syntax correctness and memorize commands, creating a significant cognitive load before seeing any tangible output.

4.2.1.2 AFTER: AI-Assisted Approach

In an AI-assisted classroom, both the instructor and students can concentrate immediately on the purpose and design of the website rather than on implementation details. The activity transitions into a creative and analytical exercise centered on communication goals, audience needs, and content organization.

The instructor guides the process with conceptual questions and planning prompts:

1. **Planning Discussion (20 minutes):** "What is the purpose of your website? Who is your intended audience? What key information should visitors find immediately? Sketch a rough layout on paper showing main sections and content hierarchy."
2. **Content Development (30 minutes):** "Draft the key text for your website. Organize your content into logical sections

(About, Projects, Contact, etc.). Select 2–3 images that complement your message."

3. **Design Considerations (15 minutes)**: "What colors reflect the tone of your message? Find examples of websites with layouts you find effective. What functional elements (navigation, forms, etc.) will your site need?"

4. **AI Collaboration for Implementation (30 minutes)**: "Now that we have our design plan, let's use AI to help implement it. Open ChatGPT or a similar tool and provide this prompt:

   'I'm creating a personal portfolio website with sections for [list your sections]. The site should use [describe color scheme] and include [describe functional elements]. Can you provide the HTML and CSS code for this site?'

5. **Understanding the Code (15 minutes)**: "Review the AI-generated code. Ask the AI to explain any parts you don't understand. For example: 'What does the viewport meta tag do?' or 'How does the CSS flexbox in the navigation work?'"

6. **Customization (20 minutes)**: "Modify the generated code to include your specific content. Ask the AI for help with any modifications like: 'How can I add a contact form to this page?' or 'How do I make the images responsive?'"

7. **Deployment Guidance (15 minutes)**: "To publish your site, ask the AI:

   'How do I deploy this website using GitHub Pages? I've never used Git or GitHub before. Please provide step-by-step instructions for complete beginners.'

9. **Troubleshooting with AI (as needed)**: "If you encounter any issues, describe the problem to the AI: 'I'm getting this error message when trying to push to GitHub...' or 'My images aren't displaying correctly...'"

10. **Reflection (15 minutes)**: "Write a brief reflection: How did your implementation compare to your initial design? What did you learn about the relationship between design planning and technical implementation? How did the AI assist your creative process?"

In this approach, neither the instructor nor the students need prior coding knowledge. The focus shifts to communication design, content strategy, and problem-solving—disciplinary skills that non-STEM faculty already possess. The tool handles syntax details and technical implementations while students engage with higher-order learning objectives.

The contrast between these two approaches demonstrates the realignment enabled by machine assistance. The traditional approach front-loads technical knowledge, delaying meaningful application until students have mastered syntax basics. The cognitive load falls heavily on memorization and rule-following before creativity can emerge. The assisted approach inverts this sequence, allowing immediate engagement with meaningful design challenges while deferring technical implementation details to the tool. This does not eliminate learning about code—instead, it contextualizes that learning within purposeful creation. Students still develop an understanding of HTML, CSS, and deployment concepts, but they learn them at the point of need rather than as prerequisite knowledge. This approach particularly benefits non-STEM contexts in three ways. First, it aligns with disciplinary priorities, keeping the focus on communication, design, and content rather than technical mechanics. Second, it builds confidence through early success, as students can produce professional-looking websites in their first session. Third, it creates authentic learning scenarios that mirror contemporary professional practice, where assisted coding is increasingly commonplace.

4.2.2 Activity 2: Data Visualization Project (Advanced Level)

4.2.2.1 BEFORE: Traditional Coding Instruction

In a conventional programming course, creating interactive data visualizations would be considered an advanced topic, typically introduced only after students had mastered programming fundamentals, data structures, and basic web development. The instructor would need extensive knowledge of JavaScript, data manipulation libraries, and visualization frameworks.

The activity might unfold over several weeks with detailed technical instruction:

1. Prerequisites: Ensure students understand JavaScript fundamentals including variables, functions, arrays, objects, and DOM manipulation

2. Introduction to data formats: Teach JSON structure and parsing

3. Setting up the development environment: Provide students with terminal commands to install dependencies, set up a development server, and anticipate troubleshooting

4. Data loading and parsing: Sections from JavaScript textbook or online resources detailing syntax for these functions

5. Creating basic visualizations with a detailed explanation of the D3.js library: extensive time spent learning to navigate D3 documentation and use correct syntax from documentation in appropriate files

6. Adding interactivity with event listeners: Similar instructions as above

7. Implementing transitions and animations: Similar instructions as above

8. Deploying the visualization to a web server: Instructor support to troubleshoot and provide help with infrastructure most likely required for student success

This approach would require the instructor to understand complex JavaScript concepts, the D3.js library's unique data binding approach, SVG manipulation, and asynchronous programming. Students would need to master these technical details before they could apply them to their own data analysis questions, creating a high barrier to entry for non-STEM disciplines.

4.2.2.2 AFTER: AI-Assisted Approach

In an AI-assisted classroom, creating sophisticated data visualizations becomes accessible to non-STEM instructors and students by shifting the focus to data interpretation, visual communication principles, and discipline-specific analysis rather than implementation details. The instructor guides the process through conceptual frameworks and analytical questions:

1. **Data Selection and Research Question (30 minutes)**: "What dataset is relevant to your research question? What specific aspects of this data do you want to visualize? What patterns or relationships are you hoping to discover or communicate?"

2. **Visualization Strategy (25 minutes)**: "What type of visualization would best represent your data? Consider bar charts for comparisons, line charts for trends over time, scatter plots for relationships between variables, etc. Sketch how you envision the final visualization."

3. **Data Preparation Discussion (20 minutes)**: "Let's discuss how your data needs to be structured for visualization. Does it

need cleaning, filtering, or aggregating? What variables will be mapped to visual elements (x-axis, y-axis, color, size)?"

4. **AI Collaboration for Data Preparation (25 minutes)**: "Using your dataset, ask the AI:

   'I have a CSV file with the following columns: [list columns]. I want to visualize [specific aspect] to show [research question]. How should I prepare this data for visualization? Are there any transformations I should make?'"

5. **Visualization Implementation (30 minutes)**: "Now, ask the AI to help create the visualization:

   'Can you help me create an interactive [chart type] visualization of this data using D3.js? I want to show [specific aspects] and include interactive features like [tooltip/filtering/zooming]. Please provide complete code that I can run in a web browser, including explanations of key components.'"

6. **Understanding the Visualization (20 minutes)**: "Review the code provided by the AI. Ask questions about specific sections:

   'Can you explain how the data binding works in this visualization?'

   'What does this scale function do?'

   'How is interactivity being implemented?'"

7. **Customization for Disciplinary Needs (30 minutes)**: "Modify the visualization to better align with your specific research questions by asking the AI:

   'How can I modify this visualization to emphasize [specific pattern or relationship]?'

   'Can you help me add annotations to highlight [specific data points of interest]?'

   'How can I incorporate disciplinary conventions for [field] visualizations?'"

8. **Deployment and Sharing (15 minutes)**: "Ask the AI:

   "What's the simplest way to share this interactive visualization with colleagues? Can you provide instructions for publishing it online using GitHub Pages?'"

9. **Critical Analysis and Interpretation (25 minutes)**: "Write an analysis of what your visualization reveals about your research question. What patterns emerged? What limitations exist in this visual representation? How would you improve it in future iterations?"

In this approach, both the instructor and students can create sophis-ticated, interactive data visualizations without needing to master JavaScript or D3.js beforehand. Attention remains on data interpreta-tion, analytical thinking, and visual communication—skills that align with disciplinary expertise in non-STEM fields. The tool handles the complex technical implementation while the humans work on asking meaningful questions, interpreting results, and refining visualizations to effectively communicate insights. This makes advanced data visu-alization techniques more widely available, making them accessible to researchers and students across all disciplines.

These two activity translations—one beginner level and one advanced—demonstrate how AI assistance fundamentally changes programming education in non-STEM contexts. The change is not simply about making coding "easier" but about redirecting cognitive attention to higher-order thinking skills that align with disciplinary expertise.

Several key principles emerge from these translations:

1. **Conceptual First, Implementation Second**: Both activities pri-oritize conceptual understanding (design thinking, data anal-ysis) before technical implementation, inverting the traditional sequence.
2. **Point-of-Need Learning**: Technical concepts are introduced contextually when they become relevant to the task at hand, rather than as prerequisites.
3. **Discipline-Centered Approach**: The primary focus remains on disciplinary questions and objectives, with technology serving as a means rather than an end.
4. **Scaffolded AI Collaboration**: Students learn to craft effective prompts and engage critically with generated solutions, devel-oping an important meta-skill for the AI era.
5. **Authentic Problem-Solving**: Activities mirror real-world workflows where professionals increasingly collaborate with tools to solve complex problems.

This translation approach enables non-STEM faculty to confidently integrate computational thinking into their courses without becom-ing programming experts themselves. It allows students to engage with meaningful, discipline-specific programming projects from day one, bypassing the traditional syntax-first barrier that has limited cod-ing education to technical disciplines. In the sections that follow, we will explore specific strategies for implementing this approach across different non-STEM contexts, addressing common challenges, and assessing student learning when assistance is part of the instructional design. This activity framework acknowledges that non-STEM faculty don't need to become coding experts to implement computational thinking in their courses. Instead, faculty can position themselves as co-explorers with students, modeling effective collaboration with tools while maintaining disciplinary knowledge and critical thinking.

This reflective assessment activity marks a critical departure from how we conceptualized the role of faculty in computational education in the past. Unlike traditional programming contexts—where instructors needed years of technical training before guiding students—the assisted framework positions faculty as expert facilitators of learning processes rather than repositories of syntax knowledge. By honestly assessing their own computational thinking skills and developing strategies for collaboration, non-STEM faculty can confidently venture into territories previously reserved for computer science specialists. What makes this approach revolutionary is its acknowledgment that subject-matter expertise combined with critical thinking remains the true north star of education, while technical implementation details become increasingly automatable. As we move into deployment practices in the next section, this foundational recognition continues: meaningful learning happens when disciplinary questions drive technological implementation, not when technology dictates the boundaries of disciplinary inquiry. The assistant becomes a bridge between conceptual understanding and technical execution, allowing both instructor and student to focus on the "why" rather than merely the "how."

4.3 Deployment Skills as a Foundational Step

Reorienting programming instruction around immediate, real-world applications rather than isolated syntax drills has proven to reduce cognitive overload and encourage deeper engagement with computational concepts (Haindl & Weinberger, 2024). The traditional programming pedagogy places deployment near the end of the learning sequence—a capstone achievement after students have mastered syntax, debugging, and algorithmic problem-solving. This sequencing creates an artificial barrier that delays the most motivating aspect of programming: seeing one's creation live in the world where others can interact with it. This approach is particularly problematic in non-STEM contexts, where students may never reach the deployment stage due to the technical prerequisites demanded by traditional instruction.

Through the inversion of this sequence—making deployment the starting point rather than the destination—we reshape programming education from an exercise in syntax memorization to a process of creative problem-solving with immediate, tangible outcomes.

Instead of asking novices to memorize syntactical rules upfront, educators can lead with functional projects that illustrate how coding solves tangible problems. This approach aligns with constructivist learning theories, suggesting that knowledge retention improves when learners explore concepts within meaningful contexts (Ausubel, 2012). By initially framing coding as a pathway to building a basic web application, automating tasks, or analyzing a dataset, students see firsthand how computational thinking becomes an invaluable asset across diverse fields—from business analytics to digital humanities (Jung, 2020). In conventional programming courses, students might spend weeks learning HTML tags, CSS properties, and JavaScript functions before ever publishing anything on the web. This creates an artificial separation between learning and application that contradicts how professionals actually work in the field. Through real-world project work, the traditional emphasis on error-free syntax morphs into a process of iterative testing and refinement, better mirroring the realities of modern software development (Ding et al., 2024). For non-STEM disciplines, this syntax-first approach presents an almost insurmountable barrier. Faculty in fields like history, literature, or marketing rarely possess the technical expertise to guide students through complex syntax learning, creating a situation where computational thinking remains inaccessible precisely where it could be most impactful.

Coding tools serve as gateways to computational thinking, inviting newcomers to engage with logical problem-solving while sidestepping the discouragement that often accompanies syntax memorization. Platforms like GitHub Copilot, Vercel v0, and Replit with its Ghostwriter coding assistant have enhanced the learning experience by offering suggested code snippets and automating routine tasks—preserving early enthusiasm that might otherwise be extinguished by trivial syntax errors. In the classroom, this creates opportunities for deeper learning; instructors can design exercises where students critically evaluate and refine generated solutions, simultaneously developing conceptual mastery and essential analytical capabilities. This approach reframes programming as an inherently creative discipline that emphasizes exploration and problem-solving, illustrating how computational thinking directly addresses real-world challenges rather than existing as an isolated technical skill to be conquered.

The deployment-first approach directly addresses the central problem identified in earlier chapters: the artificial delay between learning and application that diminishes motivation and relevance, particularly for non-STEM students. By making immediate publication and sharing of work the starting point, we create a context where technical details gain purpose and meaning. Syntax is learned not as an abstract set of rules, but as a means to improve something already functioning in the world.

4.3.1 Before/After Translation: Simple Personal Website Deployment

4.3.1.1 BEFORE: Traditional Approach

In a conventional introduction to web development, instructors would typically begin with HTML basics, requiring students to memorize tags and attributes before moving to CSS properties and selectors. JavaScript would be introduced only after these basics were mastered, often well into the second half of the course. The deployment process would be relegated to perhaps the final week, treated as an advanced topic requiring command-line expertise.

The traditional syllabus might look like:

1. **Weeks 1–2:** HTML structure and semantics
2. **Weeks 3–4:** CSS styling and layout
3. **Weeks 5–6:** Basic JavaScript functionality
4. **Weeks 7–8:** Forms and data validation
5. **Week 9:** Introduction to version control
6. **Week 10:** Deployment concepts

Students would be required to write all code manually, with assessment centering on syntactic correctness and adherence to technical standards. This approach assumes that deployment is a reward for mastering coding rather than a motivational starting point. The instructor would need to provide detailed technical explanations covering:

- HTML document structure and validation
- CSS selectors and the cascade
- JavaScript syntax and DOM manipulation
- Git commands and workflow
- Server configuration and hosting options

This approach creates significant cognitive load for both the instructor and the student, requiring extensive technical knowledge before any meaningful creation can be shared.

4.3.1.2 AFTER: AI-Assisted Deployment-First Approach

In an AI-assisted, deployment-first classroom, the very first project begins with publication. Non-STEM instructors guide students through conceptualizing and planning a personal website, focusing on content strategy, audience needs, and communication goals—areas where disciplinary expertise already exists. A revised syllabus might look like:

1. **Day 1:** Website planning and content development
2. **Day 2:** AI-assisted implementation and initial deployment
3. **Week 2:** Understanding HTML structure through iterative refinement
4. **Week 3:** Exploring CSS through design modifications
5. **Week 4:** Adding interactive elements as needed for content goals
6. **Weeks 5–10:** Progressive enhancement based on project needs

The instructor facilitates discussions around purpose, audience, and content organization—conceptual skills that transfer from their disciplinary expertise. When implementation questions arise, both the instructor and students leverage AI assistance:

"I want to create a responsive navigation menu for my portfolio site that collapses on mobile screens. Can you provide the HTML, CSS, and JavaScript for this, explaining the key concepts?"

This approach allows non-STEM faculty to confidently guide computational projects without becoming coding experts themselves. Students experience the satisfaction of having a live website from the first week while gradually developing technical understanding through purposeful refinement rather than abstract exercises. Assessment changes from syntax correctness to effective problem-solving, communication clarity, and thoughtful iteration based on user feedback. This aligns with how professionals in the field actually work, where deployment is not the final step but an ongoing process of refinement and enhancement.

By positioning deployment as a foundational step rather than an advanced skill, we create a context where technical learning becomes immediately relevant. This approach particularly benefits non-STEM disciplines, where the focal point is using technology to communicate disciplinary content rather than mastering technology for its own sake. When students deploy their work early, they encounter authentic technical challenges with inherent motivation to solve them. A student whose personal portfolio is live but displays incorrectly on mobile devices has genuine motivation to understand responsive design principles. A history student whose interactive timeline is visible to the public but loads slowly has a real incentive to learn about web performance optimization.

4.3.2 Before/After Translation: Collaborative Repository Management

4.3.2.1 BEFORE: Traditional Approach

In conventional programming education, version control and collaborative workflows would be introduced only after students had mastered basic coding skills. Instructors would need to provide detailed technical training on Git concepts and commands, requiring students to memorize a complex syntax for version control operations. A traditional collaborative project might require students to:

1. Install Git and configure their local environment
2. Learn command-line operations for repository management
3. Understand branching models and merge strategies
4. Master conflict resolution through manual editing
5. Implement protected branches and code review protocols

This approach assumes technical expertise that non-STEM faculty rarely possess and creates significant barriers to implementing collaborative programming projects in disciplines where the focus should be on content rather than tools. The instructor would need to troubleshoot complex technical issues like merge conflicts, authentication problems, and repository misconfigurations—areas far removed from their disciplinary expertise.

4.3.2.2 AFTER: AI-Assisted Collaborative Approach

In an AI-enhanced environment, collaborative version control becomes accessible to non-STEM contexts by centering the conceptual benefits of collaboration rather than the technical mechanics. The instructor designs a collaborative project where students jointly develop a resource repository, digital exhibition, or interactive publication related to course content. The central framing remains on disciplinary knowledge while introducing collaborative digital creation:

1. Students begin with a planning document outlining responsibilities and contribution areas
2. The instructor creates an initial repository structure using AI assistance
3. Students use AI to help navigate repository operations:

"I need to update the economic data visualization in our group project without affecting my teammate's historical analysis section. Can you explain how to create a branch, make my changes, and request a review?"

4. When technical challenges arise, AI provides just-in-time guidance:

5. "I'm seeing a merge conflict in our project. Can you explain what this means and guide me through resolving it step by step?"

This approach allows non-STEM faculty to implement sophisticated collaborative digital projects without becoming Git experts themselves. Students learn valuable collaboration skills contextualized within disciplinary content creation, with the assistant providing technical breakdowns when needed. Assessment centers on effective collaboration, thoughtful integration of diverse perspectives, and contribution quality rather than technical command proficiency. This better reflects professional collaborative environments where tools serve the collaborative process rather than defining it.

4.3.3 Before/After Translation: CI/CD Pipeline Implementation

4.3.3.1 BEFORE: Traditional Approach

Continuous Integration/Continuous Deployment (CI/CD) pipelines represent advanced DevOps concepts traditionally reserved for upper-level computer science courses or professional development contexts. In conventional programming education, instructors would need extensive knowledge of:

- Build systems and dependency management
- Testing frameworks and automation
- Server configuration and environment variables
- YAML syntax for pipeline configuration
- Containerization technologies like Docker
- Cloud service provider interfaces

Students would spend weeks learning these complex systems before implementing even a simple automated workflow. The technical prerequisites would effectively make this content inaccessible to non-STEM contexts, regardless of how valuable the concepts might be.

The traditional approach would require detailed technical documentation and step-by-step guides for:

- Setting up testing frameworks
- Configuring build processes
- Managing environmental secrets
- Defining deployment targets

4.3.3.2 AFTER: AI-Assisted CI/CD Approach

In an AI-assisted classroom, the conceptual benefits of automated testing and deployment can be introduced without requiring deep technical expertise. Non-STEM faculty can guide students in understanding why continuous integration matters for collaborative work while using AI to handle implementation details. The instructor frames the activity around a disciplinary question: "How can we ensure our collaborative digital project maintains consistent quality as multiple contributors make changes?" Students explore the concept through a simplified workflow:

1. The class discusses quality standards relevant to their discipline (data accuracy, citation formatting, visual consistency, etc.)
2. Students collaborate to define "tests" for these standards in plain language
3. Using AI assistance, these plain-language requirements are translated into automated checks:

   "I want to create an automated check that verifies all external links in our digital history exhibit are working. Can you help me set up a GitHub Action that tests links whenever changes are made to the repository?"

4. Students experience the benefits of automation when their changes trigger the checks:

   "The automated check found two broken citations in my section. Help me see how this helps maintain quality across our collaborative project."

This approach allows non-STEM contexts to benefit from advanced CI/CD concepts without requiring technical expertise. The focus remains on quality standards relevant to the discipline, with AI handling the technical implementation. Assessment evaluates students' understanding of quality-assurance processes and how automation supports collaborative work rather than technical configuration skills. This better aligns with how professionals use these tools—as a means to ensure quality and consistency rather than technical exercises.

The integration of early project deployment into introductory programming courses represents a significant pedagogical change that challenges traditional methodologies. By reconceiving assessment to consider problem-solving and communication rather than syntax mastery, this approach aligns programming education with the realities of modern software development and the needs of non-STEM disciplines. Conventional instruction typically reserves project deployment for advanced learners who have mastered syntax, debugging, and algorithmic problem-solving; however, postponing public exposure neglects opportunities for early engagement and real-world contextualization. Early deployment shows that isolated coding exercises evolve into a comprehensive process that produces tangible outcomes, bridging the gap between theory and applied practice. This approach enables students to experience the complete software development lifecycle, encompassing workflow management, iterative refinement, and version control. The immediate publication of projects engenders a sense of accomplishment and motivates learners by demonstrating the direct impact of their work. Educators who implement early deployment create an environment in which programming is perceived as a dynamic, evolving discipline rather than a series of abstract tasks. Early exposure to deployment practices also demystifies the technical aspects of public hosting and collaborative development.

Integrating public project sharing into the curriculum further promotes a comprehensive understanding of the software development lifecycle. By requiring students to publish their work on platforms such as GitHub Pages, Netlify, or Vercel, educators encourage learners to engage with aspects of hosting, accessibility, and user interface design that extend beyond mere code composition. Public deployment also transforms assignments into opportunities for receiving iterative feedback from peers, instructors, and external audiences, enhancing both technical and design skills. This iterative feedback loop reinforces the importance of maintainability and continuous improvement within software projects. Moreover, the public sharing of work encourages a collaborative atmosphere that mirrors professional development environments and cultivates critical communication skills. Educators who adopt this strategy can support learners' appreciation of the real-world implications of their coding efforts and understand the importance of user-centric design.

Introducing version control systems—particularly GitHub—early in the curriculum enhances both technical literacy and collaborative competency. Early exposure to Git-based workflows allows students to appreciate the importance of tracking changes, managing repositories, and engaging in collaborative development. Educators who break down this instruction by beginning with individual repositories and gradually progressing to team-based projects support a structured pathway to mastering these indispensable tools. The systematic introduction of branching, pull requests, and code reviews not only aligns academic practices with industry standards but also instills disciplined coding habits from the outset. Such early mastery of version control systems reinforces iterative refinement and effective project management. By integrating these practices, instructors prepare learners for the collaborative demands of modern software development environments, where version control is a primary component. This structured approach enables technical skills to be developed in tandem with critical problem-solving and teamwork competencies.

Deploying projects on contemporary platforms such as Netlify and Vercel further moves programming instruction into a practice-oriented discipline. These streamlined deployment solutions reduce configuration barriers and allow students to focus on translating code into publicly accessible applications. Engaging with both front-end and back-end components, learners gain a holistic perspective on full-stack development and the practical challenges associated with scalability, security, and continuous integration. Early hands-on experience with these platforms demystifies the deployment process and emphasizes the tangible outcomes of programming efforts. This experiential learning cultivates an entrepreneurial mindset that encourages innovation and creative problem-solving. Educators who incorporate these modern deployment tools prompt students to consider real-world issues and iterate rapidly based on user feedback. Such assignments bridge the gap between theoretical knowledge and applied technical skills, equipping learners for professional environments.

Embedding early project deployment and public sharing within the curriculum yields multifaceted benefits that extend beyond technical mastery. Students develop a pronounced sense of ownership and pride as they witness their work evolve into publicly accessible applications, thereby increasing overall engagement and motivation. The iterative process of deployment and feedback collection not only enhances technical skills but also cultivates critical soft skills, such as reflective practice and effective communication. Integrating deployment-related assessments—ranging from personal portfolio development to dynamic web application construction—provides an environment where learners experience every stage of the software development lifecycle. This comprehensive approach reinforces the interconnectedness of theoretical instruction and practical application, better preparing students for the evolving demands of the digital era. Assignments that emphasize real-world deployment processes validate the significance of continuous improvement and collaborative coding practices.

For non-STEM contexts, the deployment-first approach offers a revolutionary entry point to programming education. By inverting the traditional sequence—starting with meaningful publication and working backward to technical understanding—we create a learning environment where:

1. Disciplinary content remains central rather than being subordinated to technical requirements
2. Students experience immediate success and relevance, motivating deeper exploration
3. Technical concepts are introduced when they serve a clear purpose rather than as abstract prerequisites
4. Faculty can guide computational thinking without needing to master syntax details
5. Assessment focuses on problem-solving, communication, and iterative improvement—skills that align with disciplinary priorities

This approach does not diminish technical learning—it contextualizes it within meaningful application, making programming accessible to disciplines that have previously been excluded from computational practices.

4.4 Introducing Organizational Thinking Earlier

Introducing organizational thinking early in programming education is paramount for cultivating a systematic mindset that underpins professional software development. Traditional curricula frequently postpone instruction in organizational practices—ranging from maintaining clean file structures to proficient command-line navigation—until advanced projects necessitate such skills. This delay often leaves students ill-equipped to manage complex workflows, resulting in confusion and inefficiency when scaling projects. Early exposure to organizational principles not only enhances code quality but also instills habits essential for planning, modular design, and long-term maintainability. By integrating these practices at the outset, educators facilitate the development of a disciplined approach that mirrors the operational demands of professional software engineering. This approach is particularly valuable in non-STEM contexts, where students and instructors may already possess strong organizational thinking from their disciplinary training— historians organize archives, literary scholars create taxonomies of texts, and sociologists structure research data. By leveraging these existing strengths as entry points to programming, we create bridges between disciplinary expertise and computational thinking.

The conventional programming curriculum treats organizational skills as advanced concepts that follow syntax mastery—students first learn to write code, then later learn how to organize it effectively. This sequencing creates artificial barriers, particularly for non-STEM disciplines where organizational thinking may actually precede coding ability. By inverting this relationship—making organization a precursor to implementation—we build on existing strengths while creating foundations for technical learning.

4.4.1 Before/After Translation: Command-Line Introduction

4.4.1.1 BEFORE: Traditional Approach

In conventional programming education, command-line interfaces are typically introduced as technical prerequisites, requiring memorization of commands, flags, and syntax patterns. Students might encounter terminal operations only when they become necessary for specific technical tasks like package installation or deployment—often weeks or months into a course.

A traditional approach might include:

1. Introduction to terminal concepts and command syntax
2. Memorization of common commands (cd, ls, mkdir, rm, etc.)
3. Understanding flags and options for command modification
4. Learning path structures and navigation patterns
5. Mastering file permission concepts and modification commands
6. Introduction to package managers and installation procedures

This approach treats command-line proficiency as a technical skill to be mastered through rote memorization rather than as an organizational framework for understanding computer systems. The instructor would need to provide detailed technical instructions and troubleshoot syntax errors across different operating systems. Students would be expected to remember exact command syntax, with assessments often focusing on command recall rather than conceptual understanding. This creates a significant cognitive load, particularly for non-STEM students who may have limited exposure to command-based interfaces.

4.4.1.2 AFTER: AI-Assisted Approach

In an AI-assisted classroom, command-line introduction centers on the conceptual understanding of file system organization while using AI to provide just-in-time syntax support. This approach frames terminal use as an organizational tool rather than a technical barrier. The instructor designs an activity that introduces file system concepts through guided exploration:

1. Students begin by discussing how they organize their own digital files and folders
2. The instructor introduces the concept of hierarchical file systems as an organizational pattern
3. Students draw diagrams of file organization for a hypothetical project
4. Using AI assistance, students learn to navigate and manipulate this structure:

   "I want to create a project folder with separate directories for data, analysis, and visualization. Can you show me the commands to create this structure, explaining what each command does?"

5. When students need to perform specific operations, AI provides contextualized guidance:

   "How do I find all files containing the word 'climate' in my research data folder and copy them to a new analysis directory?"

This approach allows non-STEM faculty to introduce file system organization without needing to master command syntax themselves. Attention moves from memorizing commands to understanding organizational principles—an approach that builds on existing strengths in many non-STEM disciplines. Assessment centers on students' ability to design logical organizational structures and articulate their organizational thinking rather than command recall. This better aligns with how professionals actually use command-line interfaces—as tools for implementing organizational strategies rather than as technical exercises. Many novice programmers initially depend on graphical user interfaces, which, while accessible, may inadvertently cultivate habits that are less transferable to professional environments. In contrast, mastering the command line is critical for achieving faster, more flexible workflows that support essential tasks such as version control, remote server management, and package installation. Embedding command-line instruction within early project-based assignments demystifies terminal operations and encourages learners to adopt text-based workflows from the beginning. Instructors can introduce foundational commands—such as ls, cd, mkdir, touch, nano, git, and npm—to build confidence and proficiency. This early focus not only streamlines subsequent development tasks but also equips students with the practical tools necessary for navigating diverse computing environments. Command-line fluency becomes a vital asset as learners progress to more sophisticated development challenges. Emphasizing these skills from the outset supports the objective where students are prepared to engage with advanced technical concepts and industry-standard tools.

4.4.2 Before/After Translation: Project Structure Development

4.4.2.1 BEFORE: Traditional Approach

In conventional programming education, project structure and organization are typically taught after students have mastered basic syntax and programming concepts. This sequencing assumes that organization follows implementation rather than precedes it—a notion that contradicts professional best practices. A traditional approach might include:

1. Learning programming basics through single-file scripts
2. Introduction to functions and basic modularity
3. Advanced concepts of module systems and import mechanics
4. Introduction to package dependencies and management
5. Refactoring exercises to transform monolithic code into modular structures

This approach often leads to students developing inefficient organizational habits that must later be unlearned. The instructor would need to provide detailed technical guidance on module syntax, import systems, and packaging standards—areas that vary significantly across programming languages. Students would encounter organizational concepts only after developing potentially problematic coding practices, creating a situation where refactoring becomes more challenging than proper initial organization would have been.

4.4.2.2 AFTER: AI-Assisted Approach

In an AI-assisted classroom, project structure and organization become starting points rather than afterthoughts. This approach recognizes that thoughtful organization should precede implementation—a principle that aligns with disciplinary practices in many non-STEM fields. The instructor guides students through organizational planning before any code is written:

1. Students begin by mapping the conceptual components of their project
2. The class discusses the separation of concerns and logical grouping
3. Students design folder structures and file naming conventions based on project needs
4. Using AI assistance, students implement these structures:

   "I'm creating a data analysis project that will include data collection, preprocessing, analysis, and visualization components. Can you help me create an appropriate project structure with separate modules for each component and explain how these will interact?"

5. When implementation questions arise, AI provides guidance that reinforces organizational principles:

   "How should I structure my code to separate the data processing logic from the visualization components so that other researchers can easily reuse parts of my project?"

This approach allows non-STEM faculty to teach sound organizational practices without requiring deep technical knowledge of module systems. The framing instead pivots to conceptual organization—an area where many non-STEM disciplines already possess sophisticated frameworks. Assessment evaluates students' ability to design logical project structures that facilitate collaboration, maintenance, and reuse rather than thinking about technical implementation details. This better reflects professional practice where organization drives implementation rather than following it.

The integration of scaled-down deployment pipelines and disciplined file organization further enhances early organizational thinking. Many courses reserve deployment and systematic file structuring for later stages, yet these practices are indispensable for understanding the complete software development lifecycle. Embedding simple continuous integration (CI) and continuous deployment (CD) pipelines into introductory coursework allows students to observe firsthand how code transitions from a local environment to production. Tools such as GitHub Actions, Netlify, and Vercel facilitate automated testing and deployment, thereby demystifying the process and reinforcing the iterative nature of development. Concurrently, effective file organization—through the use of structured directories (e.g., src, public, assets, config), consistent naming conventions (camelCase for variables, PascalCase for classes, kebab-case for filenames), and comprehensive documentation via README.md files—enables learners to manage complexity as projects expand. These foundational practices prevent the pitfalls associated with monolithic codebases and promote scalable design.

4.4.3 Before/After Translation: Documentation Practices

4.4.3.1 BEFORE: Traditional Approach

In conventional programming education, documentation is often treated as an afterthought—a task to complete after the "real work" of coding is finished. When taught, it frequently focuses on technical syntax for documentation tools rather than effective communication strategies. A traditional approach might include:

1. Introduction to documentation formats and standards
2. Learning Markdown or other documentation syntax
3. API documentation tools and patterns
4. Generating documentation from code comments
5. Repository documentation best practices

This approach positions documentation as a technical skill rather than a communication practice. The instructor would need to provide detailed guidance on documentation syntax and tools—areas that may be outside their expertise in non-STEM contexts. Students often perceive documentation as busywork rather than an integral part of the development process, leading to inadequate or afterthought documentation practices that fail to serve future users (including their future selves).

4.4.3.2 AFTER: AI-Assisted Approach

In an AI-assisted classroom, documentation becomes an extension of disciplinary communication practices rather than a technical requirement. This approach recognizes that effective documentation is essentially about clear communication—a strength in many non-STEM disciplines. The instructor frames documentation as knowledge preservation and transmission:

1. Students begin by analyzing examples of good and poor documentation from their perspective as users

2. The class discusses principles of clear communication in their disciplinary context

3. Students outline documentation needs for their project based on intended audiences

4. Using AI assistance, students implement documentation that meets these needs:

   "I've created a data visualization tool for historical population trends. Can you help me write documentation that explains both the technical aspects (how to use the tool) and the methodological considerations (data sources, limitations) in a format appropriate for a README file?"

5. When technical questions arise, AI provides guidance that maintains focus on communication:

   "How should I document the data preprocessing steps in my project so that other researchers can understand my methodological choices and reproduce my results?"

This approach allows non-STEM faculty to teach documentation as an extension of disciplinary communication practices rather than a technical skill. The focus changes to effective knowledge sharing—an area where many non-STEM disciplines excel. Assessment evaluates students' ability to communicate project purpose, usage, and limitations clearly rather than focusing on documentation syntax. This better reflects how documentation functions in professional environments—as a communication tool rather than a technical artifact.

Ultimately, this iterative approach aligns academic practices with the professional workflows encountered in real-world development. A curriculum that consistently reinforces real-world practices—emphasizing command-line efficiency, structured file layouts, collaborative workflows, and continuous deployment—ensures that students not only write code but also think, organize, and operate like seasoned developers from day one. For non-STEM contexts, the AI-assisted approach to organizational thinking offers particular advantages:

1. It leverages existing disciplinary strengths in knowledge organization and classification
2. It reduces technical barriers to implementing sound organizational practices
3. It positions organization as a creative and analytical activity rather than a technical requirement
4. It creates natural bridges between disciplinary methodologies and computational approaches

By reimagining organizational thinking as an entry point rather than an advanced topic, we create pathways for non-STEM disciplines to engage with programming in ways that build on their existing strengths. This inversion doesn't diminish the importance of organization—rather, it elevates it from a technical afterthought to a foundational framework that guides implementation. The organizational frameworks introduced through this approach translate directly to professional environments where clear structure, effective documentation, and collaborative workflows are essential for successful projects. By positioning these elements as starting points rather than advanced topics, we prepare students for real-world development practices from their first engagement with programming. In the AI era, organizational thinking takes on even greater importance as implementation details become increasingly automated. When an assistant can generate code based on prompts, the critical human contribution is redirected toward effective organization, clear specification, and thoughtful integration— precisely the skills this approach develops from the outset.

4.5 Troubleshooting as a Critical Thinking Exercise

Troubleshooting in programming education is often narrowly conceptualized as the correction of syntax errors, yet professional software development demands a broader, more nuanced approach. Traditional pedagogical models frequently position error correction as a reactive process, wherein students merely address surface-level mistakes. In contrast, a reimagined framework treats troubleshooting as a critical thinking exercise—a deliberate, analytical process that underpins deeper computational literacy. This encourages learners to engage not only with immediate errors but also with complex integration challenges, system dependencies, and logical inconsistencies that arise in real-world projects. By reorienting debugging as a structured method for deconstructing problems and verifying solutions, educators facilitate the development of skills that are essential for long-term technical proficiency and resilience. Such an approach imbues troubleshooting with cognitive significance, transforming it into a mechanism for cultivating systematic problem-solving and reflective analysis. The resultant mindset enables students to appreciate that debugging is integral to the software development lifecycle rather than an isolated corrective measure. This reconfiguration is particularly significant in the context of API integration—perhaps the most valuable and simultaneously challenging aspect of modern programming for non-STEM disciplines. APIs (Application Programming Interfaces) connect different software systems, allowing historians to access digital archives, sociologists to retrieve social media data, or literature scholars to analyze linguistic patterns across vast text corpora. Yet traditional approaches to API integration require extensive technical knowledge—authentication protocols, request formatting, response parsing, and error handling—creating an almost insurmountable barrier for non-specialists.

The ability to troubleshoot API integration challenges represents a perfect case study for our "before/after" approach. When API troubleshooting is treated as a syntax-centric technical task, it remains inaccessible to most non-STEM contexts. When reimagined as a critical thinking exercise with AI assistance providing technical breakdowns of material, it becomes a powerful tool for disciplinary inquiry accessible to all fields.

4.5.1 Before/After Translation: API Integration Troubleshooting

4.5.1.1 BEFORE: Traditional Approach

In conventional programming education, API integration is typically introduced after students have mastered programming fundamentals, data structures, and networking concepts. Troubleshooting API issues requires extensive technical knowledge across multiple domains:

1. Understanding HTTP request/response mechanisms
2. Mastering authentication protocols (API keys, OAuth, JWT)
3. Parsing complex JSON or XML responses
4. Managing asynchronous operations and promises
5. Implementing error handling for network failures

6. Debugging cross-origin resource sharing (CORS) issues

7. Handling rate limiting and request throttling

A traditional approach would require the instructor to provide detailed technical instruction on:

- Setting up development environments with appropriate libraries
- Configuring authentication credentials
- Constructing properly formatted API requests
- Parsing and transforming response data
- Implementing comprehensive error handling
- Troubleshooting network and server issues

This approach creates significant barriers for non-STEM contexts, where both instructors and students lack the technical prerequisites. As a result, the valuable data and services accessible through APIs remain largely unavailable for disciplinary inquiry in non-technical fields.

4.5.1.2 AFTER: AI-Assisted Approach

In an AI-assisted classroom, API integration becomes accessible to non-STEM contexts by focusing on the conceptual understanding of information exchange while using AI to handle technical implementation details. The instructor designs activities centered on disciplinary questions that can be explored through API-accessible data:

1. Students begin by identifying data sources relevant to their disciplinary questions

2. The class discusses the concept of APIs as standardized information exchange protocols

3. Students formulate specific questions they want to answer using external data

4. Using AI assistance, students implement API integration:

   "I want to analyze climate data for historical periods in specific geographic regions for my environmental history project. I found the NOAA Climate Data API that seems relevant. Can you help me understand how to access this API, what data is available, and how I might request specific information for my research question?"

5. When troubleshooting is needed, AI provides contextualized assistance:

"I'm getting an error when trying to access this historical newspaper API. The message says 'Unauthorized.' What might be causing this, and how can I fix it?"

This approach allows non-STEM faculty to guide API integration projects without needing to master the technical details themselves. The focus remains on disciplinary questions and data interpretation—areas where faculty expertise already exists. Students learn to formulate effective queries to both the API and the assistant, developing critical thinking about information access and validation while the tool handles syntax-level implementation. When errors occur, troubleshooting becomes an exercise in problem formulation and hypothesis testing rather than technical debugging. Assessment centers on students' ability to formulate meaningful questions, interpret returned data, and draw disciplinary insights rather than on technical implementation details. This better reflects how APIs should function in non-STEM contexts—as windows to valuable data rather than as technical challenges. In professional settings, developers and writers must navigate complex version histories, source control systems, and collaborative workflows. APIs add another layer of complexity, requiring careful monitoring of versioning, deprecation notices, and documentation changes. Smart platforms facilitate structured interaction with these systems, allowing students to focus on the conceptual understanding of inter-system communication rather than syntactical details. Through integrating API exploration into project-based learning, educators provide students with practical experience in accessing external resources and services—a pivotal skill for contemporary research and application development.

Encouraging debugging as a logical problem-solving exercise is essential for transitioning students away from ad hoc, trial-and-error methodologies. Novice programmers often resort to random code modifications, a practice that may yield ephemeral fixes but ultimately obscures the underlying causes of errors. Faculty can counteract this tendency by promoting hypothesis-driven reasoning that requires learners to methodically isolate issues. Structured strategies—such as interpreting compiler and runtime error messages, breaking problems into smaller test cases, and tracing program execution—equip students with the analytical tools necessary to diagnose and resolve issues systematically. Moreover, the stepwise elimination of variables reinforces the importance of isolating the root cause of a problem, rather than merely masking its symptoms. Instructors may further enhance this process by integrating self-explanation prompts, which require students to articulate their thought processes before implementing code changes. This reflective practice reinforces the cognitive processes underlying effective debugging and supports a mindset oriented toward continuous improvement.

4.5.2 Before/After Translation: Debugging Methodology

4.5.2.1 BEFORE: Traditional Approach

In conventional programming education, debugging methodology is typically taught through syntax-dependent exercises where students identify and fix errors in given code snippets. This approach assumes technical knowledge of

1. Programming language syntax and common errors
2. Debugging tools and breakpoint mechanics
3. Stack trace interpretation
4. Variable state inspection
5. Step-through execution processes

A traditional debugging activity might provide students with broken code and instructions to

- Identify syntax errors using IDE error highlighting
- Set breakpoints at strategic locations
- Watch variable values during execution
- Step through code line by line
- Interpret stack traces when exceptions occur

This approach frames debugging as a technical skill requiring specialized tools and knowledge, rather than as an analytical thinking process. The instructor would need to provide detailed guidance on debugging tools and error interpretation across different programming environments. Students without deep syntax knowledge struggle to make progress, as traditional debugging assumes the ability to recognize correct from incorrect code patterns—a challenge for non-specialists.

4.5.2.2 *AFTER: AI-Assisted Approach*

In an AI-assisted classroom, debugging methodology is reimagined as an exercise in systematic problem-solving and hypothesis testing—skills that transfer from many disciplinary contexts.

The instructor designs activities that focus on analytical approaches to troubleshooting:

1. Students begin by discussing problem-solving methodologies in their disciplinary context

2. The class explores how these methodologies can be applied to computational problems

3. Students practice formulating clear problem statements and hypotheses

4. Using AI assistance, students implement debugging strategies:

   "My data visualization isn't displaying correctly. The graph shows all zero values even though I know my dataset contains positive numbers. Can you help me think through what might be causing this issue and how to diagnose it systematically?"

5. When technical details are needed, AI provides contextualized guidance:

   "Based on your description, this could be a data type conversion issue. Let's test this hypothesis by examining how the data is being read from the source. Can you show me the code that loads the data?"

This approach allows non-STEM faculty to teach debugging as analytical thinking rather than technical syntax correction. The focal point moves to methodical problem-solving—a skill that transfers to many disciplinary contexts. Students learn to articulate problems clearly, form testable hypotheses, and interpret results—skills that extend beyond programming to general critical thinking. The tool provides technical support while students develop stronger analytical frameworks. Assessment evaluates students' problem-solving approach, hypothesis formulation, and logical reasoning rather than their technical debugging skills. This better reflects the cognitive value of debugging as a thinking exercise rather than merely a technical necessity.

To illustrate how troubleshooting can be reframed as a critical thinking exercise, we present a practical activity that encourages students to document and reflect on their debugging processes. This activity, which instructors might call "Debugging Diaries," for their students, will challenge students to analyze errors systematically, formulate hypotheses, and develop solutions through a structured approach that emphasizes metacognition and analytical reasoning.

4.5.3 Before/After Translation: Error Diagnosis and Communication

4.5.3.1 BEFORE: Traditional Approach

In conventional programming education, error diagnosis and communication are often treated as technical skills requiring specialized knowledge of the following:

1. Error code interpretation across different environments
2. Exception class hierarchies and inheritance patterns
3. Logging frameworks and configuration
4. Debugging tool interfaces and functionality
5. Technical vocabulary for describing program behavior

A traditional approach might involve teaching students to:

- Recognize common error patterns in specific languages
- Use technical terminology for precise error description
- Configure logging at appropriate levels
- Generate and interpret crash reports
- Document errors using standardized formats

This approach treats error communication as a technical skill rather than a general communication competency. The instructor would need extensive knowledge of language-specific error patterns and debugging tools—expertise that non-STEM faculty rarely possess. Students often struggle to translate between technical error messages and meaningful problem descriptions, limiting their ability to seek help or document issues effectively.

4.5.3.2 AFTER: AI-Assisted Approach

In an AI-assisted classroom, error diagnosis and communication are reimagined as extensions of disciplinary communication practices, with AI bridging the gap between natural language descriptions and technical details. The instructor designs activities that emphasize clear problem articulation:

1. Students begin by analyzing how they describe problems in their disciplinary context
2. The class discusses principles of effective problem description (specificity, context, expected vs. actual outcomes)
3. Students practice describing computational issues in natural language
4. Using AI assistance, students refine their error communication:

   "When I try to analyze this dataset, I get an error. The program was working yesterday, but today it stops and displays a red message. I didn't change anything intentional."

   AI (speculated output): "Your description helps me understand that something unexpected happened. To diagnose this more effectively, could you tell me:

   a. What specific action triggers the error?
   b. What is the exact text of the error message?
   c. What were you expecting to happen instead?"

5. Students learn to iterate their problem descriptions based on feedback:

   "I was trying to load data from the census_data.csv file into my visualization. When I click 'Load Data,' nothing happens for about 10 seconds, then a message appears saying 'Failed to parse CSV: unexpected end of file.' I expected the data to load and show population trends in the graph."

This approach allows non-STEM faculty to teach effective error communication without requiring technical expertise. The focus pivots to clarity and precision in problem description—skills that transfer from many disciplinary contexts. Students develop the ability to communicate effectively about technical issues—a valuable skill regardless of whether they are communicating with assistants, technical support, or colleagues. The tool provides feedback on what additional information would help diagnosis, teaching students to provide more effective problem descriptions over time. Assessment evaluates students' ability to communicate problems clearly and respond to requests for clarification rather than their technical vocabulary. This better reflects how error communication functions in professional environments—as a bridging practice between technical and non-technical stakeholders.

The integration of assisted debugging strategies represents another frontier in modern programming education, offering real-time insights that can enhance efficiency when used judiciously. Contemporary tools such as GitHub Copilot, ChatGPT, and Replit Ghostwriter provide suggestions and code corrections that can accelerate the identification of errors. However, without careful guidance, students may develop a habit of passively accepting generated fixes rather than engaging critically with the debugging process. Faculty should emphasize that the tools are intended to complement, not replace, human reasoning. Key strategies include validating generated solutions against the original code intent, comparing multiple recommendations before implementation, and prompting the assistant to explain underlying errors rather than simply proposing fixes. This approach encourages learners to maintain an active role in the debugging process, ensuring that they remain engaged with the logic and structure of their code. By integrating assisted strategies responsibly, educators can enhance the efficiency of troubleshooting while reinforcing the importance of critical analysis.

4.5.4 Before/After Translation: System Integration Troubleshooting

4.5.4.1 BEFORE: Traditional Approach

In conventional programming education, system integration troubleshooting is typically reserved for advanced courses or professional settings, requiring expertise in:

1. Network protocols and architecture
2. Database connection management
3. Authentication and security systems
4. Microservice communication patterns
5. Distributed system debugging

A traditional approach would involve teaching students to:

- Configure network analysis tools
- Set up monitoring for service communications

- Trace requests across system boundaries
- Debug timing and race conditions
- Implement logging across distributed systems

This approach positions integration troubleshooting as an advanced technical specialization requiring deep expertise across multiple domains. The instructor would need extensive knowledge of systems architecture and distributed computing—far beyond what could be expected in non-STEM contexts. The complexity of traditional system integration troubleshooting effectively makes these skills inaccessible to non-specialists, despite their growing importance in an increasingly interconnected digital landscape.

4.5.4.2 AFTER: AI-Assisted Approach

In an AI-assisted classroom, system integration troubleshooting becomes accessible by centering on the conceptual understanding of system interactions while using AI to navigate technical implementation details. The instructor designs activities that emphasize conceptual system models:

1. Students begin by mapping the components of their project and how they interact
2. The class discusses potential points of failure in connected systems
3. Students create diagrams showing data flow between components
4. Using AI assistance, students diagnose integration issues:

   "My project combines a data collection component that retrieves information from a historical archive API, a processing component that analyzes text patterns, and a visualization component that displays results. The visualization is showing no data, even though I can confirm the API is returning results when tested separately. How can I systematically troubleshoot where the breakdown is occurring?"

5. When technical implementations are needed, AI provides guided assistance (speculated output):

   "Let's test whether data is successfully moving between your components. Can you add some logging statements at these key transfer points to track the data's journey through your system? Here's how you might implement that..."

This approach allows non-STEM faculty to guide integration troubleshooting without requiring deep technical expertise. The focal point moves to a conceptual understanding of system interactions—an area where disciplinary knowledge about information flow may already provide relevant frameworks. Students learn to think systematically about connected components and information transfer—concepts that apply broadly across many disciplines. The tool provides technical implementation details while students develop stronger conceptual models of system interaction. Assessment evaluates students' ability to map system components, identify potential failure points, and develop systematic testing strategies rather than their technical debugging skills. This better reflects how integration troubleshooting functions in professional environments—as a systematic analysis process supported by technical tools.

A critical evolution in troubleshooting pedagogy involves moving the locus from merely fixing errors to understanding complex integration challenges. In professional software development, errors are not confined to syntax but extend to issues such as dependency conflicts, API integration failures, scalability bottlenecks, and performance inefficiencies. Exposing students to system-level challenges early in the curriculum provides them with a realistic perspective on the multifaceted nature of software projects. Educators can introduce scenarios involving library and package management challenges—such as handling outdated dependencies or missing modules—and offer guidance on debugging API requests, managing authentication failures, and validating data formats. Such comprehensive exposure equips learners with the ability to anticipate and mitigate integration issues before they escalate. Emphasizing the interplay between disparate components of a system encourages a holistic approach to problem-solving, where the focus redirects from isolated error correction to maintaining robust, interdependent software architectures. This methodology not only prepares students for real-world challenges but also instills an appreciation for the systemic nature of modern programming.

4.5.5 Troubleshooting as the Foundation for Computational Literacy

Using troubleshooting as an entry point to broader computational literacy deepens students' understanding of foundational programming concepts. Far from being a mere technical necessity, debugging serves as a cognitive exercise that strengthens pattern recognition, algorithmic reasoning, and problem decomposition. Through structured troubleshooting, students recognize recurring errors across projects, grasp how small code changes affect program logic, and develop systematic approaches to finding root causes. This iterative process builds resilience and self-sufficiency—qualities vital in both research and industry. When woven naturally into the learning process, troubleshooting becomes a lens for exploring software behavior, making coding more approachable and encouraging proactive problem-solving. Instructors enrich this experience by examining historical software failures, drawing valuable lessons from the challenges faced by industry veterans. For non-STEM contexts, the AI-assisted approach to troubleshooting offers particular advantages:

1. It positions error resolution as an analytical thinking process rather than a technical skill, building on existing disciplinary strengths in critical inquiry
2. It reduces technical barriers to engaging with sophisticated systems like APIs and integrated applications
3. It teaches transferable problem-solving frameworks that apply across technical and non-technical domains
4. It develops precise communication skills for describing problems and solutions—a valuable capability in any field

Through reimagining troubleshooting as a critical thinking exercise with these smart tools providing technical support, we alter what was once an exclusionary technical skill into an accessible entry point for computational thinking across all disciplines. The approach outlined in this section does not diminish the importance of technical understanding—rather, it contextualizes technical details within broader analytical frameworks. Students still learn about error types, system interactions, and debugging processes, but they learn them as applications of general critical thinking rather than as isolated technical skills. Reframing troubleshooting as a critical thinking exercise empowers students to develop a comprehensive and methodical approach to debugging that extends far beyond mere syntax correction. By encouraging structured debugging techniques, integrating assistive strategies responsibly, and expanding the framing to include complex integration challenges, educators prepare students for the dynamic realities of professional software development. This holistic approach not only enhances technical proficiency but also cultivates essential cognitive skills such as logical reasoning, pattern recognition, and problem decomposition. By normalizing errors as an integral aspect of the iterative development process, instructors create an environment where students are motivated to continually refine their strategies and learn from each debugging experience. Ultimately, viewing troubleshooting as a powerful entry point to broader computational literacy reshapes it from a mundane corrective task into a foundational component of a developer's skill set.

4.6 A Flipped Pedagogical Model: Revising Bloom's Taxonomy

Traditional undergraduate curricula often adopt a bottom-up progression, requiring students to master foundational skills before engaging in real-world problem-solving. In programming education, this structure manifests as a prolonged focus on syntax memorization, debugging drills, and algorithmic exercises before learners tackle meaningful applications. However, current software development practices—particularly those involving assisted coding—do not conform to this stepwise approach. Rather than relying on memorized syntax, industry professionals leverage collaborative tools, online documentation, and automated solutions to streamline their workflow. This traditional sequence creates a significant barrier for non-STEM disciplines, where neither faculty nor students possess the technical foundation presumed necessary for meaningful programming work. The conventional wisdom has been that at least one party—either teacher or student—must master programming basics before computational thinking can be effectively incorporated into disciplinary contexts. This assumption has effectively excluded many fields from the benefits of computational approaches.

A flipped pedagogical model addresses this disconnect by emphasizing higher-level, real-world problem-solving from the outset. Instead of reserving complex, industry-relevant projects for the final stages of a course, educators can guide learners toward advanced applications early on while using assistants and automation to support basic syntax and debugging skills. This approach not only mirrors professional coding contexts but also encourages student engagement and aligns with modern development workflows (Shaik et al., 2023). Therefore, revising Bloom's Taxonomy to prioritize big-picture thinking over low-level skill acquisition offers a practical way to structure this flipped model (Table 4.2). By beginning with tasks tied to evaluation, application, and synthesis—and allowing the machine to facilitate the more mechanical aspects of coding—students build conceptual understanding and develop adaptive, problem-solving mindsets. Research demonstrates that tackling higher-order challenges first can improve knowledge retention and equip learners with the agility needed to navigate complex coding environments (Premana et al., 2023).

TABLE 4.2

Bloom's Revised Taxonomy for Programming Education

Bloom's Revised Taxonomy Level	Student Activity	Practical Reason	Pedagogical Reason	Learning Outcome
Create	Students start by creating and deploying AI-assisted projects to see real-world applications immediately.	Real-world applications provide immediate relevance, improving motivation and engagement before syntax mastery.	Starting with creation fosters intrinsic motivation, ensuring students see coding as a problem-solving tool, not just rules to memorize.	Students develop real-world problem-solving skills, confidence in deploying applications, and ability to iterate on AI-assisted projects.
Evaluate	Students critique and evaluate generated solutions, comparing efficiency, security, and scalability.	Industry professionals continuously review and optimize existing code rather than writing from scratch.	Evaluation and critique reinforce higher-order cognitive skills, promoting deeper learning and professional readiness.	Students improve critical thinking, code evaluation skills, and the ability to optimize and refine AI-generated code.
Analyze	Students analyze AI-assisted outputs by debugging, stress-testing, and optimizing solutions.	Debugging and optimizing AI-generated solutions mimic real-world software development workflows.	Breaking down complex AI-generated outputs strengthens computational literacy and logical reasoning.	Students strengthen debugging skills, system analysis, and workflow efficiency, ensuring they can troubleshoot complex software challenges.
Apply	Students apply programming knowledge in structured tasks, working with APIs, version control, and automated testing.	Working with APIs, version control, and automation reflects modern software engineering practices.	Applying knowledge through structured real-world tasks helps students bridge theoretical concepts with industry expectations.	Students gain hands-on experience in modern software development practices, such as version control, automation, and API integration.

(Continued)

TABLE 4.2 (CONTINUED)

Bloom's Revised Taxonomy for Programming Education

Bloom's Revised Taxonomy Level	Student Activity	Practical Reason	Pedagogical Reason	Learning Outcome
Understand	Students develop understanding through guided AI explanations, structured pseudocode, and problem decomposition.	Structured explanations and problem decomposition reinforce computational thinking before syntax.	Guided explanations break down learning, ensuring students develop strong conceptual foundations before diving into syntax.	Students develop computational thinking and structured problem-solving skills before engaging with complex syntax.
Remember	Students use AI to structure learning, retrieving syntax explanations and debugging support as needed.	Syntax retrieval and debugging support allow students to focus on problem-solving instead of rote memorization.	AI support allows for adaptive learning, reducing frustration and improving retention of programming concepts.	Students achieve syntax fluency while maintaining a strong focus on logical reasoning and problem decomposition.

4.6.1 Before/After Translation: Implementing a Flipped Taxonomy

4.6.1.1 BEFORE: Traditional Approach

In conventional programming education, Bloom's Taxonomy is applied in its traditional sequence, with remembering and understanding preceding application and creation:

1. **Remember**: Students memorize syntax rules, command structures, and language constructs
2. **Understand**: Students explain programming concepts and interpret code examples
3. **Apply**: Students implement basic algorithms and solve structured problems
4. **Analyze**: Students examine code for errors and inefficiencies
5. **Evaluate**: Students assess different implementation approaches
6. **Create**: Students design and develop original programming solutions

This approach requires extensive technical foundations before students engage in meaningful creation. A typical course might include:

- Weeks of syntax exercises and code memorization
- Quizzes testing recall of language rules and structures
- Simple implementation exercises with predefined parameters
- Increasingly complex algorithms with instructor-provided scaffolding
- Limited original creation only in the final weeks of the course

The instructor would need to provide detailed syntax instruction and gradually introduce concepts in a predetermined sequence. This approach assumes that understanding must precede application, which must precede creation—a sequence that delays meaningful engagement and often leads to high attrition rates, particularly in non-STEM contexts. Students spend significant time on low-level details before experiencing the satisfaction of creating functional applications, often becoming discouraged before reaching the more engaging aspects of programming.

4.6.1.2 AFTER: AI-Assisted Flipped Taxonomy Approach

In an AI-assisted classroom, Bloom's Taxonomy is deliberately inverted, beginning with creation and evaluation before delving into lower-level details:

1. **Create**: Students immediately begin designing and developing meaningful applications
2. **Evaluate**: Students critically assess different approaches and solutions
3. **Analyze**: Students examine the structure and function of code components
4. **Apply**: Students implement specific functions or features as needed
5. **Understand**: Students explore the concepts underlying their implementations
6. **Remember**: Students reinforce syntax and structures through repeated application

This sequence makes creation the entry point rather than the destination. A revised course might include:

- Day 1: Students design and deploy a simple application using AI assistance
- Week 1: Students evaluate different implementation approaches for their projects
- Week 2: Students analyze code structure and component relationships
- Week 3: Students apply specific techniques to enhance their applications
- Throughout: Technical concepts and syntax are introduced contextually as needed

The instructor guides conceptual understanding and problem-solving approaches while assistants provide syntax support and implementation assistance. This approach assumes that meaningful creation provides context and motivation for understanding technical details—an assumption particularly well-suited to non-STEM contexts. In practice, this might look like:

1. Students begin by designing a data visualization for their disciplinary research:

   "I want to create an interactive timeline showing the relationship between economic factors and literary movements in 19th century Britain. Can you help me create this visualization and explain the key components of the code?"

2. Students evaluate different visualization approaches:

"I notice this visualization uses D3.js while another example used Chart.js. What are the trade-offs between these
approaches for my historical timeline?"

3. Students analyze the structure of their implementation:

"Can you explain how the data loading component connects to
the visualization rendering in this code? I want to understand
the overall architecture."

This approach allows non-STEM faculty to guide programming projects without requiring extensive technical expertise. Primary attention
remains on disciplinary questions and conceptual understanding—areas
where faculty already possess expertise. Assessment likewise shifts to
students' ability to solve meaningful problems, evaluate approaches critically, and develop conceptual understanding rather than syntax memorization. This better reflects professional practice where problem-solving
and conceptual understanding take precedence over recall.

In traditional programming education, students are typically introduced to coding through rigorous syntax drills, rule-based exercises,
and debugging tasks before they are allowed to engage in applied
problem-solving. This approach imposes a high cognitive load, as
students must simultaneously master low-level syntax and high-level
problem-solving, often leading to frustration and disengagement
(Kiesler, 2020). However, emerging pedagogical frameworks argue for
a top-down approach—where computational thinking is introduced
before syntax rules—aligning with best practices in cognitive learning
theory and Bloom's Revised Taxonomy (Sobral, 2021). Computational
thinking, which encompasses breaking down problems, structuring
workflows, and logical reasoning, provides a conceptual framework
for problem-solving in coding before students grapple with syntax
intricacies. Research indicates that students who first engage with
abstract computational thinking demonstrate greater problem-solving
resilience and adaptability when they later transition to syntax-heavy
programming tasks (Masapanta-Carrión & Velázquez-Iturbide, 2018).
In contrast, when students begin with rote memorization of syntax,
they struggle to contextualize programming as a problem-solving
tool and instead view it as a strict rule-based activity with little real-
world relevance. Thus, by reversing the traditional approach, instructors can introduce syntax in context—only when necessary to support
the completion of meaningful applications. This structured learning
approach allows students to spend more time on the "why" before the
"how," developing conceptual understanding first and learning syntax
as a tool rather than an obstacle (Premana, Widiana, & Wibawa, 2023).
The integration of tools such as GitHub Copilot and Replit Ghostwriter
further reinforces this approach by enabling students to experiment

with code structure, receive contextualized suggestions, and learn syntax through applied experience rather than through isolated exercises (Zhang, Wong, Giacaman, & Luxton-Reilly, 2021).

From an instructional standpoint, faculty should prioritize computational thinking exercises using pseudocode, flowcharts, and algorithmic decomposition before transitioning to programming syntax. Research supports this model, demonstrating that curricula structured according to Bloom's Revised Taxonomy enhance conceptual knowledge retention and promote deeper cognitive engagement (Gunarso et al., 2024). When students begin coding with a conceptual understanding of workflows and logic, they engage in programming as a creative and analytical process rather than a mechanical task of syntax memorization. This pedagogical change aligns programming education with modern software development practices, where professional developers do not rely on rote memorization of syntax but instead utilize generative documentation, collaborative coding environments, and computational problem-solving techniques (Velázquez-Iturbide, 2021). By pivoting the focus toward higher-order thinking first, educators not only reduce early-stage frustration but also equip students with essential problem-solving skills that remain relevant across evolving programming languages and industry practices.

4.6.2 Before/After Translation: Project-Based Learning Implementation

4.6.2.1 *BEFORE: Traditional Approach*

In conventional programming education, project-based learning is typically reserved for advanced courses after students have mastered programming fundamentals. The traditional approach requires students to:

1. Complete weeks or months of syntax and algorithm exercises
2. Build small, isolated programming components
3. Study existing codebases to understand structure
4. Progressively tackle larger, more complex assignments
5. Eventually design and implement a capstone project

This sequence assumes that substantial technical knowledge must precede meaningful project work. A typical progression might include:

- Basic syntax exercises and quizzes
- Small algorithm implementations

- Structured labs with predefined outcomes
- Guided modifications to existing projects
- Semi-structured projects with significant constraints
- Final capstone project with more freedom

The instructor would need to provide detailed technical guidance at each stage, carefully sequencing concepts and providing extensive feedback on implementation details. This approach assumes that students must "learn to code" before they can "code to learn"—a sequence that delays the application of programming to disciplinary questions. Students often struggle to connect these technical exercises to their disciplinary interests, leading to disengagement, particularly in non-STEM contexts where the disciplinary relevance may not be immediately apparent.

4.6.2.2 AFTER: AI-Assisted Project-First Approach

In an AI-assisted classroom, project-based learning becomes the starting point rather than the destination. From day one, students work on projects relevant to their disciplinary interests, with AI providing technical scaffolding as needed. The flipped approach guides students through:

1. Defining a meaningful project related to their disciplinary interests
2. Creating a high-level design and implementation plan
3. Using AI assistance to implement core functionality
4. Iteratively enhancing and refining the project
5. Learning technical concepts contextually as they become relevant

This sequence makes disciplinary relevance the driving force from the beginning. A revised progression might include:

- Day 1: Project conceptualization and initial implementation with AI assistance
- Week 1: Functional prototype deployment and testing
- Week 2: Feature enhancement and refinement
- Week 3: Performance optimization and user experience improvements

- Throughout: Technical concepts introduced when needed to support project goals

The instructor guides conceptual development and disciplinary application, while AI provides implementation support. This approach assumes that meaningful projects provide context and motivation for technical learning—an assumption well-aligned with constructivist learning theory. In practice, this might look like:

1. A history student begins by creating a digital archive visualization:

   "I want to create an interactive map showing migration patterns during the Industrial Revolution, using data from historical census records. Can you help me set up this project and explain the key components I'll need?"

2. As the project develops, technical concepts are introduced contextually:

   "I notice my visualization is slow when displaying all data points. Can you explain what might be causing this performance issue and how I might optimize it?"

3. Refinement focuses on disciplinary goals rather than technical perfection:

   "I want to make the connection between economic factors and migration patterns more clear in my visualization. How might I modify the display to emphasize this relationship?"

This approach allows non-STEM faculty to guide programming projects without requiring extensive technical expertise. The central consideration remains disciplinary questions and insights—areas where faculty already possess expertise. Assessment evaluates students' ability to apply programming to meaningful disciplinary questions, their iterative refinement process, and their conceptual understanding rather than technical perfection. This better reflects how programming functions as a tool for inquiry in non-technical disciplines.

Given this change in programming education, particularly in how foundational concepts are taught, there is a move away from traditional programming curricula, which often require students to memorize syntax, debug manually, and build programs from scratch, which can create unnecessary barriers to learning (Sobral, 2021). Tools such as GitHub Copilot, ChatGPT, and Replit Ghostwriter now provide real-time code generation, syntax correction, and debugging support, allowing students to focus on higher-order problem-solving skills rather than rote memorization (Masapanta-Carrión & Velázquez-Iturbide, 2018). In fact, one of the most significant benefits of foundational learning is its ability to automate and streamline lower-order tasks, such as error handling and boilerplate code generation. Traditionally, students encounter frustration when syntax errors prevent them from grasping programming logic (Gunarso et al., 2024). The interface mitigates this issue by offering real-time debugging suggestions that not only correct errors but also provide contextual explanations for why a fix is necessary. This approach facilitates the activity of debugging, not as an isolated skill but an integral part of the learning process, reinforcing conceptual understanding rather than simply correcting mistakes (Zhang, Wong, Giacaman, & Luxton-Reilly, 2021). One such strategic use outlined in Chapter 3 involves presenting generated code snippets as case studies for deeper learning. Instead of requiring students to write every line of code from scratch, faculty can provide pre-generated functions or algorithms and ask students to analyze, optimize, or adapt the provided solutions (Gunarso et al., 2024). This approach mirrors professional software development, where developers frequently modify existing code rather than writing entirely new implementations. Faculty can further refine this strategy by introducing inefficiencies or subtle errors into generated snippets, prompting students to identify performance bottlenecks and security vulnerabilities (Zhang et al., 2021).

4.6.3 Before/After Translation: Assessment Approaches

4.6.3.1 *BEFORE: Traditional Approach*

In conventional programming education, assessment primarily focuses on technical accuracy and syntax correctness, often through:

1. Syntax quizzes and terminology tests
2. Algorithm implementation exercises
3. Debugging assignments with predefined errors
4. Time-limited coding examinations
5. Final projects evaluated primarily on technical criteria

This approach assumes that technical mastery should be the primary focus of assessment. A typical assessment pattern might include:

- Weekly syntax quizzes testing recall of language rules
- Mid-term examination requiring implementation of specific algorithms
- Lab assignments with detailed technical requirements
- Final project with extensive technical rubrics focusing on code quality

The instructor would need to develop detailed grading rubrics for technical correctness, code efficiency, and adherence to syntax conventions. This approach primarily assesses what students can produce without assistance—a model increasingly disconnected from professional practice where collaboration and tool use are standard. Students often spend the most time meeting technical requirements rather than solving meaningful problems, leading to shallow learning centered on passing assessments rather than developing transferable skills.

4.6.3.2 AFTER: AI-Assisted Assessment Approach

In an AI-assisted classroom, assessment shifts from technical recall and production to critical thinking, problem-solving, and effective tool use:

1. Problem decomposition and analysis
2. Solution design and evaluation
3. AI collaboration and prompt engineering
4. Iterative refinement and reflection
5. Application to disciplinary questions

This approach recognizes that in professional contexts, effectiveness is measured by problem-solving ability rather than recall. A revised assessment pattern might include:

- Project planning documents evaluating problem analysis
- Decision journals documenting solution design choices
- Annotated AI interactions showing thoughtful collaboration
- Iterative project versions demonstrating refinement
- Reflection papers connecting technical implementation to disciplinary insights

The instructor evaluates student thinking processes, problem-solving approaches, and effective collaboration with the tool rather than considering time spent exclusively on code production. This approach assesses how students would actually work in professional environments—with tools, collaboration, and iterative refinement. In practice, this might look like:

1. Students submit a problem analysis document:

   "The challenge I'm addressing is analyzing sentiment patterns in historical correspondence during the Civil War period. This requires processing unstructured text data, identifying sentiment indicators, and visualizing changes over time..."

2. Students document their collaboration process:

   "I initially asked the AI to suggest approaches for sentiment analysis on historical texts, but the suggestions were too modern-focused. I refined my prompt to specify 19th-century language patterns and received more appropriate recommendations..."

3. Students reflect on connecting technical implementation to disciplinary insights:

   "The sentiment visualization revealed unexpected patterns in communication between military leaders and civilian authorities. This technical implementation allowed me to identify a shift in tone that occurred approximately two months before a major strategic change..."

This approach allows non-STEM faculty to assess meaningful learning without requiring deep technical expertise. The focus remains on thinking processes and disciplinary applications—areas where faculty already possess evaluative expertise. Assessment criteria emphasize problem-solving effectiveness, critical thinking, disciplinary relevance, and reflective practice rather than technical perfection. This better reflects how programming functions as a tool for inquiry and how AI-assisted programming functions in professional contexts.

Programming assessments traditionally emphasize rote memorization of syntax and theoretical knowledge, rather than evaluating problem-solving ability, collaboration, and code optimization. AI-assisted education necessitates a change in assessment methodologies, centering on:

1. Problem decomposition over coding from scratch—Students should be assessed on their ability to break down complex challenges into structured, logical solutions before writing code (Masapanta-Carrión & Velázquez-Iturbide, 2018).

2. Collaboration and version control over individual submission correctness—Industry professionals rarely work in isolation; therefore, assessments should evaluate teamwork, version control fluency, and collaborative problem-solving (Zhang et al., 2021).

3. Algorithmic reasoning and efficiency optimization over syntax recall—Rather than rewarding students for memorizing syntax rules, evaluations should prioritize how efficiently students optimize AI-generated solutions or analyze different implementation strategies (Premana et al., 2023).

Through restructuring programming assessments to mirror real-world industry expectations, educators make space for students to develop immediately transferable skills. This strategy aligns with Bloom's Revised Taxonomy, which places application, analysis, and evaluation above rote memorization (Gunarso et al., 2024). Simultaneously, the flipped pedagogical model represents a break from conventional, syntax-focused instruction, favoring instead an industry-aligned, assisted, and problem-driven approach. By foregrounding real-world applications, iterative learning, and augmented problem-solving, students experience meaningful coding challenges from the outset rather than waiting for advanced courses to tackle industry-relevant projects (Sobral, 2021). Rather than viewing these tools as a shortcut that bypasses foundational learning, this model leverages their ability to strengthen computational thinking, ensuring that learners master critical evaluation, error diagnosis, and collaborative problem-solving (Premana et al., 2023). Here, they serve as a cognitive partner, enabling students to concentrate on higher-order reasoning while automating lower-level tasks such as syntax checks and routine debugging. Reversing the traditional learning hierarchy thus positions graduates to tackle modern development environments with agility and competence (Masapanta-Carrión & Velázquez-Iturbide, 2018). Ultimately, this change extends beyond the adoption of new tools—offering an essential reimagining of how programming is taught, assessed, and aligned with current industry standards.

For non-STEM contexts, this flipped taxonomy approach offers particular advantages:

1. It builds on existing strengths in critical thinking and disciplinary knowledge

2. It reduces technical barriers to engaging with programming as a tool for inquiry

3. It positions programming as an extension of disciplinary methods rather than a separate technical skill

4. It creates natural connections between programming concepts and disciplinary questions

Through inverting Bloom's Taxonomy for programming education, we create pathways for disciplines that have formerly been excluded from computational thinking to engage meaningfully with programming from day one. This inversion does not diminish the importance of technical understanding—rather, it contextualizes technical details within meaningful application, making programming accessible to all fields.

4.7 AI-Assisted Curatorial Approaches to Coding and Writing

The increased integration of these smart tools into both coding and writing instruction demands a reconceptualization of how students create, refine, and adapt content. Formerly, programming has been associated with logical structure and precise syntax, while writing has emphasized narrative flow and clarity. However, assistive tools—such as GitHub Copilot, ChatGPT, and Replit Ghostwriter—are blurring the boundaries between these traditionally distinct domains, enabling students to approach both as iterative, parallel processes. Rather than relying solely on one to generate content, students must learn to refine, adapt, and edit the automated output, thereby developing critical evaluation skills that complement their technical proficiency. This curatorial approach not only maintains student intellectual ownership over their work but also positions the tool as a collaborative agent rather than a passive content generator. As a result, learners are encouraged to integrate computational and narrative thinking in a manner that reflects the complexities of contemporary creative and technical practices.

This redirect from "creation from scratch" to "curation of AI-generated content" represents an essential change in how we approach programming education, particularly in non-STEM disciplines. Traditional teaching models assumed that students must master technical skills before applying them to meaningful projects—an assumption that effectively excluded many disciplines from computational practices. The curatorial approach inverts this relationship, allowing students to begin with high-level concepts and disciplinary questions while using these smart systems to support implementation details. For non-STEM faculty, this transition offers a revolutionary opportunity. Rather than needing to become programming experts themselves, they can leverage their existing strengths in critical analysis, conceptual organization, and evaluation—applying these skills to generative code just as they would to any other text or creative work. The role of the instructor changes from technical expert to facilitator of critical thinking about both the process and products of such a collaboration.

4.7.1 Before/After Translation: AI-Powered Code Review

4.7.1.1 BEFORE: Traditional Approach

In conventional programming education, code review is typically introduced as an advanced topic after students have mastered programming fundamentals. The traditional approach requires extensive technical knowledge:

1. Understanding language-specific best practices and style guides
2. Identifying common coding anti-patterns and vulnerabilities
3. Evaluating algorithmic efficiency and complexity
4. Assessing code structure and organization
5. Providing technically precise feedback

A traditional code review assignment might require students to:

- Study language-specific style guides and conventions
- Memorize common anti-patterns and security vulnerabilities
- Learn specialized vocabulary for describing code issues
- Practice giving technically accurate feedback
- Apply detailed rubrics, focusing on technical correctness

This approach positions code review as a technical skill requiring deep programming knowledge rather than as an analytical thinking exercise. The instructor would need extensive programming expertise to model effective review practices and evaluate student performance.

Students without strong technical foundations struggle to participate meaningfully in code review, seeing it as an advanced task beyond their capabilities rather than as an extension of general critical thinking.

4.7.1.2 AFTER: AI-Assisted Curatorial Approach

In an assisted classroom, code review is reimagined as a curatorial practice where students apply critical thinking to evaluate, refine, and improve generated code—skills that transfer from many disciplinary contexts.

The instructor frames code review as an extension of general critical analysis:

1. Students begin by discussing evaluation criteria in their disciplinary context
2. The class explores how similar analytical approaches apply to code evaluation
3. Students generate AI-assisted code for a disciplinary project
4. Students conduct a systematic review of the generated code:

   "I asked the AI to create a text analysis function for identifying rhetorical patterns in historical speeches. Can you help me evaluate this code to ensure it correctly implements the rhetorical theory concepts we've studied in class? I'm particularly concerned with how it distinguishes between different types of appeals."

5. Students develop their curatorial judgment through guided practice:

   "The AI suggested this approach for visualizing network relationships in my sociological data. What questions should I ask to evaluate whether this implementation aligns with established sociological frameworks for understanding community connections?"

This approach allows non-STEM faculty to guide code review without requiring deep technical expertise. The attention transitions to conceptual alignment, analytical clarity, and disciplinary relevance—areas where disciplinary faculty already possess evaluative expertise. Students learn to approach code as a text to be critically evaluated against disciplinary standards, developing transferable review skills while engaging meaningfully with computational implementations of disciplinary concepts. Assessment is centered on students' analytical reasoning, evaluative clarity, and ability to connect technical implementations to disciplinary frameworks rather than technical correctness. This better reflects how code review functions as a thinking process rather than merely a technical validation.

One of the most significant benefits of assisted learning is its ability to personalize educational pathways based on individual student progress. Traditional curricula often follow a one-size-fits-all sequence that expects every student to master concepts at the same pace. In contrast, intelligent systems can dynamically adjust lesson difficulty, suggest alternative resources, and provide tailored feedback to meet each student's unique needs. This adaptive model allows learners to focus on areas that require further development while accelerating through topics they have already mastered. For instance, a learning assistant might recommend additional debugging exercises for students grappling with logical errors, while suggesting optimization challenges for those who have demonstrated proficiency in syntax basics. Such personalized pathways not only enhance engagement but also support a more efficient, individualized learning process.

4.7.2 Before/After Translation: AI-Assisted Writing-Code Integration

4.7.2.1 BEFORE: Traditional Approach

In conventional education, programming and writing are typically taught as separate disciplines with distinct methodologies, skills, and outcomes. The traditional approach maintains strict boundaries between:

1. Writing courses focused on rhetoric, structure, and style
2. Programming courses focused on syntax, algorithms, and efficiency
3. Separate assignments with different evaluation criteria
4. Different faculty with specialized expertise in each domain
5. Distinct pedagogical approaches and assessment methods

This separation reflects historical disciplinary boundaries but fails to recognize the deep connections between computational and narrative thinking. When interdisciplinary projects are attempted, they typically require:

- Advanced students who have already completed coursework in both domains
- Team-based approaches where technical and writing specialists collaborate
- Extensive faculty expertise spanning both disciplines
- Complex coordination between different departments and programs

This approach effectively excludes most students from meaningful integration of programming and writing, particularly in non-STEM disciplines where programming expertise may be limited. The instructor would need dual expertise or team-teaching arrangements to guide such integration. Students experience programming and writing as seemingly different activities requiring different skill sets, limiting their ability to see connections and transfer insights between domains.

4.7.2.2 AFTER: AI-Assisted Curatorial Approach

In an AI-assisted classroom, programming and writing are reimagined as parallel curatorial processes where students apply similar critical thinking skills to refine and enhance both code and narrative—with AI providing implementation support across domains. The instructor guides students to recognize fundamental similarities in the curatorial process:

1. Students begin by examining revision processes in writing and programming
2. The class discusses how selection, arrangement, and refinement apply to both domains
3. Students develop integrated projects that combine narrative and computational elements
4. Using AI assistance, students implement and refine both components:

   "I'm creating a digital humanities project analyzing character relationships in Victorian novels. I need both a narrative analysis of key relationship patterns and a visualization component showing character interaction networks. Can you help me develop both components in parallel, ensuring they complement each other conceptually?"

5. Students develop curatorial judgment across both domains:

   "The AI generated this code visualization and this written analysis of my network data. How might I refine both to ensure they present a coherent argument about community structure? Are there aspects of my written analysis that should be more clearly reflected in the visualization, or insights from the visualization that should be incorporated into my analysis?"

This approach allows faculty from any discipline to guide integrated projects without requiring expertise in both domains. At the same time, the focus shifts to conceptual coherence, analytical clarity, and effective communication—areas where disciplinary faculty already possess expertise. Students learn to approach both code and writing as different expressions of the same analytical thinking, developing transferable curatorial skills while creating meaningful integrated projects that serve disciplinary goals. Assessment evaluates how effectively the computational and narrative elements complement each other in advancing disciplinary inquiry rather than treating them as separate technical exercises. This better reflects how integrated communication functions in professional contexts where multiple modalities work together to convey complex ideas. Another key advantage of integrating these tools is their facilitation of iterative development through real-time, context-aware feedback. Just as professional developers rely on version control and continuous integration to refine software through multiple iterations, students should view both coding and writing as processes that benefit from ongoing revision. Generative revision tools can pinpoint inefficiencies in code or ambiguities in written text, enabling learners to test and improve their work dynamically. By embedding automated feedback loops into assignments, educators cultivate habits of continuous refinement, reinforcing the value of incremental improvement over immediate perfection. This process encourages students to approach their work as evolving drafts, subject to regular enhancement through careful analysis and revision.

This new approach to the curation of content also offers the distinct advantage of merging programming and composition into a unified creative process. Both disciplines require the logical structuring of ideas, the establishment of coherent narratives, and the systematic refinement of outputs through revision. By teaching students to evaluate generated code with the same critical lens used to assess AI-generated writing, educators encourage cross-disciplinary literacy that enhances both technical and communicative skills. For example, a student refining an assisted function might apply similar principles as when revising an essay—identifying redundancies, ensuring clarity, and improving overall efficiency. This unified approach strengthens computational thinking while also honing the ability to critically evaluate generated language and reasoning—a crucial skill in an era of widespread generative integration. Additionally, AI-assisted curation enhances inclusivity and accessibility by accommodating diverse learning styles and language backgrounds. Students who struggle with traditional instruction methods benefit from AI's capacity to provide customized explanations, translations, and structured materials that simplify complex tasks. AI-driven environments also offer multimodal feedback—delivering explanations via text, audio, or interactive formats—thus adapting to individual preferences and needs. This flexibility enables all students to engage meaningfully with challenging programming and writing assignments, regardless of their initial proficiency levels.

The role of these platforms as a curatorial assistant extends beyond individual assignments to encompass the management of large-scale projects. In professional settings, developers and writers must navigate complex version histories, source control systems, and collaborative workflows. Platforms such as GitHub Copilot for coding and Grammarly for writing facilitate structured revisions by enabling students to track their progress and coordinate changes over time. Their integration into project-based learning enables educators to provide students with practical experience in iterative development methodologies and collaborative problem-solving. This approach facilitates an environment where learners can be well-prepared for real-world challenges, where managing revisions and maintaining organized workflows are critical. Despite its many advantages, the integration into educational settings must be accompanied by a critical approach to generated content. Overreliance without proper evaluation can lead to misconceptions, inefficiencies, and ethical concerns related to authorship and intellectual integrity. Educators must emphasize the importance of verifying generated recommendations, urging students to apply their own reasoning before incorporating these suggestions into their work. One effective strategy is to require learners to annotate generated solutions, explaining why they accept or reject certain recommendations—a process that reinforces metacognition and critical engagement.

For non-STEM disciplines, the curatorial approach offers particular advantages:

1. It leverages existing strengths in critical analysis and evaluation
2. It positions coding as an extension of scholarly judgment rather than a separate technical skill
3. It acknowledges the value of selection and refinement—central activities in many humanities and social science disciplines
4. It creates natural connections between computational thinking and disciplinary methodologies

The reimagining of both programming and writing as curatorial processes facilitated by these new tools creates entry points for fields that have been excluded from computational practices. This approach does not diminish the importance of technical understanding—rather, it contextualizes technical details within disciplinary frameworks, making programming accessible to all fields. The curatorial model also better reflects contemporary professional practices across disciplines. In fields from journalism to business, law to healthcare, professionals increasingly work with generated content—selecting, refining, and integrating machine outputs into human-directed projects. By teaching students to curate rather than merely create, we prepare them for workplaces where human-AI collaboration is becoming the norm. Thus, integrating assisted curation into educational practices equips students with the ability to manage, refine, and critically engage with generated content across disciplines, positioning AI as an enhancement to human intelligence and encouraging iterative, adaptive, and cross-disciplinary fluency.

Reflecting on the recommendations in this chapter, integrating new tools into programming education calls for a wholesale reevaluation of traditional teaching methods, moving beyond rote syntax drills and toward real-world application, iterative learning, and assisted problem-solving (Table 4.3). Through the reorientation of instruction around practical coding scenarios and modern industry workflows, educators can cultivate stronger computational thinking skills and enable students to refine their coding proficiencies with structured, automated support.

Early in the learning process, having students deploy their projects supports real-world relevance and familiarizes them with professional coding habits. When learners begin publishing their work within the first weeks of a course, they acquire immediate exposure to version control, continuous integration, and iterative refinement. This approach replaces delayed introductions to deployment with tangible practice, letting students see the real impact of their code from the outset and reinforcing the notion that coding extends well beyond isolated classroom exercises. A further change involves prioritizing conceptual and higher-order thinking before syntax mastery. Rather than insisting that learners memorize language rules before engaging with problem-solving, educators can guide them in analyzing and designing solutions, using a tool to assist with syntax and debugging. This flipped approach reduces cognitive overload, emphasizes big-picture reasoning, and aligns with Bloom's Revised Taxonomy by placing application, analysis, and evaluation at the forefront of the learning experience.

Platforms such as GitHub Copilot, ChatGPT, and Replit Ghostwriter serve as catalysts for automating lower-order tasks, allowing students to consider and spend more time on logic development and critical problem-solving. However, integrating AI literacy into coursework is

TABLE 4.3

Programmatic Revisions in Programming Education

Key Revision	Implementation Strategy	Expected Outcome
Early Deployment for Real-World Relevance	Introduce project deployment within the first few weeks, using GitHub, Netlify, or Vercel.	Students develop real-world coding habits early and understand software deployment as an iterative process.
Prioritizing Higher-Order Thinking Before Syntax Mastery	Start with conceptual problem-solving and computational thinking before syntax-heavy tasks.	Learners engage with programming as a problem-solving tool, developing a strong foundation in logic and structure.
Using AI to Automate and Streamline Foundational Learning Tasks	Use AI-assisted tools for debugging, syntax correction, and boilerplate generation to accelerate learning.	Students focus on high-order programming concepts while AI handles lower-order technical details.
Aligning Coursework with Industry Practices	Embed agile development, peer code reviews, and continuous integration into coursework.	Graduates are better prepared for industry workflows, teamwork, and modern software development practices.
Moving Assessments from Syntax Recall to Problem-Solving and Optimization	Move beyond correctness-based grading to assess problem decomposition, iterative refinement, and efficiency optimization.	Assessments align with industry demands, reinforcing critical thinking and collaborative skills.
Fostering AI-Assisted Curation in Coding and Writing	Merge coding and writing as iterative refinement processes, teaching students to critique and optimize generated content.	Students become proficient in structuring, refining, and debugging AI-assisted work across disciplines.
Integrating Iterative Learning Models	Encourage students to refine and enhance their work through multiple submission cycles with feedback loops.	Students develop resilience, adaptability, and a habit of refining their work to professional standards.
Developing AI Literacy and Critical Evaluation Skills	Require students to annotate AI-generated solutions, explaining modifications and verifying correctness.	Graduates demonstrate AI literacy, ensuring ethical and effective use of AI in development.
Ensuring Personalized Learning Pathways	Utilize platforms that adapt to individual learning progress, suggesting targeted exercises based on skill level.	Students receive individualized learning experiences, reducing frustration and improving engagement.

essential. Learners must learn to scrutinize, refine, and validate outputs instead of relying blindly on automated suggestions. Structured assignments can require them to justify the modifications they make to generated code, ensuring they exercise computational reasoning and maintain intellectual ownership of their work. Programming education should also reflect modern software development practices, embedding agile workflows, version control platforms, and collaborative coding environments directly into course activities. Rather than relying on single-submission assessments that focus on correctness alone, instructors can adopt incremental development and ongoing feedback cycles. This mirrors professional standards, where code undergoes continuous refinement and peer review, and prepares students for the rapid pace and adaptability expected in industry.

For non-STEM disciplines, the assisted curatorial approach offers a revolutionary entry point to programming education. By reframing both programming and writing as processes of thoughtful selection, refinement, and integration of generated content, we create accessible pathways for disciplines where technical syntax has been a barrier. This approach builds on existing strengths in critical thinking and analytical evaluation while using these automated solutions to bridge the gap between disciplinary knowledge and technical implementation. The future of programming education lies not in teaching students to code from scratch in isolation but in preparing them to collaborate effectively with their personal assistant—directing, refining, and integrating machine-generated content into meaningful disciplinary work. By embracing this curatorial model, we expand access to computational thinking across all fields while better preparing students for professional environments where human-AI collaboration is increasingly the norm.

References

Ausubel, D. P. (2012). *The acquisition and retention of knowledge: A cognitive view.* Springer Science & Business Media.

Barlaskar, E. (2020). *User-centric cloud application management* (Doctoral dissertation). Queen's University Belfast.

Bessen, J. (2022). *The new goliaths: How corporations use software to dominate industries, kill innovation, and undermine regulation.* Yale University Press.

Bretthauer, D. (2001). Open source software: A history. *Information Technology and Libraries, 21,* 3–10.

Bright, W., Alexandrescu, A., & Parker, M. (2020). Origins of the D programming language. *Proceedings of the ACM on Programming Languages, 4(HOPL),* 1–38.

Campbell-Kelly, M., & Garcia-Swartz, D. D. (2015). *From mainframes to smartphones: A history of the international computer industry.* Harvard University Press.

Ceri, S., Fraternali, P., Bongio, A., Brambilla, M., Comai, S., & Matera, M. (2003). *Morgan Kaufmann series in data management systems: Designing data-intensive Web applications.* Morgan Kaufmann.

Ceruzzi, P. E. (2003). *A history of modern computing.* MIT Press.

Collen, M. F., & Kulikowski, C. A. (2015). The development of digital computers. In M. F. Collen & C. A. Kulikowski (Eds.), *The history of medical informatics in the United States* (pp. 3–73). Springer.

Ding, H., Fan, Z., Guehring, I., Gupta, G., Ha, W., Huan, J., ... & Zhou, H. (2024, August). Reasoning and planning with large language models in code development. In *Proceedings of the 30th ACM SIGKDD Conference on Knowledge Discovery and Data Mining* (pp. 6480–6490).

Edwards, B. (2024, October 30). Google CEO says over 25% of new Google code is generated by AI. *Ars Technica.* https://arstechnica.com/ai/2024/10/google-ceo -says-over-25-of-new-google-code-is-generated-by-ai/#:~:text=Adventures %20in%20Augmentation-,Google%20CEO%20says%20over%2025%25%20of %20new%20Google%20code%20is,AI%20to%20continue%20that%20tradition

Farley, D. (2021). *Modern software engineering: Doing what works to build better software faster.* Addison-Wesley Professional.

Gunarso, G., Syamsudin, M. S., Nursalman, M., Nurdin, E. A., & Fitri, A. (2024). Computational bibliometric analysis of research on bloom digital taxonomy and critical thinking. *AL-ISHLAH: Jurnal Pendidikan, 16*(1), 616–629.

Haigh, T., & Ceruzzi, P. E. (2021). *A new history of modern computing.* MIT Press.

Haindl, P., & Weinberger, G. (2024). Does ChatGPT help novice programmers write better code? Results from static code analysis. *IEEE Access, 12,* 114146–114156.

Jadhav, A., Kaur, M., & Akter, F. (2022). Evolution of software development effort and cost estimation techniques: Five decades study using automated text mining approach. *Mathematical Problems in Engineering, 2022*(1), 5782587.

Jung, H. (2020). A study on the current state of artificial intelligence-based coding technologies and the direction of future coding education. *The International Journal of Advanced Culture Technology, 8*(3), 186–191.

Khan, F. H., Pasha, M. A., & Masud, S. (2021). Advancements in microprocessor archi-tecture for ubiquitous AI—An overview on history, evolution, and upcoming challenges in AI implementation. *Micromachines, 12*(6), 665.

Kiesler, N. (2020, June). Towards a competence model for the novice programmer using bloom's revised taxonomy-an empirical approach. In *Proceedings of the 2020 ACM Conference on Innovation and Technology in Computer Science Education* (pp. 459–465).

Koti, A., Koti, S. L., Khare, A., & Khare, P. (2024). 1335 beyond the paradigm: Unraveling the limitations of object-oriented programming. *Multifaceted approaches for Data Acquisition, Processing & Communication,* 95.

Masapanta-Carrión, S., & Velázquez-Iturbide, J. Á. (2018, February). A systematic review of the use of bloom's taxonomy in computer science education. In *Proceedings of the 49th ACM Technical Symposium on Computer Science Education* (pp. 441–446).

Mishra, A., &Otaiwi, Z. (2020). DevOps and software quality: A systematic mapping. *Computer Science Review, 38,* 100308.

Mockus, A., Fielding, R. T., &Herbsleb, J. D. (2002). Two case studies of open source software development: Apache and Mozilla. *ACM Transactions on Software Engineering and Methodology (TOSEM), 11*(3), 309–346.

Ogundipe, D. O., Odejide, O. A., &Edunjobi, T. E. (2024). Agile methodologies in digital banking: Theoretical underpinnings and implications for customer satisfaction. *Open Access Research Journal of Science and Technology, 10*(2), 021–030.

Premana, D. N. D., Widiana, I. W., & Wibawa, I. M. C. (2023). Improving conceptual knowledge in elementary school students with revised bloom's taxonomy-oriented learning activities. *Thinking Skills and Creativity Journal, 6*(1), 9–18.

Shaik, T., Tao, X., Li, L., Dann, C., Sun, Y., & Sun, Y. (2023). Advancing educational content classification via reinforcement learning-integrated Bloom's taxonomy. *2023 3rd International Conference on Digital Society and Intelligent Systems (DSInS)* (pp. 8–13).

Sobral, S. R. (2021). Bloom's taxonomy to improve teaching-learning in introduction to programming. *International Journal of Information and Education Technology, 11*(3), 148–153.

Tabarés, R. (2021). HTML5 and the evolution of HTML; tracing the origins of digital platforms. *Technology in Society, 65,* 101529.

Velázquez-Iturbide, J. Á. (2021, November). An analysis of the formal properties of bloom's taxonomy and its implications for computing education. In *Proceedings of the 21st Koli Calling International Conference on Computing Education Research* (pp. 1–7).

Zhang, J., Wong, C., Giacaman, N., & Luxton-Reilly, A. (2021, February). Automated classification of computing education questions using Bloom's taxonomy. In *Proceedings of the 23rd Australasian Computing Education Conference* (pp. 58–65).

5

Practical Examples and Case Studies in Non-STEM Classrooms

The foundational redirect in coding education detailed in Chapter 4—where smart tools enable both non-STEM instructors and students to engage with programming without prior expertise—finds concrete expression through the case studies presented in this chapter. Rather than merely documenting current adoption of emergent generative technologies, these examples illustrate how the pedagogical inversion outlined previously transforms education across disciplines. Through the repositioning of assistive tools as not merely supplements to traditional learning but as collaborative partners that restructure the educational experience, the low-code, no-code, and assisted programming approaches detailed here demonstrate how computational thinking becomes accessible to all fields. Each case study reveals how disciplines from sociology to literature, history to business can now integrate coding across curricula without requiring either instructors or students to possess specialized technical knowledge. The assignments presented don't simply add technology to existing pedagogical models—they reconceptualize teaching and learning by prioritizing disciplinary inquiry, problem-solving, and conceptual understanding while allowing the generative support tool to manage technical implementation details. This chapter provides concrete examples of how programming education can evolve from an exclusionary technical skill to an accessible, domain-specific tool for creative and analytical expression across all academic disciplines.

5.1 Framing the Role of AI in Supporting Practical Learning

The integration of artificial intelligence into programming education represents a dramatic change in how coding is taught and applied across disciplines, moving from syntax-driven instruction to concept-driven learning that prioritizes problem-solving over technical prerequisites. Traditional pedagogical models that emphasized writing precise syntax and developing logical structures from scratch created artificial barriers between technical and non-technical fields, effectively excluding many disciplines from the benefits of computational thinking. Assisted coding dismantles these barriers

DOI: 10.1201/9781003637738-5

by enabling a more dynamic learning experience where neither instructors nor students need prior programming expertise to engage meaningfully with code (Zhou et al., 2023). Similarly, low-code and no-code platforms eliminate the historical requirement that at least one party—either teacher or student—possess coding knowledge, allowing all disciplines to integrate software creation through intuitive, visual interfaces (Bull & Kharrufa, 2023).

This broadened access to programming extends far beyond computer science classrooms, reconceiving how computational thinking is taught and applied across the entire academic landscape. Evolving generative tools are now enabling instructors in business, healthcare, and humanities to incorporate programming into their curricula despite having no prior coding experience (Zawacki-Richter et al., 2019). The critical insight is that code generation does not merely make programming "easier"—it inverts the traditional learning sequence, allowing students to engage immediately with meaningful disciplinary questions while the assistant handles technical implementation. This inversion enables faculty to focus on their disciplinary expertise rather than struggling to master programming syntax (Ebert et al., 2023). As we transition to this new educational model, students must learn not just to generate code but to critically evaluate and refine generated outputs. Professional developers increasingly collaborate with such tools to accelerate workflows and generate efficient solutions, positioning them as a partner rather than a replacement (Sailer & Petrič, 2019). Effective programming education must therefore emphasize the role of students as curators of generated content, teaching them to approach generative code critically rather than accepting it passively (Zhou et al., 2023). This parallels the move from "creation from scratch" to "curation of AI-generated content," where faculty guide students in applying disciplinary judgment to evaluate and refine machine outputs.

Beyond coding tasks, assistive tools are reshaping how software is deployed, maintained, and integrated into broader technological systems—all areas where non-STEM disciplines can now participate without specialized training. Automated testing, continuous integration, and deployment pipelines increasingly rely on the tech to enhance reliability and reduce human error, making previously advanced topics immediately accessible to beginners (Sailer & Petrič, 2019). This directly supports a "deployment-first" approach, where students experience the satisfaction of publishing functional applications from day one rather than waiting until after mastering syntax. By introducing students to these industry-standard workflows early in their learning journey, educators prepare them for careers where augmented deployment plays a central role (Nazaretsky et al., 2021). The change extends beyond programming instruction, as tools make computational methods accessible to non-programmers through natural language commands and intuitive interfaces (Bull & Kharrufa, 2023). This accessibility does not eliminate the need for critical thinking—rather, it moves attention from syntax mastery to conceptual understanding and problem-solving, exactly as outlined in our reimagining of Bloom's Taxonomy (Ebert et al., 2023). Students must develop the ability to critically engage with these technologies, understanding their capabilities and limitations while maintaining control over the decision-making process. The pedagogical priority becomes teaching students to direct tools effectively while centering on disciplinary questions rather than technical details (Zawacki-Richter et al., 2019).

As these rapidly evolving tools continue to reshape educational practices, programming instruction must evolve beyond rote memorization of syntax toward a flipped pedagogical model based on conceptual understanding, problem-solving, and strategic thinking (Zhou et al., 2023). Smart learning environments offer opportunities to personalize instruction and provide real-time feedback, but these benefits must be balanced with developing students' independent reasoning skills (Ray et al., 2020). The challenge for educators is not simply to incorporate these tools but to fundamentally restructure learning sequences so that creation and evaluation precede detailed technical understanding—allowing non-STEM disciplines to engage with programming from day one (Nazaretsky et al., 2021). The effective integration into programming education depends on thoughtful instructional design that positions these tools as collaborative partners rather than substitutes for human judgment (McInnes et al., 2024). Faculty must develop strategies that encourage students to use the tools as part of an iterative learning process, continuously refining both their understanding and their outputs (Zhou et al., 2023). This requires abandoning linear instructional models in favor of more flexible, adaptive approaches where students explore different problem-solving methods with generative assistance (Nazaretsky et al., 2021). By designing assignments that incorporate assisted programming alongside disciplinary inquiry, educators create learning experiences that better prepare students for a world where human-AI collaboration is increasingly the norm (Zawacki-Richter et al., 2019).

5.2 First-Year Sociology: AI-Augmented Data Analysis and Visualization

Introductory sociology courses increasingly leverage assistive coding tools to enable immediate, practical engagement with large datasets, effectively uncovering social trends and patterns without prior programming expertise. Historically, sociology curricula highlighted theoretical discussions about the potential of computational methods but provided limited practical opportunities for students to directly analyze data (Schneider, 2019). Manual coding approaches, typically dependent on proficiency in programming languages such as Python, presented technical barriers that limited meaningful data analysis to students with specialized backgrounds. The rise of low-code and no-code platforms has significantly reduced these barriers, enabling immediate access to sophisticated computational analyses without requiring syntax mastery. Students can now quickly process extensive datasets, identify significant correlations, and detect anomalies without technical constraints (Davies et al., 2020).

This shift aligns with a "flipped Bloom's Taxonomy," emphasizing creative and evaluative skills before detailed technical understanding. Sociology courses now prioritize cultivating critical data literacy and interpretive abilities—areas where instructors already hold deep expertise—rather than focusing on developing programming skills. Consequently, sophisticated computational analyses are accessible to all sociology students, regardless of their previous experience with technology. Intelligent platforms allow instructors without coding experience to integrate computational methodologies effortlessly into their courses (Purnomo, 2024), offering intuitive interfaces for interactive visualization, statistical testing, and sentiment analysis (Baiburin et al., 2024).

Positioning these platforms as collaborative partners rather than technical hurdles enables students to actively engage with live social datasets from diverse sources such as news, government reports, and social media, empowering them to test hypotheses and refine research questions dynamically (Hong et al., 2022). Natural language processing features further enhance accessibility by automating qualitative analyses, including sentiment evaluation and topic modeling—tasks historically reserved for technically proficient students (Hernández-Lugo, 2024). This development does not reduce the necessity for sociological expertise but rather reorients it toward disciplinary interpretation and conceptual rigor, facilitating computational projects led by sociology instructors based on their scholarly knowledge.

The assignment in Table 5.1 exemplifies this method by introducing data visualization as a foundational step in developing computational thinking, rather than treating it as an advanced skill contingent upon prior technical knowledge. Students engage directly in meaningful tasks, such as creating interactive dashboards and visualizations tied to sociological research, instead of beginning with syntax-focused drills or traditional programming exercises. Utilizing intuitive low-code/no-code platforms, the assignment directs students to build interactive dashboards that visually represent significant social trends. These platforms handle technical complexities, allowing students to concentrate on selecting pertinent social indicators and interpreting the resulting data patterns.

The assignment adopts a curatorial strategy, asking students to critically evaluate outputs from automated analyses alongside their own interpretations. Students are tasked with comparing visualizations generated through assistive technologies with manually created alternatives, thoroughly documenting their reasoning and scrutinizing the limitations and biases present in automated methods (Sailer & Petrič, 2019). This positions students actively

TABLE 5.1

Data Visualization for Social Trend Analysis

Field	Details
Title	Data Visualization for Social Trend Analysis
Description	In this assignment, students analyze a dataset on urban demographics or social mobility using low-code/no-code platforms to generate interactive dashboards and automated visualizations.
Grading	**Total: 100 points** - Data analysis and accuracy: 30 points - Quality and interactivity of visualizations: 30 points - Reflective commentary comparing AI-assisted and manual approaches: 20 points - Clarity, organization, and documentation of the final submission: 20 points
Learning Outcomes	- Develop foundational data literacy and analytical skills in a sociological context. - Understand how tools facilitate efficient data visualization and coding. - Compare traditional coding methods with AI-assisted approaches to appreciate their respective strengths and limitations. - Critically evaluate how low-code/no-code platforms can popularize access to data analysis and generate sociological insights.
Step-by-Step Instructions (with Tools and URLs)	**Step 1:** Access the provided dataset on urban demographics (e.g., City Demographics Dataset). **Step 2:** Choose a low-code/no-code platform to import and analyze the dataset. Recommended platforms include: - Google Data Studio - Tableau Public - Microsoft Power BI **Step 3:** Use the chosen platform to generate interactive visualizations (e.g., dashboards, charts) that highlight key social trends and patterns. **Step 4:** If additional data manipulation is required, use a coding tool such as GitHub Copilot or ChatGPT to generate and refine necessary code snippets. **Step 5:** Compare the outputs from the AI-assisted approach with any manually coded solutions (if available) and document the differences. **Step 6:** Prepare a comprehensive report (3–5 pages) that details your analysis process, rationale behind your visualization choices, and a critical reflection on the effectiveness of AI tools versus manual coding techniques in sociological research. *(Continued)*

TABLE 5.1 (CONTINUED)

Data Visualization for Social Trend Analysis

Field	Details	
What to Turn In	- A link to the published interactive dashboard (or screenshots if publishing is not feasible). - A written report (3–5 pages) that includes: - An explanation of your data analysis process. - A comparative discussion of AI-assisted versus manual coding approaches. - Reflections on the role and impact of AI tools in sociological data analysis. - Supplementary materials such as code snippets or annotated notes documenting your process.	

Criteria	Description	Points
Data Analysis and Accuracy	Identifies relevant social indicators and manipulates data accurately. Demonstrates thorough analysis of trends within the dataset.	30
Visualization Quality and Interactivity	Develops an interactive, well-designed dashboard using a low-code/no-code platform. Visualizations clearly communicate key social trends.	30
Reflective Commentary and Critical Analysis	Provides a detailed comparative discussion of AI-assisted versus manual coding approaches. Critically evaluates limitations, biases, and sociological insights.	20
Documentation and Process Explanation	Offers clear, comprehensive documentation of the decision-making process, including rationale for visualization choices and tool usage.	10
Submission Completeness and Presentation	Submits all required components (dashboard link/screenshots, report, annotated notes, and supplementary code snippets) in a well-organized format.	10

as curators rather than passive users of computational outputs, empowering them to effectively direct automated tools toward sociological inquiries while maintaining analytical oversight. Such a pedagogical shift allows introductory sociology students to simultaneously acquire technical familiarity and apply sociological theories, removing the need to choose between coding proficiency and theoretical understanding. With technical obstacles minimized, assisted coding enables deeper student engagement with the interpretative dimensions of sociological research, facilitating integration between computational results and established theoretical frameworks (Zhou et al., 2023).

The integration of these technological solutions further encourages interdisciplinary collaboration, enabling students to combine computational methods seamlessly with sociological analysis, irrespective of specialized training. This interdisciplinary environment mirrors professional contexts, where diverse expertise collaboratively addresses complex issues. Thus, automated tools serve as connectors between technical proficiency and sociological insight, preparing students for future environments in which computational literacy and disciplinary expertise are closely integrated.

As these technologies advance, their application in sociology education will broaden, opening new avenues for investigating social phenomena through computational simulations. Future sociology curricula will increasingly incorporate these simulations, allowing students to explore social behaviors and policy impacts within virtual scenarios. These technological resources will augment, rather than replace, traditional sociological methods, enhancing students' capability to apply theoretical frameworks to empirical data and refining their analytical and critical thinking within disciplinary contexts. Embracing this conceptual-first pedagogical model renders sociology education more interactive, inclusive, and methodologically varied. Students can immediately engage with advanced computational methods, free from initial coding or statistical computing hurdles, ensuring that all sociology students, irrespective of their technical experience, can effectively leverage data analysis to address sociological questions and thrive in a data-intensive world.

5.3 Sophomore Literature: Using LLMs to Scaffold Literary Analysis

LLMs are reshaping how students engage with textual analysis in literature courses, providing accessible computational methods that complement and enhance traditional close-reading practices without requiring specialized technical backgrounds. Historically, sophomore-level English Literature classes focused heavily on manual annotation and careful textual analysis, exploring narrative structure, thematic elements, symbolism, and stylistic devices across literary works ranging from Shakespearean plays to contemporary fiction (Albay, 2017). These courses traditionally demanded meticulous critical reading, exploration of nuanced meanings, and contextual analysis within broader historical and cultural frameworks (Raj et al., 2023). Student success relied primarily on their ability to synthesize varied critical perspectives and articulate well-supported interpretations through detailed essays (Alice et al., 2024). Although intellectually rigorous, this conventional approach relied entirely on human analytical capabilities with minimal technological intervention. Consequently, the significant technical barriers associated with computational textual analysis often isolated literary scholarship from technological methodologies, traditionally necessitating coding proficiency unavailable in many literature departments.

The integration of LLMs significantly lowers these barriers, opening up access to computational textual analysis for students and faculty regardless of technical proficiency. Literature faculty no longer need programming expertise, nor must students acquire coding skills before utilizing computational methods. LLM-driven literary analysis platforms facilitate thematic identification, characterization analysis, and stylistic evaluations seamlessly without prior technical knowledge (Liu & Wang, 2024). This model aligns with a collaborative approach, allowing technological tools to manage complex computational tasks while enabling students and faculty to concentrate on critical literary interpretation. Capabilities such as sentiment analysis, topic modeling, and comparative text analyses provided by the tools allow students to investigate literary works from broader analytical perspectives, uncovering intertextual and thematic patterns less visible through conventional close-reading methods (Saddhono et al., 2024).

Furthermore, adopting these writing tools in literature courses also fosters adaptive learning environments, where technological platforms personalize student interactions with texts. Such systems monitor and respond dynamically to students' interpretive engagement, identifying areas requiring additional support and recommending targeted readings or alternative analytical strategies (Raj et al., 2023). Some models even automate essay prompt generation, summarize complex critical theories, and deliver immediate writing feedback, effectively reducing cognitive load and allowing students greater freedom to engage deeply with argumentation and critical synthesis (Alice et al., 2024). This realignment empowers literature instructors to leverage computational analysis based on their disciplinary expertise, eliminating the prerequisite of technical skills and thus broadening pedagogical possibilities.

The assignment detailed in Table 5.2 embodies a novel pedagogical approach, employing generative models as dynamic guides for literary analysis accessible to all students, irrespective of technical background. By introducing literary passages into platforms such as ChatGPT, students obtain

TABLE 5.2

LLM Literary Analysis and Annotation

Field	Details
Title	LLM-Enhanced Literary Analysis and Annotation
Description	In this assignment, students will select a passage from a literary text and use a large language model (LLM) such as ChatGPT to generate a thematic summary and stylistic analysis. They will then perform a close reading of the passage, manually annotate key literary elements, and compare the AI-generated output with their own analysis. This exercise aims to scaffold traditional literary analysis with AI-assisted insights, demonstrating how computational tools—grounded in coding and algorithmic processes—can support and enhance humanistic inquiry.
Grading	**Total: 100 points** - Quality of generated analysis vs. manual analysis and comparison: 30 points - Depth of critical reflection on the use of tools and potential biases: 30 points - Clarity and coherence of written annotations and reflective report: 20 points - Completeness of documentation (including screenshots and process notes): 10 points - Professional presentation and submission format: 10 points
Learning Outcomes	- Develop the ability to use tools (e.g., ChatGPT) for generating literary analysis. - Enhance close reading and manual annotation skills to identify themes, stylistic devices, and narrative structures. - Critically compare generated insights with human interpretation to evaluate the strengths and limitations of automated analysis. - Gain an understanding of how computational thinking and coding underpin the functionality of these tools.
Step-by-Step Instructions (with Tools and URLs)	**Step 1:** Select a passage (200–500 words) from a literary text studied in class. **Step 2:** Access ChatGPT at https://chat.openai.com and input the selected passage. Request a thematic summary and stylistic analysis from the AI. **Step 3:** Manually annotate the passage using a text editor or annotation tool such as Hypothesis to identify key literary elements (themes, motifs, stylistic devices, etc.). **Step 4:** Compare the generated analysis with your manual annotations. Create a comparison chart that outlines similarities, differences, and potential biases in the output. **Step 5:** Write a reflective report (3–5 pages) that details your analytical process, discusses the efficacy of the tool, and evaluates how AI-assisted analysis aligns with or diverges from traditional close-reading techniques. Highlight aspects where computational methods (i.e., underlying coding and algorithmic processes) contributed to or detracted from your analysis. **Step 6:** Organize all supporting materials (comparison chart, annotated passage screenshots, ChatGPT output screenshots) as part of your submission.

(Continued)

TABLE 5.2 (CONTINUED)

LLM Literary Analysis and Annotation

Field	Details
What to Turn In	- A reflective report (3–5 pages) detailing the analytical process, comparisons, and reflections on assisted versus manual analysis. - The annotated passage (either digital file or screenshots). - A comparison chart summarizing the generated analysis and manual annotations. - Screenshots or export files showing the ChatGPT output from https://chat.openai.com. - Supplementary documentation that details your decision-making process throughout the assignment.

Criteria	Description	Max Points	Weight (% of Total)	How Met (Criteria Explanation)
Quality of AI vs. Manual Analysis	Compares the AI-generated thematic summary and stylistic analysis with manual close-reading annotations. Evaluates clarity, accuracy, and depth in identifying literary elements.	30	30%	Met by providing a well-organized comparison chart and a clear discussion in the reflective report that highlights both convergences and divergences between the two approaches.
Critical Reflection on AI Tool Usage	Provides a deep critical analysis of the benefits and limitations of AI-assisted analysis, including discussion of potential biases and how computational methods underpin the tool's functionality.	30	30%	Evidenced by an insightful reflection that not only evaluates AI-generated output but also discusses the role of underlying coding and algorithmic processes, with specific examples.
Clarity and Coherence of Written Work	Presents a well-structured and articulate reflective report, with clear annotations and logical organization that supports the overall argument.	20	20%	Demonstrated by a coherent report that integrates analysis, reflective commentary, and evidence from the comparison chart, ensuring that the narrative is both engaging and academically rigorous.

(Continued)

TABLE 5.2 (CONTINUED)

LLM Literary Analysis and Annotation

Field		Details
Documentation and Process Explanation	10	10%	Includes comprehensive documentation of the analytical process, such as screenshots, annotated passages, and detailed process notes.	Achieved by submitting all required supporting materials, organized in a manner that clearly details each step of the assignment, from data input to final reflection.
Submission Completeness and Presentation	10	10%	Ensures that all required components are submitted in a professional, organized, and visually appealing format.	Met by a complete package that includes the reflective report, annotated materials, comparison chart, and supporting screenshots, all presented in a clear and professional format.

initial thematic analyses and stylistic insights, forming a foundational analytical framework that they subsequently refine via critical reflection and detailed textual examination. This method fosters a curatorial skill set, challenging students to actively juxtapose machine-generated insights with their own interpretations, effectively discerning the alignment and discrepancies between computational and human analyses. Consequently, students develop the ability to critically evaluate the inherent limitations and potential biases of automated textual methodologies, gaining insight into both the strengths and boundaries of these computational approaches. This educational strategy reframes generative models as analytical collaborators rather than replacements or technical impediments, thereby seamlessly integrating traditional close-reading practices with computational textual analysis.

Looking forward, advancements in generative models and computational methods promise deeper, more personalized avenues for literary scholarship. Potential developments could include sophisticated tools capable of producing literary criticism, adaptive and customized learning experiences, and interactive simulations that enable dialogs with literary characters. These innovative possibilities would significantly extend capabilities for historical contextualization, intricate intertextual analyses, and advanced narrative modeling, empowering literature students to explore new scholarly terrains previously inaccessible without specialized technological skills. Furthermore, evolving digital annotation platforms might support real-time collaborative literary analysis, facilitating shared insights, comparative interpretations, and collective scholarly dialogs across diverse student cohorts. Importantly, these enhanced analytical tools reinforce traditional literary expertise by broadening the methodological scope, ensuring literature students and educators are well-equipped to navigate and meaningfully integrate computational advancements into humanistic inquiry.

5.4 Junior-Level History: Mapping and Annotating Historical Trends with AI Tools

Historical research and visualization are being transformed through AI-driven mapping and annotation tools that allow students to create sophisticated digital timelines and spatial analyses without mastering programming languages first. Traditionally, junior-level history courses immersed students in primary and secondary sources to interpret complex historical narratives, but the technical barriers to computational analysis meant that digital approaches remained inaccessible to most history classrooms. Students were challenged to engage critically with archival materials and historical documents, but sophisticated digital mapping, visualization, and computational analysis remained out of reach without specialized technical training (Baiburin et al., 2024). This traditional approach created an artificial divide between historical expertise and computational methods. Historical inquiry emphasized close reading and qualitative analysis, while computational tools demanded programming skills that most history faculty and students lacked. The integration now disrupts this framework, eliminating the historical requirement for technical expertise and making computational methods accessible to all history students and faculty. Rather than requiring history professors to become coding experts before incorporating digital methods, new tools now enable the analysis of large corpora of texts and spatial data without prerequisite programming knowledge (Fritsche & Münster, 2024). This approach directly mirrors an "AI as collaborative partner" framework, where technology handles technical implementation while humans focus on disciplinary interpretation.

NLP models can now be applied to digitized historical archives to classify texts, recognize named entities, and cross-reference sources within expansive datasets—tasks previously restricted to those with programming backgrounds (Fritsche & Münster, 2024). These technologies facilitate discourse analysis by tracking language evolution, examining ideological changes, and identifying patterns in political rhetoric over time, making computational methods accessible to history classrooms without requiring coding expertise (Ni, 2024). Similarly, digital humanities platforms that leverage mapping technologies allow students to overlay historical data onto geographical spaces, revealing migration patterns, economic changes, and political conflicts in visually compelling ways without demanding technical skills from either instructors or students (Pajares et al., 2023). The advancement of optical character recognition (OCR) and handwriting recognition systems further exemplifies this increased accessibility, automating the transcription of historical documents and reducing the labor-intensive nature of manual data entry (Luther et al., 2024). AI handles routine technical tasks while students practice higher-order thinking—in this case, historical interpretation and synthesis rather than document transcription.

The assignment outlined in Table 5.3 exemplifies a contemporary educational model by integrating computational tools into historical analysis without requiring extensive technical expertise. Students undertake the creation of a digital timeline, mapping significant events within a selected historical period, immediately engaging in meaningful analytical tasks. Employing accessible, low-code visualization platforms such as Google My Maps or Tableau Public, students directly construct interactive timelines that visually represent the chronology and geographical contexts of historical events. This method prioritizes conceptual engagement and interpretative analysis, as students curate data sets from archival sources and apply intuitive visualization technologies. Furthermore, generative language models like ChatGPT assist students by providing initial annotations contextualizing each historical event, thus functioning as analytical collaborators within the research process. Students critically assess and refine these automated annotations, applying their own historical insight and methodological rigor.

TABLE 5.3

Digital Timeline of Historical Events

Field	Details
Title	Digital Timeline of Historical Events: Mapping and Annotating Trends
Description	In this assignment, students select a specific historical period and compile a dataset of key events from reputable archival sources. Using a low-code platform such as Google My Maps (https://www.google.com/mymaps) or Tableau Public (https://public.tableau.com), students create an interactive digital timeline that maps these events. They then use ChatGPT (https://chat.openai.com) to generate preliminary annotations for each event, which are subsequently refined and verified manually. This exercise emphasizes traditional coding practices—such as data structuring, logic-based filtering, and iterative refinement—while demonstrating how AI tools can augment historical research and digital curation.
Learning Outcomes	• Develop digital literacy in the context of historical data analysis. • Acquire skills in data organization, visualization, and interactive dashboard creation using low-code platforms. • Critically compare AI-generated annotations with manually curated research. • Understand and apply foundational coding principles to enhance historical inquiry.
Step-by-Step Instructions	**Step 1:** Select a specific historical period and compile a dataset of significant events from primary and secondary archival sources. **Step 2:** Using a low-code platform, either Google My Maps or Tableau Public, import the dataset and design an interactive timeline that visually represents the sequence and spatial distribution of events. **Step 3:** Input excerpts or descriptions related to each event into ChatGPT to generate initial AI-driven annotations that summarize the context and significance of the events. **Step 4:** Manually review and refine the AI-generated annotations, cross-checking with your research to ensure accuracy and relevance. Emphasize traditional coding practices such as logical data structuring and filtering during this process. **Step 5:** Document your process in detail, including the criteria used for event selection, your methodology for integrating AI outputs, and the rationale behind manual refinements. **Step 6:** Prepare a reflective report (3–5 pages) discussing the integration of AI and manual curation, analyzing the benefits and limitations of AI-assisted annotation, and exploring how coding principles support modern historical analysis.
What to Turn In	• A link to the published interactive digital timeline or screenshots if publishing is not feasible. • A reflective report (3–5 pages) that outlines your process, comparative analysis of AI-generated versus manually refined annotations, and insights on the application of coding principles in historical research. • Supplementary documentation, including annotated screenshots and process notes detailing your decision-making.
Grading: Total Points	**100 Points Total**

(Continued)

TABLE 5.3   (CONTINUED)

Digital Timeline of Historical Events

Field	Details
Grading Rubric: Data Analysis and Accuracy	**Description:** Evaluates the selection of significant historical events, the organization of data, and the accurate integration of AI-generated annotations with manual research. **Max Points:** 30 **Weight:** 30% **How Met:** Demonstrated through precise event selection, coherent data structuring, and error-free annotation verification.
Grading Rubric: Visualization Quality and Interactivity	**Description:** Assesses the design, clarity, and interactivity of the digital timeline created on the low-code platform. **Max Points:** 30 **Weight:** 30% **How Met:** Met by creating a visually engaging and user-friendly interactive timeline that effectively represents historical data and trends.
Grading Rubric: Reflective Analysis and Critical Evaluation	**Description:** Measures the depth of the reflective report, including the critical comparison of AI-generated and manual annotations, and the discussion of underlying coding and data processing principles. **Max Points:** 20 **Weight:** 20% **How Met:** Evidenced by a comprehensive analysis that discusses the benefits, limitations, and potential biases of AI-assisted annotation, supported by insights into computational thinking and coding practices.
Grading Rubric: Documentation and Process Explanation	**Description:** Evaluates the completeness and clarity of the documentation, including annotated screenshots and detailed process notes. **Max Points:** 10 **Weight:** 10% **How Met:** Achieved by providing thorough documentation that clearly outlines each step of the assignment, including justifications for decisions made and a clear record of the integration process.
Grading Rubric: Submission Completeness and Presentation	**Description:** Assesses the overall organization, professionalism, and completeness of the final submission. **Max Points:** 10 **Weight:** 10% **How Met:** Demonstrated by a complete and well-organized submission that includes all required components and is presented in a professional, accessible format.

The pedagogical model further emphasizes reflective practice, requiring students to document their methodologies, selection criteria, and the analytical rationales behind their refinement of generated annotations. By actively comparing machine-produced outputs with manually curated historical information, students cultivate a critical awareness of both the strengths and limitations inherent in computational historical analysis. This reflective component positions students as active directors of computational methods, reinforcing their analytical autonomy and encouraging a deeper engagement with historical inquiry.

Looking forward, the role of computational technologies in history education promises further innovation through sophisticated applications such as virtual reality (VR) simulations and interactive digital reconstructions of historical events. Emerging advancements could facilitate immersive, first-hand experiences of historical scenarios without the technical complexities traditionally associated with VR development (Hutson, 2024; Ni, 2024). Moreover, conversational models based on historical texts may soon enable dynamic interactions with representations of historical figures, promoting deeper understanding through dialog-based and role-playing pedagogical techniques (Hutson et al., 2024; Pope & Ma, 2024). Such computational enhancements will complement traditional historical research methods, offering students multimodal and interdisciplinary avenues of exploration previously inaccessible without specialized technological skills. As with the earlier examples, this integrated approach equips students with traditional skills they would learn, robust historical research competencies, and proficiency in directing computational methodologies toward meaningful and innovative historical investigations.

Senior-level business administration capstone courses are rapidly evolving as intelligent systems enable students to create interactive analytics dashboards and execute sophisticated strategic models without extensive technical training, thus prioritizing strategic business insights and practical decision-making. Historically, these advanced courses have emphasized strategic management, project planning, and real-world decision-making through methods like case studies, business simulations, and consulting collaborations with industry partners (Knott et al., 2018). The curriculum traditionally fosters critical thinking, strategic leadership, and interdisciplinary teamwork, equipping students with the data-driven decision-making skills vital in contemporary business environments (Mackenzie & DiStefano, 2018; Alstete & Beutell, 2020).

Previously, significant technical barriers to advanced data analytics and software execution meant that student business projects often remained theoretical rather than fully implemented. Students typically outlined strategies and theoretical plans without the practical realization of these concepts in functional software, primarily due to the limited technical proficiency among business faculty and students. The integration of sophisticated computational tools has transformed this model, effectively removing traditional prerequisites for technical expertise, thus democratizing advanced computational capabilities. These innovative platforms offer predictive analytics, risk assessment automation, and data-driven strategic insights, all without requiring prior coding knowledge from faculty or students (Gerçek & Erkin, 2024).

Through the deployment of synthetic intelligence-driven platforms—including business simulations, advanced financial modeling tools, and market research software—students can seamlessly analyze market trends, test strategic scenarios, and refine resource allocation strategies without preliminary programming training (Alkaabi, 2021). This represents a crucial reversal of the conventional educational approach, enabling immediate, meaningful engagement with strategic business analytics while automated systems manage technical execution.

The most impactful applications within business education include project management and operational deployment. Automated project management systems utilize advanced algorithms to forecast project timelines, efficiently allocate resources, and optimize workflow, obviating the necessity for students to grasp complex programming details (Gerçek & Erkin, 2024). Additionally, computationally enhanced risk management tools empower students to conduct comprehensive evaluations of project risks, competitor strategies, and economic conditions, all without extensive statistical training. Entrepreneurial education similarly benefits from automation platforms, which perform SWOT analyses, customer segmentation, and business plan development, thereby enabling students to craft sophisticated market entry strategies without technical proficiency (Washuta & Bass, 2019). In finance-specific scenarios, intelligent financial modeling tools analyze historical market data, forecast revenue streams, and manage investment portfolios, providing valuable practical exposure to predictive modeling previously reserved for technically skilled professionals (Alkaabi, 2021).

The assignment outlined in Table 5.4 illustrates a progressive shift in educational methodology by tasking students with developing an interactive Business Analytics Dashboard, utilizing computational tools to visualize and interpret key performance indicators for strategic decision-making. Rather than mandating prior programming proficiency, the assignment employs accessible, low-code visualization platforms like Tableau Public or Microsoft Power BI, allowing students to engage immediately with sophisticated analytical techniques. Students begin the process by selecting relevant business datasets, importing them into intuitive analytical environments, and visually interpreting complex metrics relevant to strategic business contexts. Further integration is achieved through automated coding assistants such as GitHub Copilot, alongside generative language tools like ChatGPT, which help generate preliminary code snippets necessary for data cleaning and transformation.

These computational assistants function as analytical collaborators, facilitating technical aspects while allowing students to prioritize strategic business interpretation. Students critically evaluate machine-generated outputs against manually refined results, documenting their methodologies comprehensively—detailing data selection rationales, platform configurations, and strategic optimization choices. A reflective report accompanying each dashboard requires students to articulate the advantages and limitations of computational assistance clearly, emphasizing how these technologies enhance traditional business analytics practices through integrated computational thinking.

TABLE 5.4

Business Analytics Dashboard

Field	Details
Title	AI-Driven Business Analytics Dashboard: A Capstone Project
Description	In this assignment, students develop an interactive dashboard that integrates low-code/no-code platforms with AI-powered coding tools to analyze and visualize key business performance data. Students will compile a dataset of essential business KPIs—such as revenue, expenses, and profit margins—and use AI-driven methods to reshape and interpret the data. The project emphasizes the integration of computational thinking with strategic decision-making, demonstrating how coding can enhance traditional business analytics and inform effective business strategy.
Learning Outcomes	- Develop advanced data literacy skills within a business context. - Understand the role of low-code/no-code platforms in augmenting traditional coding methods. - Create interactive dashboards to visualize and analyze business performance metrics. - Critically assess the benefits and limitations of AI-driven analytics for strategic planning. - Integrate computational methods with business decision-making and ethical considerations.
Step-by-Step Instructions	**Step 1:** Select or obtain a dataset focused on key business KPIs (e.g., revenue, expenses, profit margins) from a provided source or online database (e.g., Business KPI Dataset). **Step 2:** Import the dataset into a low-code/no-code analytics platform, such as Tableau Public (https://public.tableau.com) or Microsoft Power BI (https://powerbi.microsoft.com). **Step 3:** Use an AI-powered coding tool like GitHub Copilot (https://github.com/features/copilot) or ChatGPT (https://chat.openai.com) to generate initial code snippets for data cleaning, transformation, and analysis. **Step 4:** Develop interactive visualizations—such as dashboards, charts, and graphs—that highlight trends, correlations, and anomalies within the dataset. **Step 5:** Manually refine the visualizations by adjusting parameters, applying filters, and verifying the accuracy of the data representation. **Step 6:** Write a reflective report (3–5 pages) detailing your methodology, comparing AI-assisted outputs with manual coding adjustments, and discussing the strategic and ethical implications of AI in business decision-making. **Step 7:** Compile all supporting documentation, including screenshots of the dashboard, annotated code snippets, and detailed process notes, to accompany your final submission.
What to Turn In	- A link to the published interactive dashboard or a set of screenshots if publishing is not feasible. - A reflective report (3–5 pages) that details the analysis process, compares AI-assisted and manual coding approaches, and provides insights on the integration of AI in business analytics.- Supplementary documentation, including annotated code snippets, screenshots, and process notes.

(Continued)

TABLE 5.4   (CONTINUED)

Business Analytics Dashboard

Field	Details
Grading Rubric	**Total: 100 Points** **Data Analysis and Accuracy (30 Points, 30%):** Evaluates the precise selection, structuring, and analysis of the business dataset. Points are awarded for accurate data manipulation and insightful analysis that informs strategic decisions. **Visualization Quality and Interactivity (30 Points, 30%):** Assesses the design, clarity, and interactivity of the dashboard. Points are given for creating a visually engaging, functional, and user-friendly dashboard that effectively communicates key business trends. **Reflective Analysis and Critical Evaluation (20 Points, 20%):** Measures the depth and quality of the reflective report, including the critical comparison between AI-assisted and manual methods, and discussion of strategic and ethical considerations in AI-driven analytics. **Documentation and Process Explanation (10 Points, 10%):** Evaluates the completeness and clarity of the supporting documentation, including annotated code snippets and process notes that detail the step-by-step methodology. **Submission Completeness and Presentation (10 Points, 10%):** Assesses overall organization, professionalism, and the inclusion of all required components in the final submission.

This educational approach expands traditional business curricula, simultaneously building technical familiarity and strategic business acumen without forcing a choice between the two. As computational tools become integral to the business landscape, course content will increasingly transition from manual data handling to strategic planning, model evaluation, and real-time analytics interpretation. Students will cultivate expertise in directing computational systems toward substantial business challenges, effectively preparing for professional environments marked by human-computational collaboration (Knott et al., 2018). Advanced business curricula will further emphasize interdisciplinary collaboration, integrating strategic management expertise with advanced analytics powered by computational platforms. Real-world, industry-based projects may incorporate dynamic market data analysis and predictive modeling, facilitating real-time strategic refinement. Faculty roles will increasingly evolve toward guiding and mentoring, equipping students to synergize computational insights with informed human judgment, thus preparing graduates for dynamic, innovation-driven professional contexts (Mackenzie-Ruppel & DiStefano, 2018). Students acquire both traditional business competencies and proficiency in leveraging computational methodologies toward impactful strategic inquiry, ensuring readiness for evolving professional ecosystems where analytical technologies and strategic human decision-making coexist seamlessly.

5.6 Graduate Digital Humanities: Literate Programming for Textual and Data Research

Graduate programs in digital humanities (DH) are increasingly integrating computational methods into humanistic research through advanced programming systems, enabling scholars to engage deeply with textual and data analysis without extensive prior programming experience. Traditionally, DH programs sought to combine computational analysis with humanities scholarship, equipping students to visualize, interpret, and curate digital artifacts through interdisciplinary approaches (Rushmeier & Chen, 2022). These programs typically merged data science, archival management, textual analytics, and computational historical research, aiming to provide both technical expertise and critical theoretical insights. However, conventional models often faced considerable barriers, requiring either technically proficient entrants or substantial coding training for humanities students before meaningful engagement could occur. Consequently, programs frequently offered only superficial computational exposure or segregated technical and humanities scholarship into distinct academic tracks, preventing authentic interdisciplinary integration (Augst & Engel, 2022).

The introduction of advanced computational systems substantially reduces these historical barriers, democratizing access to sophisticated computational methodologies for humanities scholars irrespective of their programming backgrounds. Humanities faculty no longer need extensive coding knowledge; instead, intelligent computational platforms serve as active partners, managing complex technical processes and allowing scholars to concentrate on interpretive, theoretical questions. Historically, DH curricula required intensive workshops to teach programming languages like Python or R alongside humanities content, often resulting in significant pedagogical tension and limited depth of integration (Augst & Engel, 2022). Faculty frequently relied on technical collaboration models to navigate the challenges of simultaneously developing students' technical and humanistic skills (Kaminska, 2022).

With computational tools now effectively managing the technical intricacies, DH pedagogy is transitioning toward immediate, meaningful application of computational analysis to humanistic inquiries. Instead of prolonged foundational programming training, students can now directly engage computational methodologies to address relevant disciplinary questions. Computational assistants thus enable humanities scholars to maintain a robust focus on conceptual frameworks and critical theory, while benefiting from sophisticated textual analysis and visualization capabilities. This approach prepares students for future academic and professional environments characterized by seamless integration between computational

TABLE 5.5

Literary Analysis with Custom API Integration

Field	Details
Title	Literary Analysis with Custom API Integration
Description	In this assignment, graduate digital humanities students will harness AI agents and custom API integration to analyze a corpus of literary texts. Students will select a corpus from a digital archive such as Project Gutenberg, clean and structure the dataset using Python libraries (e.g., Pandas), and then use OpenAI's GPT-4 API to generate preliminary textual analyses (e.g., thematic summaries and keyword extraction). Following this, they will build a custom API using FastAPI to aggregate and refine the AI-generated outputs. Visual Studio Code, along with the REST Client extension and Postman, will be used to test and debug the API. The final deliverable is a digital research paper that embeds code snippets, documents the API interactions, and includes a reflective commentary comparing AI-assisted outputs with manual refinements. This assignment demonstrates the interplay between traditional coding practices and AI-driven automation, reinforcing computational methods in digital humanities research (Augst & Engel, 2022; Kaminska, 2022).
Learning Outcomes	- Develop advanced data curation and cleaning skills using Python (Pandas).- Gain proficiency in integrating AI agents (via GPT-4 API) for literary analysis.- Learn to build and test custom APIs using FastAPI and related tools.- Enhance skills in iterative refinement, critical evaluation, and reflective writing in a digital research context.- Understand how AI-driven automation complements traditional coding practices in digital humanities.
Step-by-Step Instructions	**Step 1**: Select a corpus of literary texts from Project Gutenberg (https://www.gutenberg.org). **Step 2**: Use Python and the Pandas library (https://pandas.pydata.org) to clean, structure, and prepare the dataset for analysis. **Step 3**: Access OpenAI's GPT-4 API via https://platform.openai.com and write code to input excerpts from the corpus to generate thematic summaries and extract key literary elements. **Step 4**: Build a custom API using FastAPI (https://fastapi.tiangolo.com) in Visual Studio Code. Utilize the REST Client extension (https://marketplace.visualstudio.com/items?itemName=humao.rest-client) and test endpoints using Postman (https://www.postman.com). **Step 5**: Optionally, incorporate additional scholarly insights using Deep Research (https://deepresearch.ai) to augment your analysis. **Step 6**: Write a comprehensive digital research paper (3–5 pages) that embeds code snippets, documents your API interactions, and provides a reflective commentary on the process, discussing the interplay between AI-generated outputs and manual coding refinements.

(Continued)

TABLE 5.5 (CONTINUED)

Literary Analysis with Custom API Integration

Field	Details
What to Turn In	- A link to the final published digital research paper or a PDF copy with embedded code snippets and documentation. - A complete API documentation package, including code files, annotated screenshots of API tests (via Visual Studio Code and Postman), and process notes. - A reflective report integrated into the research paper that critically evaluates the benefits and limitations of using agents versus manual refinement in literary analysis.
Grading Rubric	**Total: 100 Points** **Data Preparation and Dataset Quality (25 Points, 25%)** *Description:* Evaluate the quality of the dataset selected, the thoroughness of data cleaning, and the structuring of the corpus using Python and Pandas. *How Met:* Demonstrated by clear, error-free code and well-organized data ready for analysis. **AI Integration and API Functionality (25 Points, 25%)** *Description:* Assess the effective use of GPT–4 API for preliminary analysis and the successful development and testing of a custom API using FastAPI, Visual Studio Code, and Postman. *How Met:* Evidenced by a fully functional API and robust code integration that streamlines the AI-assisted analysis. **Reflective Analysis and Critical Evaluation (30 Points, 30%)** *Description:* Measure the depth and quality of the reflective commentary, including comparisons between AI-generated outputs and manual refinements, and a discussion of the interplay between AI automation and traditional coding practices. *How Met:* Evidenced by a well-articulated reflective report that integrates theoretical insights and practical observations. **Documentation and Process Explanation (10 Points, 10%)** *Description:* Evaluate the completeness and clarity of supporting documentation, including annotated code snippets, screenshots, and process notes. *How Met:* Achieved through thorough, well-organized documentation that clearly outlines each step of the assignment. **Submission Completeness and Presentation (10 Points, 10%)** *Description:* Assess overall organization, professionalism, and adherence to submission guidelines. *How Met:* Demonstrated by a complete, well-presented final package that includes all required components in an accessible format.

technologies and humanistic research, fostering interdisciplinary capabilities essential to innovative scholarship.

The assignment detailed in Table 5.5 illustrates a contemporary pedagogical approach in DH graduate education, empowering students to utilize computational agents and API integrations for sophisticated literary analyses without demanding extensive preliminary programming skills. Students initially select a literary corpus and employ computational resources such as Python's Pandas library to structure their datasets. Notably, automated assistance supports the technical components of data cleansing and preparation, enabling students to maintain their primary concentration on interpretative analyses. Leveraging advanced models such as OpenAI's GPT-4 API, students conduct preliminary textual analysis to generate comprehensive summaries, identify thematic patterns, and propose initial interpretive insights. This automation lays the groundwork for advanced interpretative tasks, shifting the educational emphasis from technical coding details to critical appraisal and refinement of automated analyses.

Further depth is introduced as students construct customized APIs using frameworks like FastAPI—an endeavor traditionally requiring considerable technical knowledge but now achievable through computational assistance. Students utilize intuitive tools such as Visual Studio Code and Postman for API testing and iterative development, achieving complex functionality without extensive prior programming mastery. This pedagogical approach facilitates humanistic inquiry by allowing computational platforms to manage implementation intricacies, thereby enabling students to pursue focused theoretical and interpretive questions. Students document their processes and provide critical evaluations of interactions between automated outputs and manual scholarly refinement, developing comprehensive digital research projects. By actively directing computational processes rather than passively consuming technology-generated content, students learn to effectively align computational methods with meaningful humanities research questions. This reorientation profoundly influences DH education, removing traditional constraints and allowing simultaneous cultivation of computational familiarity and sophisticated humanistic inquiry.

Looking forward, such integrated methodologies promise profound transformation in DH graduate education, reshaping both instructional strategies and scholarly outcomes. Future curricula are likely to embrace even more complex and layered computational models, employing collaborative digital agents capable of handling extensive research workflows from data acquisition and thematic analysis to intricate visualization strategies (Augst & Engel, 2022). This progression positions students to focus on high-level theoretical synthesis and advanced analytical interpretation rather than routine technical tasks. Upcoming DH programs will increasingly prioritize computational reasoning, iterative design practices, and sophisticated algorithmic methodologies, training students to build customized digital research workflows and optimize interdisciplinary computational pipelines. Scholars will engage deeply with integrated platforms featuring natural language processing, machine learning, and geospatial analytics to produce dynamic, multimodal digital archives, fostering innovative scholarly practices and comprehensive cultural understanding (Kaminska, 2022). This evolution ensures DH remains a leader in academic innovation and technological integration, effectively overcoming historical technical barriers and significantly expanding the scope of digital humanistic scholarship.

5.7 Reflective Practices: Reasoning Traces as Pedagogical Tools across Disciplines

Reflective methodologies and reasoning documentation significantly enhance student engagement by enabling rigorous examination, evaluation, and refinement of computationally generated results across various disciplines. These structured reflections, capturing detailed decision-making processes behind computational outputs, establish essential connections between automated analysis and human critical judgment (Ikhsan et al., 2024). Such reflective exercises not only deepen students' comprehension of technological assistance but also fortify essential human cognitive skills, addressing concerns that students might uncritically accept automated outputs without sufficient intellectual interrogation. Structured exercises, like those involving critical annotation of computational results described in earlier chapters, offer concrete frameworks for interdisciplinary applications, effectively bridging automated analyses with nuanced human oversight (Lewis & Hayhoe, 2024).

Reflective computational frameworks have been effectively implemented across diverse educational contexts—including teacher training, digital humanities, and professional skill development—highlighting their role in reversing traditional educational paradigms by encouraging meaningful inquiry prior to technical mastery. Teacher education programs utilizing automated feedback systems for reflective writing foster iterative cycles of student-generated analysis and critique of machine recommendations (Solopova et al., 2023). Additionally, conversational computational tools generate Socratic questioning methods, facilitating deeper cognitive engagement by prompting justification of decisions, exploration of alternative solutions, and identification of logical inconsistencies (Lewis & Hayhoe, 2024). These tools reposition computational resources as intellectual collaborators rather than merely technical facilitators.

Professional training contexts similarly benefit from structured reflective methodologies, integrating automated feedback within learning management systems (LMS) to adaptively guide professional development and track intellectual growth over time (Mohamed et al., 2022). Case-based professional training environments leverage interactive decision frameworks and computational reasoning tools to train ethical analysis, strategic management, and diagnostic skills (Machost & Stains, 2023). Embedding reflective documentation within computational workflows ensures deeper student understanding of technological limitations, equipping learners to address errors, biases, and informational gaps in computational outputs effectively.

Collaborative learning environments represent another promising application of reasoning documentation, using advanced version control platforms that record decision-making processes and facilitate peer-to-peer discussions, allowing students to critically assess divergent perspectives and refine collaborative analytical practices (Anand & Gangmei, 2023). These approaches encourage active discourse between student insights and computational results, effectively integrating human analysis and machine-generated insights (Mohamed et al., 2022). Future educational applications promise increased personalization, adapting reflective tasks to individual learning profiles and disciplinary specificities, with computational platforms dynamically responding to student understanding levels (Kaczorowski et al., 2024). Ethical considerations embedded in reflective practices further prepare students for informed, agile navigation of automated analytical processes, reinforcing intellectual rigor and ethical sensitivity (Yorks et al., 2020).

The strategic integration of advanced computational methodologies across disciplinary curricula significantly broadens access to sophisticated analytical tools, fostering critical thinking and interdisciplinary collaboration without imposing restrictive technical prerequisites. This pedagogical evolution emphasizes iterative, reflective engagement, positioning students as active evaluators of technology rather than passive recipients (Davies et al., 2020; Mackenzie & DiStefano, 2018). Academic institutions must continue promoting innovative teaching strategies that facilitate the exploration of algorithmic interactions within disciplinary contexts, ensuring a balanced integration of automated tools and manual critical analysis (Zawacki-Richter et al., 2019; Kaminska, 2022). Ultimately, this integrated approach ensures sophisticated computational analysis remains widely accessible, enriching disciplinary inquiries through meaningful and critical technological engagement.

References

Albay, M. (2017). Intertextuality in the literature. *International Journal of Social Sciences & Educational Studies, 3*(4), 208–214.

Alice, C., Jebaselvi, C. A. E., Mohanraj, K., & Anitha, T. (2024). The rise of AI in English language and literature. *Shanlax International Journal of English, 12*(2), 53–58.

Alkaabi, K. (2021). A capstone course linking geography knowledge and entrepreneurship skills: An instructional approach to entrepreneurship education. *Review of International Geographical Education Online, 11*(4), 1467–1479.

Alstete, J. W., & Beutell, N. J. (2021). Delivery mode and strategic management simulation outcomes: On-ground versus distance learning. *Journal of International Education in Business, 14*(1), 77–92.

Anand, J., & Gangmei, E. (2023). Reflective practices: A connecting bridge between theory and practices in teacher education. *International Journal For Multidisciplinary Research.* https://doi.org/10.36948/ijfmr.2023.v05i06.9459

Augst, T., & Engel, D. (2022). Project-based learning for graduate students in digital humanities. *Qeios.* https://doi.org/10.32388/4w5txn

Baiburin, A., Berezkin, Y., Boitsova, O., Gromov, A., Kovalenko, K., Kovalyova, N., Moskvitina, A., Shirobokov, I., Sokolov, E., Stanulevich, N., & Utekhin, I. (2024). Forum 60: AI in the social sciences and humanities. *Antropologicheskij Forum.* https://doi.org/10.31250/1815-8870-2024-20-60-11-68

Bull, C., & Kharrufa, A. (2023). Generative AI assistants in software development education. *ArXiv, abs/2303.13936.* https://doi.org/10.1109/MS.2023.3300574

Davies, H. C., Eynon, R., & Salveson, C. (2020). The mobilisation of AI in education: A Bourdieusean field analysis. *Sociology, 55*(3), 539–560.

Ebert, C., Louridas, P., & Ebert, C. (2023). Generative AI for software practitioners. *IEEE Software, 40*, 30–38. https://doi.org/10.1109/MS.2023.3265877

Fritsche, K., & Münster, S. (2024). Taking up artificial intelligence as teaching and learning content in the digital humanities – topics, categorisations, and examples. *Proceedings of The International Conference on Advanced Research in Teaching and Education.* https://doi.org/10.33422/icate.v1i1.225

Gerçek, M., & Erkin, H. G. (2024). How does the use of artificial intelligence reflect on business administration and management? A perspective on knowledge production at the postgraduate level. *İş'te Davranış Dergisi, 9*(1), 1–17.

Hernández-Lugo, M. D. L. C. (2024). Artificial Intelligence as a tool for analysis in Social Sciences: Methods and applications. *LatIA, 2*, 11–11.

Hong, Y., Nguyen, A., Dang, B., & Nguyen, B. P. T. (2022). Data ethics framework for artificial intelligence in education (AIED). *2022 International Conference on Advanced Learning Technologies (ICALT)* (pp. 297–301).

Hutson, J. (2024). *Art and culture in the multiverse of metaverses: immersion, presence, and interactivity in the digital age.* Springer Nature.

Hutson, J., Huffman, P., & Ratican, J. (2024). Digital resurrection of historical figures: A case study on Mary Sibley through customized ChatGPT. *Metaverse, 4*(2), 1–22.

Ikhsan, I., Ashar, M., Mashudi, A., Ichwan, I., Kadarisman, K., & Akbar, M. (2024). Design reflective practice assessment tools for teacher on learning management system using AI ādaptive feedback. *ACEID Official Conference Proceedings.* https://doi.org/10.22492/issn.2189-101x.2024.61

Kaczorowski, T., Stockman, A., Hashey, A., & Kaczorowski, J. (2024). Early adopters: Navigating AI integration in special education teacher preparation. *Journal of Special Education Preparation.* https://doi.org/10.33043/9ca46254

Knott, M. J., Forray, J. M., & Regan, C. E. (2018). Outcomes assessment in a capstone management course: Engaging multiple stakeholders. *Organization Management Journal, 15*(3), 144–157.

Lewis, M., & Hayhoe, B. (2024). The digital Balint: using AI in reflective practice. *Education for Primary Care, 36*(5), 1–5.

Liu, W., & Wang, Y. (2024). The effects of using AI tools on critical thinking in English literature classes among EFL learners: An intervention study. *European Journal of Education, 59*(4), e12804.

Luther, K., Mohanty, V., Lee, B. C. G., & Lykourentzou, I. (2024, March). Past meets future: Human-AI interaction for digital history and cultural heritage. In *Companion Proceedings of the 29th International Conference on Intelligent User Interfaces* (pp. 127–130).

Machost, H., & Stains, M. (2023). Reflective practices in education: A primer for practitioners. *CBE—Life Sciences Education, 22*(2), es2.

Mackenzie-Ruppel, M., & DiStefano, D. (2018). Business education: Real-world capstone. In *Northeast Division of the Decisions Sciences Institue (NEDSI)*.

Mohamed, M., Rashid, R. A., & Alqaryouti, M. H. (2022). Conceptualizing the complexity of reflective practice in education. *Frontiers in Psychology, 13*, 1008234.

Nazaretsky, T., Cukurova, M., Ariely, M., & Alexandron, G. (2021, September). Confirmation bias and trust: Human factors that influence teachers' attitudes towards AI-based educational technology. In *CEUR Workshop Proceedings* (Vol. 3042).

Ni, L. B. (2024). AI-enhanced digital learning: Revolutionizing middle east history education. *Universal Library of Languages and Literatures, 1*(1). https://doi.org/10.70315/uloap.ullli.2024.0101006

Pajares, P. R., Martin, M. S., Botey, J. B., Hernández-Tornero, C., García González, R., & Monclús, G. J. (2023). AI in archival holdings and digital history: Interrelational, dialogical and cooperative interdisciplinary partnerships. *2023 IEEE International Conference on Big Data (BigData)* (pp. 6263–6264).

Pope, A., & Ma, R. (2024). Exploring Historians' critical use of generative AI technologies for history education. *Proceedings of the Association for Information Science and Technology, 61*(1), 1071–1073.

Purnomo, A. M. (2023). Bibliometric analysis of sociological research on artificial intelligence. *Jurnal Ilmu Sosial, 22*(2), 31–49.

Raj, A. V. T., Udayakumar, U., & Saravanan, D. (2023). Integrating artificial intelligence in English literature: Exploring applications, implications, and ethical considerations. *International Journal of Advanced Research in Science, Communication and Technology*, 11–15. https://doi.org/10.48175/ijarsct-12003

Rushmeier, H. E., & Chen, A. (2022). A course on the digital humanities for the premodern world. In Pintus, R. & Ponchio, F. (Eds.), Eurographics Proceedings 2022, The Eurographics Association. *GCH* (pp. 121–124).

Saddhono, K., Saputra, N., Saragih, E., Rumapea, E. L. B., Tarigan, S. N., & Hasanudin, C. (2024). AI-powered automated criticism design tool based on texts and its themes. *2024 4th International Conference on Advance Computing and Innovative Technologies in Engineering (ICACITE)* (pp. 1528–1533).

Sailer, A., & Petric̆, M. (2019). Automation and testing for simplified software deployment. In *EPJ Web of Conferences* (Vol. 214, p. 05019). EDP Sciences.

Schneider, T. (2019). Longitudinal data analysis in the sociology of education: Key concepts and challenges. In R. K. Sidhu, Y. Cheng, & J. L. Waters (Eds.), *Research handbook on the sociology of education* (pp. 133–152). Edward Elgar Publishing.

Solopova, V., Rostom, E., Cremer, F., Gruszczynski, A., Witte, S., Zhang, C., & Landgraf, T. (2023, September). PapagAI: Automated feedback for reflective essays. In *German Conference on Artificial Intelligence (Künstliche Intelligenz)* (pp. 198–206). Springer Nature Switzerland.

Washuta, N. J., & Bass, P. (2019, June). A complementary approach to implementing entrepreneurship into a mechanical engineering senior capstone course sequence. In *2019 ASEE Annual Conference & Exposition*.

Yorks, L., Rotatori, D., Sung, S., & Justice, S. (2020). Workplace reflection in the age of AI: Materiality, technology, and machines. *Advances in Developing Human Resources*, 22(3), 308–319.

Zawacki-Richter, O., Marín, V. I., Bond, M., & Gouverneur, F. (2019). Systematic review of research on artificial intelligence applications in higher education–where are the educators?. *International Journal of Educational Technology in Higher Education*, 16(1), 1–27.

Zhou, X., Liang, P., Zhang, B., Li, Z., Ahmad, A., Shahin, M., & Waseem, M. (2023). On the concerns of developers when using GitHub Copilot. *arXiv preprint arXiv:2311.01020*.

6

Looking Ahead: The Future of AI-Driven Coding Education

This chapter explores how emerging technologies are poised to reform coding education beyond their current role as assistive tools to become autonomous collaborators that reshape teaching and learning across disciplines. Building on the broadening access to programming enabled by current assistants, future systems will further dissolve traditional barriers between technical and non-technical fields by generating personalized learning experiences, facilitating high-level problem-solving, and enabling creative exploration regardless of prior coding expertise. The chapter further examines how this technology will evolve from assistants to agents capable of dynamically adjusting instructional strategies, generating tailored exercises, and providing nuanced feedback without requiring either instructors or students to possess specialized technical knowledge. It further investigates how this change will re-envision programming education from syntax memorization toward critical thinking and ethical decision-making while supporting interdisciplinary applications previously inaccessible due to technical constraints. Through this forward-looking analysis, the chapter highlights how educational institutions can prepare for a future where generative integration reshapes not just who can teach programming but the central nature of what programming education entails across the curriculum.

6.1 Beyond Assistance: AI as an Autonomous Learning Agent

Historically, intelligent systems in programming education have functioned predominantly as supportive tools—generating code snippets, recommending optimizations, and automating routine tasks. Recent developments, however, indicate capabilities significantly surpassing these basic roles. Advanced educational platforms now design personalized learning paths, create interactive coding tasks, and evaluate student outcomes using nuanced metrics beyond simple correctness (Liang et al., 2023). Future instructional systems could dynamically assess student understanding, provide adaptive challenges, and employ inquiry-driven teaching methods. This shift redefines educators as facilitators and curators of technology-mediated learning

DOI: 10.1201/9781003637738-6

rather than traditional knowledge dispensers, opening pathways for integrating ethical considerations, intercultural perspectives, and cross-disciplinary content into personalized educational modules. Although there are valid concerns about reliance on these systems, the potential for tailored, self-paced learning environments presents a substantial opportunity to transcend traditional classroom constraints.

Integration of autonomous learning systems has progressed considerably, demonstrating sophisticated abilities for independent adaptation and complex problem-solving support within educational contexts. Traditionally, digital tutors provided basic code generation and debugging support, but contemporary intelligent agents, leveraging advanced language models, reinforcement learning, and multimodal processing, now exhibit enhanced cognitive capabilities far beyond mere task automation (Wang et al., 2024). These developments facilitate the dynamic adjustment of instructional strategies, individualization of learning experiences, and autonomous generation of targeted coding exercises (Lazarin et al., 2023).

A distinguishing feature of these modern educational agents is their capacity for advanced analysis, allowing prediction of learner difficulties and provision of nuanced insights into diverse problem-solving strategies (Banjanović-Mehmedović et al., 2024). Unlike earlier tutoring platforms, reliant on static question sets, today's intelligent educational technologies utilize natural language processing and neural architectural analysis to continuously evaluate student comprehension and dynamically adjust teaching content (Goel, 2024). This adaptive responsiveness significantly improves learner engagement and retention by presenting alternative strategies, generating novel challenges, and facilitating iterative refinement based on student interactions (Liu et al., 2022). Crucially, this evolution removes prior technical knowledge requirements for both educators and learners. Future intelligent agents will function as comprehensive educational partners, guiding conceptual mastery from initial engagement without needing specialized prompting or technical expertise from users.

This potential is especially notable in disciplines historically distanced from technical methods. For instance, in literary analysis within humanities education, an intelligent educational assistant could design instructional sequences introducing analytical methods through domain-specific questions, quantifying thematic elements across literary texts before progressing to more advanced analytical techniques while keeping the interpretative focus intact. The educational implications of such developments are extensive. Imagine an introductory art history class with participants lacking technical backgrounds; an intelligent learning system could effectively guide an analysis project on Renaissance artworks by facilitating the identification and analysis of compositional trends, significantly broadening participation in sophisticated visual analyses without requiring technical instruction from educators or learners.

This will be particularly impactful in disciplinary contexts where domain expertise has been separated from computational methods. For example, in a humanities seminar on literary analysis, an autonomous agent could not only generate code for textual analysis but also design a progressive learning sequence that introduces computational concepts through disciplinary questions. The agent might start by showing students how to quantify themes across literary periods, then gradually introduce more sophisticated computational methods while maintaining focus on literary interpretation rather than coding mechanics. The educational implications of this realignment are profound. Consider a first-year art history course where neither the professor nor the students have programming backgrounds. An autonomous agent could facilitate a project analyzing compositional patterns across Renaissance paintings by:

1. Assessing students' current understanding of both art history and computational concepts
2. Generating a tailored learning sequence that introduces image analysis through disciplinary questions
3. Creating progressive exercises that build computational thinking skills through visual analysis
4. Providing personalized feedback that connects technical concepts to art historical observations
5. Adapting in real-time as students demonstrate mastery or confusion
6. Facilitating reflection on both the technical methods and disciplinary insights gained

Future autonomous educational agents, distinct from current tools reliant on explicit instructions, will actively direct and shape learning experiences, significantly expanding the accessibility of advanced analytical methods across diverse academic fields. This represents a critical next step in educational technology evolution—transitioning from supportive platforms that simply reduce technical complexity to proactive partners that actively design and adapt learning experiences according to disciplinary needs.

A particularly significant advancement in autonomous educational technologies is their capacity for multimodal analysis, enabling systems to concurrently interpret and integrate code, textual information, visual imagery, and auditory inputs (Banjanović-Mehmedović et al., 2024). This capability substantially enhances learning experiences through interactive simulations, visual programming environments, and advanced debugging interfaces. The assimilation of diverse data sources by these intelligent tutoring systems provides context-sensitive recommendations that substantially improve student proficiency in identifying errors, developing optimization techniques, and mastering software architecture principles (Goel, 2024). Multimodal analytical capabilities also support collaborative human-machine programming scenarios, wherein intelligent partners suggest immediate code refinements and structural improvements (Rosenthal & Simmons, 2023).

Emerging instructional technologies are becoming essential to educational frameworks, characterized by their autonomous collaboration abilities to guide learners through comprehensive project cycles, encompassing planning, execution, and deployment (Liu et al., 2022). Educational platforms employing reinforcement learning dynamically adjust their instructional strategies based on student interactions, fostering personalized learning pathways that progressively align with learners' skill levels (Abiri et al., 2024). This adaptive responsiveness promotes structured exploration, enhancing learner autonomy and initiative.

Additionally, modern integrated development environments (IDEs) and debugging platforms proactively identify code inefficiencies, potential security vulnerabilities, and structural optimizations (Goel, 2024). Shifting from reactive problem correction to proactive system enhancements enables students to prioritize higher-order problem-solving tasks and overall system design, diminishing the traditional emphasis on detailed debugging processes (Liu et al., 2022). Advancements in networking technologies, edge computing, and immersive extended reality (XR) experiences further promise to revolutionize the educational landscape by integrating real-time analytical and interactive coding experiences beyond conventional classroom environments (Rosenthal & Simmons, 2023).

6.2 AI-Generated Software and the Shift from Coding to Problem-Solving

The rapid advancement of intelligent development platforms has significantly altered the programmer's role, shifting their responsibilities from intricate, line-by-line coding to strategic system architecture and higher-order problem-solving. Instead of manually writing detailed code, developers increasingly act as conceptual architects who outline problem constraints, optimize solution pathways, and delegate routine software generation tasks to intelligent assistants. For example, developers crafting complex web applications might employ GitHub Copilot to quickly produce foundational code and recommend algorithmic improvements, enabling them to dedicate their efforts to overall system refinement and architectural planning (Israilidis et al., 2024). Conversational platforms like ChatGPT further enhance efficiency by providing contextual insights and relevant code examples, empowering developers to focus on ethical implications, software scalability, and system reliability rather than repetitive programming tasks (Shang & Sen, 2024).

This shift challenges traditional programming curricula, necessitating education that emphasizes problem decomposition, algorithmic logic, and intelligent debugging strategies rather than syntax memorization.

A pivotal aspect of this shift is the transformation of developers from manual coders into strategic software architects. Modern assistive environments empower programmers to clearly define problems conceptually, delegating implementation tasks—such as code generation and optimization—to autonomous assistants (Taulli, 2024). A programmer might express the requirements of a new application feature in natural language, allowing intelligent agents to create multiple viable code solutions that developers iteratively refine. This new workflow demands rigorous logical reasoning skills, precision in setting constraints, and systematic evaluation of automated outputs (Ray, 2020). Consequently, skills such as algorithmic reasoning, system architecture, and conceptual planning are becoming central to programming education, equipping students to effectively collaborate with these autonomous systems rather than merely executing prescribed coding tasks (Johanyák et al., 2023).

In classroom environments, this will manifest through new forms of assignments and assessments that center on conceptual understanding and problem formulation rather than coding execution. Rather than evaluating students on their ability to write syntactically correct code, instructors will assess how effectively students can:

1. Define precise problem specifications that guide AI-generated implementations
2. Evaluate multiple AI-proposed solutions against both technical and domain requirements
3. Refine system architectures to optimize for performance, maintainability, and ethical considerations
4. Translate disciplinary knowledge into computational frameworks that AI can implement

Educationally, this evolution will reshape how students are evaluated, focusing assessments on conceptual clarity, system design sophistication, and problem articulation rather than syntax accuracy. Assignments will require students to define explicit problem specifications guiding automated software generation, evaluate multiple solutions for alignment with technical and domain-specific requirements, optimize architectures, and translate disciplinary expertise into technical frameworks. Consider a senior political science seminar studying voter patterns: rather than training students in statistical programming, educators would teach students to define precise analytical inquiries, set data analysis parameters, instruct intelligent agents to conduct relevant statistical modeling, critically review outcomes, and draw informed political conclusions.

- Articulate precise analytical questions about voting behavior
- Define the parameters and constraints of data analysis methods
- Direct AI to implement appropriate statistical models
- Critically evaluate the outputs and refine the models
- Draw meaningful political science conclusions from the computational analysis

Intelligent assistants would handle technical execution entirely, allowing students and educators to prioritize conceptual depth and interpretative rigor.

The emergence of autonomous software generation systems further intensifies this transformation, functioning as self-guided engineers capable of executing intricate workflows, identifying optimization strategies, and enhancing software performance autonomously (Liu et al., 2022; Goel, 2024). For instance, intelligent debugging tools can automatically detect and resolve memory leaks or performance inefficiencies in enterprise-scale applications, enabling developers to concentrate on strategic planning and high-level decision-making. Multimodal technological systems, integrating textual, visual, auditory, and real-time data inputs, significantly enrich developer interactions. Developers can generate software through natural language instructions, utilize interactive visualizations for structural optimization, and receive immediate performance feedback, fundamentally redefining problem-solving methodologies (Israilidis et al., 2024; Shang & Sen, 2024).

Nevertheless, this shift toward autonomously generated software presents notable challenges, particularly concerning robust human oversight and security risks from unintentional vulnerabilities (Negri Ribalta et al., 2024). Educators must incorporate ethical coding practices and bias detection into programming curricula to ensure software integrity and compliance with industry standards (Goel, 2024). The future of software engineering education will emphasize strategic decision-making, cross-domain integration, and advanced analytical skills, moving beyond mere technical execution toward comprehensive, integrative problem-solving methodologies (Alsamhi et al., 2024). Programmers will increasingly function as strategic evaluators and architects, refining generated solutions to maintain best practices, ethical standards, and regulatory compliance (Israilidis et al., 2024).

6.3 The Role of AI in Creative and Exploratory Coding

Advanced intelligent systems are rapidly transforming creative possibilities within exploratory coding, profoundly impacting fields such as game development, digital arts, and music composition. Innovative generative platforms are now capable of procedural content creation, adaptive narrative structuring, and stylistically guided musical composition, fostering unprecedented interdisciplinary collaboration (Vear & Poltronieri, 2020). These tools facilitate co-creative interactions between artists and automated systems, effectively merging human creativity with machine-generated outputs (Ford et al., 2024). Such computationally supported brainstorming allows practitioners to explore unconventional solutions, extending beyond traditional programming limitations and significantly enhancing students' creative problem-solving skills (Sedó, 2023).

Significantly, this technological evolution democratizes creative expression by removing historical prerequisites of technical programming expertise in arts and humanities curricula. Automated creative platforms actively participate in ideation and conceptual design, reversing the traditional sequence of acquiring technical skills before creative exploration. An undergraduate music composition course, for instance, could immediately engage students in computationally supported composition. Students might initiate musical patterns based on stylistic input, explore innovative harmonic progressions, visualize musical relationships interactively, adjust compositional elements through intuitive directives, and benefit from real-time auditory feedback—without initial programming skills.

Contemporary digital development environments have evolved into intelligent co-creative assistants, capable of real-time suggestions, structural optimizations, and adaptive experimentation aligned with artistic intentions (Gioti, 2021). In game design contexts, for instance, adaptive narrative engines dynamically respond to player interactions, enriching immersive storytelling experiences and allowing flexible, real-time content adjustments (Ratican & Hutson, 2024). This interactive capacity significantly enhances exploratory creativity, replacing rigid developmental frameworks with adaptive methodologies.

Further extending these impacts, generative music systems and reinforcement learning produce compositions indistinguishable from human-created works, effectively supporting and enriching the compositional process (Agwan et al., 2023). Tools like DeepClassic and MMM-Cubase highlight the emerging collaborative potential of automated compositional environments, enabling dynamic co-creation that evolves alongside the artist's vision (Tchemeube et al., 2023; Chee, 2023). Consider how this might redesign an undergraduate music composition class. Rather than requiring students to master programming languages for algorithmic composition, a creative system could:

1. Generate initial musical patterns based on stylistic descriptions provided by students
2. Suggest unconventional harmonic progressions that stretch students' creative thinking

3. Implement interactive visualizations showing relationships between different musical elements

4. Allow real-time modification of compositional parameters through natural language directives

5. Provide immediate auditory feedback on compositional choices

6. Enable collaborative composition between multiple students and the AI system

Rapid prototyping and iterative refinement facilitated by automated exploratory platforms further accelerate creative development. Artists and developers can quickly prototype visual elements, gameplay mechanics, or narrative designs without extensive manual coding, dramatically enhancing creative workflow efficiency (Sedó, 2023; Vear & Poltronieri, 2020). Moreover, research-oriented intelligent systems, such as OpenAI's Deep Research, synthesize extensive datasets into meaningful insights, helping creators identify innovative approaches and refine methodologies.

These advancements significantly enhance collaborative workflows by adapting to established coding practices, ensuring project consistency and fostering seamless cooperation among developers, automated agents, and creative teams (Novelli & Proksch, 2022). Consequently, future educational frameworks will increasingly emphasize interdisciplinary competencies, integrating technologically enhanced programming environments, interactive storytelling platforms, and dynamic co-creative systems to nurture students' combined technical and artistic skills. Ultimately, these intelligent creative systems augment human innovation, encouraging practitioners to focus on higher-order conceptual creativity, innovative problem-solving, and novel expressive possibilities (Agwan et al., 2023).

6.4 AI-Driven Debugging and Self-Optimizing Code

The technology is also changing software debugging and optimization, significantly reducing the time developers spend on error detection and performance enhancement. Debugging tools now go beyond identifying syntax errors and runtime crashes; they detect logical inconsistencies, predict vulnerabilities, and suggest targeted optimizations in real-time (Sain et al., 2024). This capability is made possible by LLMs trained on vast repositories of source code and debugging logs, allowing them to analyze patterns and provide predictive insights into software stability (Li et al., 2024). These advancements compel a reconsideration of traditional debugging pedagogy, redirecting the focus from manual error correction to the validation and refinement of generative debugging recommendations. Future curricula will need to integrate assisted debugging techniques, teaching students how to interpret and critique automated suggestions while ensuring maintainability and security. This evolution of debugging tools represents another dimension of the educational changes that the tech is enabling across disciplines. Just as current coding assistants have made programming accessible to non-technical fields by handling implementation details, advanced debugging systems will further open up software development by automating the technical aspects of error correction and optimization. This continues the inversion of traditional programming education where debugging skills once required substantial technical expertise before meaningful application was possible.

The implications for education are particularly significant in fields where software reliability is critical, but debugging expertise has traditionally been a barrier. Consider how autonomous debugging agents might rethink a digital humanities project where students are creating an interactive archive of historical documents. Without requiring either the instructor or students to possess deep debugging knowledge, the agent could:

1. Continuously monitor the application for potential performance issues
2. Automatically detect and resolve memory leaks and security vulnerabilities
3. Optimize database queries to improve retrieval times for large document collections
4. Suggest architectural improvements to enhance user experience
5. Generate explanations of technical issues and solutions in language accessible to humanities students
6. Provide a learning layer that gradually introduces debugging concepts through practical application

This approach would allow humanities faculty to guide sophisticated digital projects without needing specialized technical debugging skills, while students could spend their time on historical analysis and user experience rather than troubleshooting technical issues. The agent would not just fix problems but would make the entire debugging process accessible to non-technical disciplines, further breaking down barriers that have restricted computational methods to technical fields. One of the most promising developments in AI-driven debugging is real-time error detection and resolution, allowing the identification of potential failures before they impact application performance. Tools like GitHub Copilot, Codeium, and ChatGPT-based debuggers now analyze code as it is being written, proactively flagging issues related to memory leaks, security vulnerabilities, and inefficient logic structures (Sain et al., 2024). Moreover, predictive analytics can anticipate likely points of failure based on historical debugging data, helping developers prevent latent defects from escalating into major software failures (Liu et al., 2022). These advancements confirm that debugging is no longer a reactive process but a continuous optimization cycle integrated into modern development workflows (Tatineni, 2024).

Moving beyond routine error correction, recent innovations in intelligent code optimization have increasingly been employed for refactoring and enhancing software efficiency without compromising functionality. Assisted refactoring systems holistically analyze existing codebases, pinpointing opportunities for modular restructuring, loop optimizations, and strategic function inlining, significantly improving software performance (Gong et al., 2025). Autonomous generative frameworks, exemplified by OpenAI's STOP (Self-Taught Optimizer), advance these capabilities further by independently refining program efficiency and execution speed through recursive learning and continuous improvement cycles (Khlaisamniang et al., 2023). Such frameworks systematically evaluate execution traces, analyze algorithmic complexity, and track memory utilization, dynamically restructuring source code to optimize runtime efficiency and minimize resource demands (Rua & Saraiva, 2024). This ongoing development underscores the expanding role of intelligent automation in software's continuous self-enhancement, enabling applications to iteratively evolve without extensive human intervention.

To address potential issues from unchecked autonomous optimization, secure sandbox environments are now integral for validating and rigorously assessing self-optimized software prior to deployment. Frameworks such as AutoDev and related generative self-healing technologies operate within controlled execution settings, verifying that machine-generated optimizations maintain essential criteria, including security, functionality, and compatibility requirements before production integration (Khlaisamniang et al., 2023). These controlled testing environments prevent overly assertive automated improvements that might adversely affect readability, maintainability, or introduce unforeseen vulnerabilities (Garcia, 2024). Consequently, automated optimization increasingly prioritizes robust, scalable, and contextually appropriate software enhancements, balancing performance objectives with safe and secure implementation practices.

In parallel, the assimilation of intelligent error detection and resolution within DevOps frameworks represents another critical evolution, automating software testing, quality control, and continuous delivery processes throughout development lifecycles. DevOps platforms infused with advanced machine learning capabilities systematically analyze system logs for anomalies, identify regressions, and consistently enforce best practices in Continuous Integration/Continuous Deployment (CI/CD) processes (Bali et al., 2024). These automated quality-assurance systems significantly reduce manual oversight during software testing and deployment stages, allowing engineers to concentrate efforts on strategic software architecture and new feature development (Ajiga et al., 2024). As self-improving optimization methods continue to mature, software engineering teams will increasingly rely upon autonomous pipelines capable of independently conducting comprehensive code reviews, enhancing system performance, and ensuring security compliance across development lifecycles (Tatineni, 2024).

Looking ahead, self-optimizing debugging and code-refinement methodologies will continue to profoundly reshape practices in software quality assurance, maintenance, and performance optimization. Future intelligent models will likely integrate sophisticated reasoning abilities, allowing deeper comprehension of higher-level software design principles and suggesting nuanced, domain-specific enhancements (Ajiga et al., 2024). Furthermore, debugging assistants may evolve into interactive coding partners that proactively engage in dynamic dialog with programmers, articulating rationales behind proposed optimizations and recommending alternative debugging pathways (Sain et al., 2024). Such developments anticipate a future in software engineering characterized by genuine human-machine collaboration, where intelligent agents actively participate in the software design and implementation process alongside human developers.

6.5 Toward AI-Driven Software Engineering: The Future of Coding Instruction

As intelligent development environments increasingly manage responsibilities once held exclusively by human programmers, the fundamental definition of software development is poised for substantial realignment. Emerging trends indicate that routine coding tasks will progressively shift to autonomous development frameworks, fundamentally reshaping the competencies required of software engineers. Rather than meticulous attention to individual lines of code, developers will emphasize strategic activities such as conceptual problem-framing, solution design, and analytical oversight (McInnes et al., 2024). Consequently, future programming education will pivot toward nurturing competencies vital for successful human-machine collaboration. Software engineers will function less as traditional coders and more as solution architects, adept at articulating precise problem constraints, developing robust solution strategies, and critically refining outputs generated by intelligent systems. For instance, a student might clearly describe a sophisticated business requirement in natural language and subsequently partner with platforms like GitHub Copilot to produce initial functional prototypes, which are then methodically refined through iterative human-driven optimization (Zawacki-Richter et al., 2019).

This educational transformation marks the culmination of shifts already initiated by existing development assistants. By entirely dissolving historical technical obstacles that previously confined software instruction to highly specialized fields, next-generation autonomous systems promise a complete reimagining of computer science education—both in terms of curriculum content and potential participants. The longstanding assumption that either educators or students must possess foundational coding knowledge is rapidly becoming obsolete, enabling computational thinking and solution-driven methodologies to permeate curricula universally across diverse academic disciplines. This reconceptualization has profound pedagogical implications beyond mere accessibility: it reshapes both the essence and objectives of software education itself. Future curricula will not prioritize technical syntax proficiency, but instead emphasize deep conceptual understanding, precise problem formulation, and rigorous evaluation of autonomously generated solutions. In doing so, educational hierarchies previously structured around technical mastery followed by application will be definitively inverted, mirroring developments already evident in contemporary intelligent platforms that allow immediate, meaningful engagement prior to technical proficiency.

To illustrate how this might manifest in practice, imagine a future environmental science program that fully integrates computational methods across its curriculum without requiring either faculty or students to possess traditional coding skills. In this program:

1. First-year students immediately use tools to analyze environmental datasets, with the tool handling all technical implementation while students focus on scientific questions

2. Faculty guide sophisticated computational projects based on their environmental expertise rather than programming knowledge

3. Courses focus on teaching students how to formulate precise environmental questions that a model can implement computationally

4. Assessments evaluate students' ability to critically evaluate generated models and refine them to better address environmental problems

5. Capstone projects involve complex environmental simulations implemented entirely through AI-human collaboration

6. Graduates emerge with deep environmental knowledge combined with the ability to direct smart systems toward meaningful computational applications

In this newly envisioned context, the traditional notion of "learning to code" undergoes a complete redefinition. Students no longer need to acquire mastery over conventional programming languages or resolve syntax-level debugging issues. Instead, they develop computational reasoning focused on addressing complex environmental challenges, employing intelligent frameworks to realize their analytical solutions, all while maintaining central attention on the environmental inquiries driving their projects. A probable outcome of this transformation will be the pervasive integration of intelligent, dynamic development environments (IDEs) that provide real-time debugging assistance, automated optimization, and adaptive educational modules. These advanced IDEs will enable students to receive immediate, contextual feedback on generated solutions while simultaneously learning to critically interpret system recommendations, facilitating a more engaging, interactive, and efficient educational experience. Consequently, the traditional role of debugging tools will evolve significantly, shifting attention from low-level syntactic corrections toward higher-order tasks, such as comprehensive system design and architectural oversight.

Such an instructional shift necessitates a corresponding evolution in educational methods. Rather than teaching software development as a collection of fragmented, low-level competencies, instructors will increasingly emphasize sophisticated system planning, deep domain-specific knowledge, and strategic integration of automated assistants. Curricula will be redesigned around project-based methodologies that engage students in complex, authentic problems demanding both human expertise and automated analytical support. Educators themselves will transition from knowledge transmitters to active facilitators, curators, and guides, mediating rich, interactive, and intelligently supported educational experiences. As the role of software engineers evolves into strategic oversight, their responsibilities will increasingly entail establishing precise problem criteria, evaluating trade-offs, and ensuring alignment between autonomously generated solutions and overall project objectives. For example, intelligent agents might propose multiple iterations of a software component, but human developers retain responsibility for critically assessing these proposals, selecting optimal versions, and integrating them into cohesive software architectures. This collaborative workflow underscores the necessity of strong conceptual understanding, analytical reasoning, and disciplined evaluative skills in an era dominated by automated software development.

The integration of emergent technologies such as VR/AR, edge computing, and advanced 5G networks will further enrich and diversify software engineering education. Future curricula may employ immersive simulations, allowing students to design, test, and deploy sophisticated intelligent systems within digitally replicated ecosystems closely mirroring real-world conditions. For instance, students might leverage augmented reality interfaces to visualize, interact with, and manage dynamic data flows within a smart city simulation, acquiring practical experience with distributed, responsive software architectures and real-time analytics. At the same time, adaptive learning methodologies have the potential to improve instructional delivery further. As these intelligent educational frameworks become increasingly refined, they will dynamically tailor instructional content and difficulty levels to match individual student performance. This customized learning approach will enable learners to progress according to their own pace and needs, addressing individual weaknesses and progressively building upon personal strengths through adaptive challenges and tailored feedback. Such personalized, self-directed educational systems will promote autonomous exploration, analytical thinking, and creative problem-solving capabilities.

Accordingly, educators must design innovative curricula that encourage interdisciplinary collaboration and maximize the potential of automated analytical tools. This involves cultivating environments where students seamlessly integrate domain-specific knowledge with algorithmically supported solutions, effectively preparing them to navigate intricate, interdisciplinary challenges. New assessment strategies, collaborative team projects, and ongoing feedback mechanisms will become central pillars of reimagined educational experiences, consistently applying theoretical insights to real-world applications. Thus, the future of software education will be characterized by developers adept at strategically guiding automated systems, just as proficient in conceptual design and critical oversight as they are in leveraging intelligent development tools. Such changes not only promise to streamline the software development process but also significantly reshape core educational competencies required of future software engineers. As educators continually adapt to these transformations, software engineering education will become increasingly dynamic, interactive, and interdisciplinary, closely aligned with the realities of an interconnected, automated technological ecosystem (McInnes et al., 2024; Zawacki-Richter et al., 2019).

References

Abiri, R., Rabiee, A., Ghafoori, S., & Cetera, A. (2024). Toward human-centered shared autonomy AI paradigms for human-robot teaming in healthcare. *arXiv preprint arXiv:2407.17464.*

Agwan, M., Nemade, M., Roy, S., & Sinha, U. (2023). The fusion of AI and music generation: A comprehensive review. *2023 6th International Conference on Advances in Science and Technology (ICAST)* (pp. 90–94).

Ajiga, D., Okeleke, P. A., Folorunsho, S. O., & Ezeigweneme, C. (2024). Enhancing software development practices with AI insights in high-tech companies. *IEEE Software Engineering Institute, Technical Report TR-2024-003.*

Alsamhi, S. H., Kumar, S., Hawbani, A., Shvetsov, A. V., Zhao, L., & Guizani, M. (2024). Synergy of human-centered AI and cyber-physical-social systems for enhanced cognitive situation awareness: Applications, challenges and opportunities. *Cognitive Computation*, 1–21.

Bali, M. K., Mehdi, A., & Hariharan, S. (2024). AI-driven DevOps transformation: A paradigm shift in software development. *2024 3rd International Conference on Sentiment Analysis and Deep Learning (ICSADL)* (pp. 117–123).

Banjanović-Mehmedović, L., Husaković, A., Ribić, A. G., Prljača, N., & Karabegović, I. (2024). Advancements in robotic intelligence: The role of computer vision, DRL, transformers and LLMs. *Artificial Intelligence in Industry 4.0: The Future that Comes True*, 94.

Chee, L. (2023). *Architecture and affect: Precarious spaces.* Routledge.

Ford, C., Noel-Hirst, A., Cardinale, S., Loth, J., Sarmento, P., Wilson, E., & Bryan-Kinns, N. (2024, June). Reflection across AI-based music composition. In *Proceedings of the 16th Conference on Creativity & Cognition* (pp. 398–412).

Garcia, R. S. (2024). *The management of context in the machine learning lifecycle* (Doctoral dissertation). University of California.

Gioti, A. M. (2021, December). A compositional exploration of computational aesthetic evaluation and AI bias. In *NIME 2021*. PubPub.

Goel, S. (2024, May). Towards building autonomous AI agents and robots for open world environments. In *AAMAS* (pp. 2743–2745).

Gong, J., Voskanyan, V., Brookes, P., Wu, F., Jie, W., Xu, J., & Wang, Z. (2025). Language models for code optimization: Survey, challenges and future directions. *arXiv preprint arXiv:2501.01277.*

Israilidis, J., Chen, W.-Y., & Tsakalerou, M. (2024). Software development and education: Transitioning towards AI-enhanced teaching. *2024 IEEE Global Engineering Education Conference (EDUCON)* (pp. 1–6).

Johanyák, Z., Cserkó, J., & Pásztor, A. (2023). AI-assisted university programming education in practice. *2023 IEEE 35th International Conference on Software Engineering Education and Training (CSEE&T)* (pp. 185–186).

Khlaisamniang, P., Khomduean, P., Saetan, K., & Wonglapsuwan, S. (2023). Generative AI for self-healing systems. *2023 18th International Joint Symposium on Artificial Intelligence and Natural Language Processing (iSAI-NLP)* (pp. 1–6).

Lazarin, N. M., Pantoja, C. E., & Viterbo, J. (2023, August). Towards a toolkit for teaching AI supported by robotic-agents: proposal and first impressions. In *Anais do XXXI Workshop sobre Educação em Computação* (pp. 20–29). SBC.

Li, Y., Huo, Y., Jiang, Z., Zhong, R., He, P., Su, Y., & Lyu, M. R. (2024). Exploring the effectiveness of llms in automated logging statement generation: An empirical study. *IEEE Transactions on Software Engineering*, 50(12), 3188–3207. https://doi.org/10.1109/tse.2024.3475375

Liang, J., Yang, C., & Myers, B. (2023). Understanding the usability of AI programming assistants. *ArXiv, abs/2303.17125.* https://doi.org/10.48550/arXiv.2303.17125

Liu, B., Mazumder, S., Robertson, E., & Grigsby, S. (2022). AI autonomy: Self-initiation, adaptation and continual learning. *ArXiv.*

McInnes, L. C., Heroux, M., Bernholdt, D. E., Dubey, A., Gonsiorowski, E., Gupta, R., & Watson, G. R. (2024). A cast of thousands: How the IDEAS Productivity project has advanced software productivity and sustainability. *Computing in Science & Engineering*, 26(1), 48–60. https://doi.org/10.1109/mcse.2024.3383799

Negri-Ribalta, C., Geraud-Stewart, R., Sergeeva, A., & Lenzini, G. (2024). A systematic literature review on the impact of AI models on the security of code generation. *Frontiers in Big Data*, 7, 1386720.

Novelli, N., & Proksch, S. (2022). Am I (deep) blue? music-making ai and emotional awareness. *Frontiers in Neurorobotics*, 16, 897110.

Ratican, J., & Hutson, J. (2024). Adaptive worlds: Generative AI in game design and future of gaming, and interactive media. *ISRG Journal of Arts, Humanities and Social Sciences, 2*(5), 1–20.

Ray, B. B., Rogers, R. R., & Hocutt, M. M. (2020). Perceptions of non-STEM discipline teachers on coding as a teaching and learning tool: What are the possibilities? *Journal of Digital Learning in Teacher Education, 36*(1), 1931.

Rosenthal, S., & Simmons, R. (2023, June). Autonomous agents: An advanced course on AI integration and deployment. In *Proceedings of the AAAI Conference on Artificial Intelligence* (Vol. 37, No. 13, pp. 15843–15850).

Rua, R., & Saraiva, J. (2024). A large-scale empirical study on mobile performance: Energy, run-time and memory. *Empirical Software Engineering, 29*(1), 31.

Sain, Z. H., Serban, R., Agoi, M. A., & Sain, S. H. (2024). Leveraging ChatGPT to enhance debugging: Evaluating AI-driven solutions in software development. *Asian Journal of Computer Science and Technology, 13*(1), 41–44.

Sedó, A. X. (2023). Discovering Creative Commons Sounds in Live Coding. *Organised Sound, 28*(2), 276–289.

Shang, S., & Sen, G. (2024). Empowering learners with AI-generated content for programming learning and computational thinking. *Journal of Computer Assisted Learning, 40*, 1941–1958.

Tatineni, S. (2024). *Integrating artificial intelligence with DevOps: Advanced techniques, predictive analytics, and automation for real-time optimization and security in modern software development.* Libertatem Media Private Limited.

Taulli, T. (2024). *AI-assisted programming: Better planning, coding, testing, and deployment.* O'Reilly Media, Inc.

Tchemeube, R. B., Ens, J., Plut, C., Pasquier, P., Safi, M., Grabit, Y., & Rolland, J. B. (2023, August). Evaluating human-AI interaction via usability, user experience and acceptance measures for MMM-C: A creative AI system for music composition. In *IJCAI* (pp. 5769–5778).

Vear, C., & Poltronieri, F. (2020). Postcards (2017) Creative AI mixed-media compositional system for live performance with a human musician.

Wang, Y., Chen, W., Han, X., Lin, X., Zhao, H., Liu, Y., & Yang, H. (2024). Exploring the reasoning abilities of multimodal large language models (mllms): A comprehensive survey on emerging trends in multimodal reasoning. *arXiv preprint arXiv:2401.06805*.

Zawacki-Richter, O., Marín, V. I., Bond, M., & Gouverneur, F. (2019). Systematic review of research on artificial intelligence applications in higher education–where are the educators? *International Journal of Educational Technology in Higher Education, 16*(1), 1–27.

7

Conclusion: Embracing Software Literacy as a Foundational Skill for the 21st Century

As artificial intelligence dissolves traditional barriers between technical and non-technical disciplines, software literacy is emerging as a universal skill accessible to all fields. This chapter synthesizes how coding assistants have redesigned education by eliminating the historical requirement that either instructors or students possess programming expertise, allowing computational thinking to flourish in previously excluded domains. It examines how this revolution creates truly adaptive curricula where creation precedes technical mastery, enabling all disciplines to leverage computational methods while still emphasizing their domain-specific questions. The chapter explores how emerging workforce demands reflect this changing educational landscape, where computational thinking and disciplinary expertise increasingly complement each other across all fields. Finally, it presents a call to action for education leaders to embrace this change in approach—where AI enables a complete reimagining of what programming education means, who can teach it, and how it integrates across the entire curriculum.

7.1 The Dissolution of Academic Boundaries

The integration of assistive coding tools has begun changing the academic landscape, dissolving traditional disciplinary boundaries that once separated computational approaches from non-technical fields. Unlike earlier technological innovations that primarily enhanced existing workflows, coding assistants have eliminated the historical requirement that either instructors or students possess programming expertise—creating unprecedented opportunities for truly interdisciplinary education. This rethinking extends far beyond simply making existing practices more efficient. Large language models have revolutionized how scholars conduct research and communicate findings by making computational methods accessible to all disciplines regardless of technical background. A historian who previously required specialized programming training to analyze archival datasets can now use assistants to implement sophisticated computational analyses, allowing sustained concentration on historical inquiries rather than coding mechanics.

DOI: 10.1201/9781003637738-7

Similarly, literature professors can guide students through computational text analysis without first requiring either themselves or their students to master programming languages. The academic implications of this new approach are profound. Research that once required collaboration between technical and non-technical domains—with computer scientists handling implementation while domain experts provided subject-matter knowledge—can now be conducted entirely within humanities and social science departments. Faculty in these fields can integrate computational approaches directly into their courses without developing programming expertise or collaborating with STEM colleagues. This increased accessibility supports a more fluid exchange of methodologies and insights across traditionally separated domains.

Universities have begun responding to this through innovative interdisciplinary initiatives. Emory University's AI minor for non-computer science majors (Walczak & Cellary, 2023) and Arizona State University's integration of AI-centered courses across departments (Dotan et al., 2024) represent early efforts to reimagine curricula for this new reality. However, these initiatives often still treat the technology as something to be added to existing disciplines rather than recognizing how it reshapes what is possible within those disciplines. The more revolutionary approach—aligned with the changes described in previous chapters—repositions computational thinking as an integral component of all disciplines rather than a separate field to be integrated. In this model, students develop computational skills not as an addition to their disciplinary expertise but as a natural extension of it. A journalism student learns to direct tools toward investigating stories through data analysis; an economics major leverages computational models to test theories without first becoming a programmer.

Faculty roles are similarly transformed. Rather than serving as technical experts or gatekeepers of computational knowledge, professors become guides who help students apply computational thinking to disciplinary questions. This move from knowledge transmission to facilitative mentorship aligns with the inversion of traditional educational hierarchies described in earlier chapters, where meaningful application precedes technical mastery. Curricular reforms increasingly reflect this evolving understanding. Universities like the University of Cincinnati are creating programs that position artificial intelligence in general not as a separate technical subject but as a foundational approach integrated across all disciplines (Ruxiang & Yue, 2023). These models eliminate artificial distinctions between "technical" and "non-technical" fields, recognizing that computational thinking—supported by smart tools—can enhance inquiry in all domains. The experiential learning approaches emerging from this redefinition go beyond simply adding technical components to non-technical disciplines. Instead, they reimagine how all students engage with knowledge creation, with assistants handling technical implementation while students concentrate on domain-specific questions. This approach broadens access to powerful computational methods previously restricted to those with specialized training.

Despite these promising developments, challenges remain. Academic integrity concerns, potential biases in generated content, and questions of authorship require thoughtful institutional responses (Ruxiang & Yue, 2023). Yet these challenges should not obscure the revolutionary potential of assistants to expand the availability of computational methods across all disciplines, breaking down barriers that have customarily restricted sophisticated digital approaches to those with specialized technical training. This dissolution of academic boundaries through these tools represents more than a technological change—it changes how knowledge is created, shared, and taught across the university. Through the elimination of the requirement that either instructors or students possess programming expertise, these tools create possibilities for interdisciplinary collaboration and innovation that were previously unimaginable, preparing graduates for a world where computational thinking and disciplinary expertise increasingly complement each other across all fields.

7.2 Envisioning Adaptive, Inclusive Curricula

The integration of coding assistants in education represents a principal redesign that goes far beyond simply making existing programming approaches more efficient. Rather than merely accelerating traditional syntax-first teaching methods, these tools enable a complete reimagining of what programming education means, who can teach it, and how it integrates across the curriculum. This eliminates the historical requirement that either instructors or students possess coding expertise before engaging with computational methods, increasing access across all disciplines. This has sparked significant debate within educational circles. Traditional perspectives, represented by scholars like Janjeva et al. (2023), emphasize the continued importance of syntax mastery and technical foundations, arguing that generated code often contains errors requiring human oversight. These critics suggest that overreliance on automated code generation might undermine students' basic understanding of programming concepts (Feng et al., 2023). From this viewpoint, the tools should supplement rather than supplant traditional programming education, maintaining emphasis on manual coding skills and technical precision (Kirova et al., 2024).

Contrasting with this conservative stance, accelerationists highlight the revolutionary potential to transform programming education completely. Citing Andrej Karpathy's observation that "The hottest new programming language is English" (Garlick & Fei, 2024), they envision a future where natural language directives replace traditional coding, making programming accessible to anyone regardless of technical background. This vision aligns with industry trends, where Google reports that over 25% of its code is now generated (Kelly, 2024), and GitHub Copilot users leave 40% of AI-generated code unmodified—suggesting that technical implementation is increasingly delegated to assistants. These contrasting perspectives reflect deeper tensions about the nature of programming education in this new generative era. However, they often frame the debate too narrowly, foregrounding whether AI will replace human programmers rather than how it opens up who can engage with computational thinking across disciplines. The more revolutionary insight—aligned with previous chapters—is that it eliminates the historical barriers that restricted computational methods to technical fields, allowing all disciplines to integrate programming approaches regardless of faculty or student technical background.

Universities have begun responding to this inevitability through various curricular innovations. Many institutions are implementing hybrid learning models that position AI as a collaborative partner rather than a technical tool. For example, MIT and the University of Toronto's AI-powered programming labs provide personalized feedback to students while maintaining faculty guidance (Johanyák et al., 2023). Carnegie Mellon has similarly integrated AI assistants into programming courses, enabling students to focus on conceptual understanding rather than syntax details (Liu & Li, 2024). These adaptations reflect a growing recognition that the technology changes not just how programming is taught but who can teach and learn it. Initiatives like the University of Florida's AI Across the Curriculum empower students in all disciplines—from business to humanities—and allow them to engage with assisted programming without requiring specialized technical training. Harvard's Data Science Initiative similarly provides non-programmers with accessible computational tools, enabling journalists, economists, and policy analysts to leverage data analysis techniques previously restricted to those with programming backgrounds.

Despite these innovations, universities still face challenges in fully embracing the potential of AI in programming education. One significant concern is overreliance on automated solutions, potentially diminishing students' independent problem-solving abilities (Johanyák et al., 2023). To address this, institutions should implement frameworks requiring students to critically evaluate and refine generated code, ensuring they remain active participants in the learning process (Bakharia & Abdi, 2024). Faculty preparedness presents another challenge, as many instructors lack training in effectively integrating AI tools into their teaching (Ciolacu et al., 2018). In response, universities like Stanford and Oxford have established faculty development programs to help instructors adapt to this new model (Chang et al., 2022). The evolution toward integrated programming education mirrors historical progressions in computing abstraction levels. Just as high-level languages like Python abstracted away the complexities of machine code, assistants now further elevate programming to a conceptual level accessible to all disciplines. This change continues the expanding availability of computational methods, making sophisticated techniques available without requiring specialized technical training (Lee, 2017). The role of programmers is similarly evolving—moving from manual code writing to strategic oversight and problem formulation. This evolution does not diminish the importance of computational thinking but elevates it to a higher conceptual level centered on problem definition, solution evaluation, and ethical considerations rather than syntax implementation (Tan et al., 2024; Weber et al., 2024).

Looking forward, programming education will likely continue evolving from syntax-dependent instruction toward concept-driven learning that prioritizes problem-solving, critical evaluation, and ethical reasoning. Generative tools will increasingly handle routine implementation details while students concentrate on higher-order thinking—defining problems precisely, evaluating alternative approaches, and ensuring solutions meet both technical and domain-specific requirements. This rethought approach to programming education does not just make existing practices more efficient—it reconsiders what programming means across the curriculum. Through the elimination of the historical requirement that either instructors or students possess coding expertise, assistants make computational methods accessible to all disciplines, creating truly adaptive, inclusive curricula that prepare students for a future where computational thinking and domain expertise increasingly complement each other in all fields.

7.3 Preparing Students for Evolving Skill Demands

The evolving landscape of programming in both industry and education now demands that students are not only adept at high-level problem-solving and AI-mediated collaboration but also well-versed in the latest intellectual property (IP) considerations. Recent developments from the U.S. Copyright Office, as outlined in the January 2025 addendum "Copyright and Artificial Intelligence, Part 2: Copyrightability," affirm that copyright protection extends only to works that demonstrate sufficient human authorship (U.S. Copyright Office, 2025). This decision reinforces the necessity of human creativity in determining copyright eligibility and clarifies that outputs produced solely by AI, without significant human input beyond mere prompt design, are not eligible for protection. As programming evolves from manual code writing to AI-driven software development, students must be prepared to navigate these legal nuances, which directly impact questions of authorship, ownership, and intellectual property rights in a rapidly changing digital world. The Copyright Office report highlights that the selection, coordination, or arrangement of generative elements by a human author may establish sufficient originality for copyright protection. This finding underscores the critical role of human editorial oversight, particularly for disciplines like art history and digital humanities, where assisted outputs are increasingly prevalent. It also calls attention to the need for ongoing scrutiny of technological advancements to determine whether future systems might eventually allow for a level of human control that satisfies copyright eligibility. In this context, students and faculty must engage in discussions about the balance between automated processes and human intervention, ensuring that the creative contribution remains substantial enough to secure intellectual property rights. Such discussions are essential in supporting an understanding of the legal and ethical dimensions of AI-assisted work in both academic and professional settings.

Looking ahead, educators must prepare students for the complex legal challenges that will arise as the abilities of these intelligent systems continue to reshape software development and creative production. Issues of ownership become particularly contentious when generated code or content is involved—for example, if a codebase is generated by a new Chinese reasoning model like DeepSeek, questions will emerge regarding jurisdiction and whether legal disputes will be resolved in U.S. courts or in China. While these matters are currently emerging and primarily affect industry, it is imperative that students are exposed to these evolving IP considerations as part of their curriculum. In response, academic institutions are developing new guidelines to govern the use of generated content in coursework and research. The Australian Research Council (ARC) has introduced policies stating that while AI can assist in grant writing and academic research, authors remain fully responsible for the intellectual content (Weller-Newton & Burgess, 2023). Similarly, institutions like Harvard and Stanford have published guidelines requiring full disclosure of AI use in academic work, ensuring transparency and accountability in research integrity. These evolving policies reflect the growing tension between disclosure of tool use and further integration into existing workflows.

The rapid emergence of generative tools has led to a reevaluation of the skill sets needed in many professional domains, moving beyond traditional programming and coding tasks to include a broader range of competencies. Whereas developers once needed deep expertise in writing optimized algorithms and debugging intricate code, employers will now increasingly require proficiency in model integration, data pipeline management, and prompt engineering—skills that leverage assistants to expedite routine processes or explore new computational possibilities (Pugačova, 2023). Alongside these technical proficiencies, organizations are seeking "power skills," a term that redefines what were once called soft skills to emphasize their strategic importance. Power skills include emotional intelligence, creative thinking, adaptability, communication, and leadership—capabilities that facilitate effective collaboration, innovation, and ethical decision-making. As the Future of Jobs Report underscores, analytical thinking, complex problem-solving, and creativity remain vital across workplaces, making the balance of technical fluency and human-centered aptitudes a core expectation for today's graduates (Hlongwane et al., 2024). In response to these evolving demands, universities are revamping their curricula to integrate AI literacy alongside power skills. The University of Florida's AI Across the Curriculum initiative, for example, weaves assisted programming, data analysis, and critical thinking across diverse fields of study, ensuring that students master computational tools while honing their communication and collaboration abilities (Jackson & Jackson, 2024). Likewise, the University of Toronto has embraced augmented case studies in its business school, requiring students to apply analytics to strategic challenges while practicing negotiation, human-centered leadership, and ethical frameworks in tandem (Hlongwane et al., 2024). These models underscore an emerging consensus in higher education: technical expertise alone is insufficient; graduates must be adept at harnessing these tools responsibly within broader social, strategic, and ethical contexts.

To meet this hybrid need more fully, institutions are exploring interdisciplinary programs that merge deep technical training with a robust grounding in human-centric competencies. Oxford University's Ethics in AI curriculum, for instance, combines philosophy, data science, and software engineering to help students navigate the moral complexities of AI-generated content while maintaining strong technical credentials (Weller-Newton & Burgess, 2023). Similarly, Arizona State University has business courses that integrate computational analysis with leadership exercises, ensuring that students cultivate both the capacity to interpret AI outputs and the strategic acumen to lead diverse teams (Chiang et al., 2012; Hannan, & Liu, 2023). A further step involves mentorship programs, where automated tutors accelerate the development of coding and data skills, while human mentors guide learners through critical thinking, collaboration, and ethical reasoning (Pugačova, 2023).

In addition to these examples, universities are increasingly integrating in-demand competencies—ranging from AI literacy to problem-solving, teamwork, and effective communication—directly into existing courses (Issa & Hall, 2024). Rather than relegating these skills to optional workshops or career services, institutions like the CUNY School of Professional Studies have woven them into the fabric of general education and liberal studies curricula (https://sps.catalog.cuny.edu/general-education). Through a rethinking of core assignments, faculty at CUNY designed "Professional Connections" projects in over fourteen courses, ensuring that students in fields such as writing or history gain explicit practice in collaboration, critical thinking, and clear communication. The University of Redlands similarly encourages faculty to embed career readiness in their teaching through a Career Faculty Fellows program (Gray, 2022). Instructors are offered small fellowships to redesign courses with embedded skill-building, allowing Redlands to close the gap for students who may not attend separate career workshops and solidifying these competencies within the regular classroom experience. Some institutions are also overhauling their entire general education model to place broader "power skills" at its core. Thomas Jefferson University's Hallmarks Core exemplifies this approach by organizing a 40-credit curriculum around competencies such as rigorous inquiry, contextual communication, global perspectives, and collaborative creation (https://www.jefferson.edu/academics/hallmarks/the-hallmarks-core-curriculum.html). As students progress, they accumulate an ePortfolio of evidence, demonstrating tangible growth in these competencies. This explicit emphasis on skill outcomes attempts to resolve the persistent disconnect in which employers report difficulty finding graduates with strong communication and problem-solving abilities—even though liberal arts education has long claimed to cultivate precisely those attributes. Through systematically tracking outputs in the Hallmarks Core, Jefferson verifies that graduates can articulate and substantiate their skill sets.

To deepen these competencies, many universities now emphasize project-based, experiential learning. Capstone projects, hackathons, and case competitions allow students to apply technical knowledge and build interpersonal skills in settings that mimic real-world workplaces (Risinamhodzi & Heymann, 2023). Ball State University, for instance, employs an escape room exercise in which students must solve puzzles collaboratively under time pressure, nurturing creative problem-solving, communication, and resilience (Jones, 2022). This approach mirrors industry team projects, ensuring that learners leave campus with not only theoretical knowledge but also practical experience in leadership, adaptability, and collaboration. Collaboration between academics and career services further boosts these efforts. At Thomas Jefferson University, a narrative-focused course integrated professional personal narratives into academic assessments, allowing students to craft compelling résumés or personal branding stories while improving their communication skills (https://catalog.jefferson.edu/course-descriptions/undergraduate/isem/). Against this backdrop of skill-oriented revisions, new interdisciplinary programs are emerging to address the growing demand for AI and data literacy across all fields. Emory University recently introduced an AI minor accessible to students in any major, offering foundational knowledge of how AI operates while exploring unintended consequences such as algorithmic bias and data privacy (https://catalog.college.emory.edu/academics/concentrations/minors/AIMIN.html). Many institutions also provide data science minors aimed at non-STEM students, reflecting the fact that all disciplines increasingly rely on analytics and technology-driven insights. In some cases, universities have established entire new degree tracks, as at the University of North Carolina Charlotte, which now offers undergraduate and graduate programs in AI, data science, and related specializations (https://inside.charlotte.edu/unc-charlotte-creates-new-ai-institute/). By pooling expertise from computing, business, liberal arts, and engineering departments, these programs reflect the reality that modern technological innovations shape—and are shaped by—domains beyond traditional computer science.

A further development is the "Computing + X" model, such as at Duke University (https://cs.duke.edu/research/computation%2Bx), which pairs computational depth with an application area, whether it be ethics, digital humanities, or linguistics. MIT's Schwarzman College of Computing, for instance, seeks to embed computing education in every discipline, producing graduates who possess both the tools of technology and the critical perspectives necessary to implement them responsibly (https://computing.mit.edu/). This fusion acknowledges industry's increasing need for "T-shaped" professionals who command breadth across multiple areas while achieving deep competence in at least one. Perhaps the most comprehensive effort to integrate AI education across entire campuses is the University of Florida's "AI University" initiative (https://ai.ufl.edu/). The goal is for every student—regardless of major—to graduate with a baseline understanding of the tools and concepts. Rather than confining AI content to computer science courses, the plan distributes AI instruction throughout all sixteen colleges. Students thus gain a cross-cutting fluency in AI and, crucially, are also exposed to discussions about ethics, transparency, bias, and human-centered design.

Momentum for these curriculum innovations aligns with wider forecasts regarding the future job market, where the most resilient skills combine technical aptitude with human-centered capabilities. According to the World Economic Forum's 2023 Future of Jobs Report, 44% of core skills will evolve over the next five years due to rapid technological disruptions (WEF, 2025). Meanwhile, LinkedIn data suggests that up to 65% of the skills in current job roles will change by 2030, thanks to automation (Modi, 2024). Rather than simply eliminating positions, these changes are reinventing them—employees must be ready to integrate novel tools and processes into their daily workflows, necessitating both digital fluency and an openness to continuous learning. Even in highly automated contexts, employers still prioritize what have traditionally been labeled "soft" skills, now recognized more accurately as power skills: analytical thinking, creativity, resilience, and the capacity for lifelong learning. WEF identifies analytical and creative thinking as the top two skills for 2025 and beyond, underscoring that human insight remains integral to problem formulation and innovative idea generation. Emotional intelligence and leadership round out these competencies, reflecting the importance of guiding teams, influencing stakeholders, and maintaining ethical workplace cultures—areas in which AI cannot substitute for human understanding (bernardmarr.com; weforum.org).

At the same time, technology literacy and AI fluency are emerging as core competencies across all industries, not just for computer science majors. A recent WEF survey highlights "technological literacy" as one of the most rapidly growing skill areas, and employers increasingly expect professionals at every level to interpret data and harness intelligent tools for decision-making (WEF, 2025). While this does not require every graduate to be an

AI developer, it does demand an awareness of how it can drive efficiency, enhance problem-solving, and complement human expertise. In this evolving landscape, those who combine conceptual savvy, interpersonal dexterity, and comfort with new technologies will be best equipped to adapt. These insights underscore why universities are revamping curricula to reflect a dual emphasis on AI literacy and power skills. New interdisciplinary programs in AI or data science, such as those at UNC Charlotte and Emory University, address the growing need for technical competencies, while broader general education overhauls—seen at Thomas Jefferson University or the University of Florida—aim to cultivate communication, creative thinking, and ethical awareness in tandem with emerging technologies. Taken together, these initiatives respond directly to forecasts suggesting that future graduates must be "T-shaped" professionals: deep enough in technical domains to leverage AI solutions but broad enough in leadership, empathy, and adaptability to excel in roles that machines alone cannot fulfill.

Moreover, the growing influence of generative interfaces in software development is dramatically changing the ways in which programming is taught, learned, and practiced. While tools today can generate functional code, automate debugging, and streamline repetitive tasks, they will not replace programmers outright. Instead, these advances are altering the nature of programmers' responsibilities. Legendary developer Steve Yegge (2023) has argued that it is those unwilling to adapt who risk becoming obsolete, while junior developers who embrace the tools can potentially outperform senior engineers who resist change. This observation recalls James Bessen's (2003, 2011, 2015) studies on the Industrial Revolution, where skilled crafters were replaced not by unskilled labor, but by workers with new machine-operating expertise. Although wages initially stagnated, productivity soared once the broader workforce learned how best to use emerging technology—a process Bessen calls "learning by doing." Employers eventually needed employees with fresh skills, giving rise to an entirely different but equally necessary form of craftsmanship. Just as nineteenth-century factory laborers had to master new machinery, modern developers must understand both the current capabilities of these systems and their constraints. They need the judgment to guide AI-driven solutions, the domain expertise to integrate these solutions into business processes, and the creativity to refine workflows or invent new applications altogether. This perspective resonates with Ethan Mollick's call to "always bring AI to the table," harnessing it for daily tasks and corporate exploration alike (O'Reilly, 2025). The challenge is ensuring that every company, team, and developer invests in continuous experimentation and skill-building, turning AI from a mere productivity tool into a powerful catalyst for innovation.

The changing face of programming is further underscored by Microsoft deputy CTO Sam Schillace, who compares the present boom to previous transitions—such as moving from desktop to internet-based systems—where the entire software stack transformed, from programming frameworks and language models to development teams and deployment strategies. He points out that while large language models automate thought at a basic level, they do not (yet) offer the type of "metacognition" required for complex tasks. Humans remain essential for context, direction, and bridging conceptual gaps. Bret Taylor, CEO of AI agent developer Sierra and former co-CEO of Salesforce, likewise notes that implementing AI thoroughly in a business setting involves rethinking user interfaces, policies, and processes. His team sees a new role emerging—"agent engineer"—who combines front-end coding skills with an in-depth understanding of the organization's key business functions (O'Reilly, 2025). Amid these changes, developers face substantial challenges in designing agents that truly add value rather than merely reproducing outdated processes. The final 30% of a complex project often requires deep debugging, domain expertise, and creative problem-solving that code-generation tools alone cannot supply. Meanwhile, the future of multi-agent collaboration remains uncertain; researchers have begun exploring "agent infrastructure" to manage accountability and standards for interactions between automated systems (O'Reilly, 2025). Despite some speculation that AI might eventually solve these problems, there is little doubt that human oversight is still required to define goals, maintain alignment with organizational objectives, and manage complex network effects. This leaves ample opportunity for programmers, product managers, and entire development teams to imagine and build new systems—just as nineteenth-century factory workers learned to improve, maintain, and invent around emerging textile machines.

As technology is amplifying the nature of programming, there is a growing need for "learning by doing," both at the individual and organizational levels, as companies and developers experiment with advanced frameworks, refine best practices, and jointly shape future standards. Many tasks that once consumed developers' time—handcrafting straightforward components or debugging basic syntax—are being automated, but these changes open broader frontiers in problem formulation, high-level design, and system integration. In an era where algorithms can handle low-level details, the skill of articulating complex problems and discerning new possibilities becomes even more valuable. Far from disappearing, programming is expanding into new terrains of cognitive labor, calling for professionals who see the tech as a superpower that requires constant iteration, discovery, and a willingness to reinvent how we build software for the decades ahead.

7.4 A Call to Action for Interdisciplinary Leadership

Academic institutions now face a pivotal decision: whether to implement incremental adjustments to existing educational models or embrace the revolutionary potential of AI to recenter teaching and learning across all disciplines. This choice extends far beyond simply incorporating new technologies into existing structures—it concerns whether universities will recognize and support the complete reimagining of what programming education means, who can teach it, and how it integrates throughout the curriculum. The traditional pace of academic change—characterized by methodical curriculum revisions and committee deliberations—appears increasingly misaligned with the rapid evolution of these capabilities (Antony et al., 2022). Many current educational structures still reflect historical divisions between technical and non-technical disciplines, perpetuating barriers that AI has effectively eliminated. As previous chapters have demonstrated, coding assistants have removed the historical requirement that either instructors or students possess programming expertise, making computational methods accessible to all fields regardless of technical background (Kellner & Gennaro, 2022). This demands a similarly revolutionary response from educational leaders. Breaking down disciplinary silos becomes not just a goal but a necessity as the tools continue to dissolve the technical barriers that separated computational approaches from non-technical fields (Werthner et al., 2023). The integration of computational methods across curricula requires more than adding coding courses to existing programs—it demands recognizing how this changes what is possible within every discipline.

Faculty and staff development represents a critical dimension of this change. Rather than narrowly considering technical training, professional development should emphasize how educators can guide computational thinking within their disciplinary contexts without needing to become programming experts themselves (Akour & Alenezi, 2022). This approach acknowledges that these intelligent systems have inverted the traditional learning sequence, allowing meaningful application to precede technical mastery across all fields. At the same time, while embracing this technological realignment, universities must simultaneously honor the enduring value of liberal arts education. The study of human history, motivation, and cultural diversity develops global competence, critical thinking, and empathy—transferable skills crucial for thriving in both personal and professional contexts (Kang & Lee, 2022; Rajaram, 2023). Research consistently confirms the importance of cognitive flexibility and emotional intelligence for academic, career, and life success (Elmoutanna & Moti, 2022; González-Pérez & Ramírez-Montoya, 2022; Mabe & Bwalya, 2022; Urhan, 2023). The revolutionary insight is that these humanistic values can now seamlessly integrate with computational approaches, as the tools eliminate the technical barriers that previously forced students to choose between developing technical skills and focusing on humanistic inquiry. Across disciplines, low-code, no-code, and assistive platforms are universalizing programming skills for students and faculty without formal computer science backgrounds. Educational leaders should actively seek ways to integrate these technologies into coursework, enabling all disciplines to adopt computational methods without the traditional barriers of learning advanced coding languages. With tools evolving rapidly, teaching "learning to learn" becomes essential. Professors should encourage students—especially those from non-technical backgrounds—to experiment with coding assistants and data visualization platforms, developing a growth mindset that extends beyond semester boundaries. Some universities provide alumni with ongoing access to online courses or certification modules, reinforcing that skill development continues throughout one's career. This approach recognizes that computational literacy, like writing or quantitative reasoning, requires continuous development rather than one-time mastery.

Industry collaborations further enhance the relevance of computational education across disciplines. Technology companies often provide micro-internships or sponsor campus competitions where diverse student teams tackle real-world challenges using accessible coding frameworks. Industry representatives might guest-lecture on best practices, ensuring that all students—regardless of major—recognize the value of computational approaches in their fields. These partnerships create feedback loops where academic innovations reflect workplace needs, and companies gain access to graduates who combine domain expertise with computational fluency. Together, these best practices point toward a comprehensive redefinition of "programming" and "technological fluency." By leveraging AI-assisted tools, educators can integrate computational thinking into any subject—from literature to health sciences—equipping all learners with the ability to apply computational approaches to disciplinary questions without first mastering technical details. This does not diminish either technical or humanistic education—instead, it creates unprecedented opportunities for integration, preparing students for a future where computational thinking and domain expertise increasingly complement each other across all fields.

As educational leaders navigate this rapidly evolving landscape, they must embrace both technological innovation and humanistic values, recognizing that AI has eliminated the historical barriers that once forced students to choose between them. By reimagining curricula around the integration of computational thinking and disciplinary expertise—made possible by such tools that handle technical implementation while humans focus on meaningful questions—universities can prepare graduates for a future where these previously separate domains increasingly complement each other in all professions.

References

Akour, M., & Alenezi, M. (2022). Higher education future in the era of digital transformation. *Education Sciences*, 12(11), 784.

Antony, J. S., Cauce, A. M., Gangone, L. M., & Nicola, T. P. (Eds.). (2022). *The college president handbook: A sustainable and practical guide for emerging leaders*. Harvard Education Press.

Bakharia, A., & Abdi, S. (2024). Shaping programming and data science education: Insights from GenAI technical book trends. *2024 IEEE International Conference on Advanced Learning Technologies (ICALT)* (pp. 116–120).

Bar-On, R., Brown, J. M., Kirkcaldy, B. D., & Thome, E. P. (2000). Emotional expression and implications for occupational stress; An application of the Emotional Quotient Inventory (EQ-i). *Personality and Individual Differences, 28*(6), 1107–1118.

Bessen, J. (2003). Technology and learning by factory workers: The stretch-out at Lowell, 1842. *The Journal of Economic History, 63*(1), 33–64.

Bessen, J. E. (2011). Was mechanization de-skilling? The origins of task-biased technical change. *Boston Univ. School of Law Working Paper* (pp. 11–13).

Bessen, J. E. (2015). *Learning by doing: The real connection between innovation, wages, and wealth*. Yale University Press.

Chang, Q., Pan, X., Manikandan, N., & Ramesh, S. (2022). Artificial intelligence technologies for teaching and learning in higher education. *International Journal of Reliability, Quality and Safety Engineering, 29*(05), 2240006.

Chiang, R. H., Goes, P., & Stohr, E. A. (2012). Business intelligence and analytics education, and program development: A unique opportunity for the information systems discipline. *ACM Transactions on Management Information Systems (TMIS), 3*(3), 1–13.

Ciolacu, M., Tehrani, A., Binder, L., & Svasta, P. (2018). Education 4.0 – Artificial intelligence assisted higher education: Early recognition system with machine learning to support students' success. *2018 IEEE 24th International Symposium for Design and Technology in Electronic Packaging (SIITME)* (pp. 23–30).

Dotan, R., Parker, L. S., & Radzilowicz, J. (2024, June). Responsible adoption of generative AI in higher education: Developing a "points to consider" approach based on faculty perspectives. In *The 2024 ACM Conference on Fairness, Accountability, and Transparency* (pp. 2033–2046).

Elmoutanna, N. & Moti, N. (2022). Soft skills from university to workplace: A literature review. *International Journal of Accounting, Finance, Auditing, Management and Economics, 3*(5–1), 187–198.

Feng, Y., Vanam, S., Cherukupally, M., Zheng, W., Qiu, M., & Chen, H. (2023). Investigating code generation performance of ChatGPT with crowdsourcing social data. *2023 IEEE 47th Annual Computers, Software, and Applications Conference (COMPSAC)* (pp. 876–885).

Garlick, R., & Fei, W. (2024). AI meets human capital (management) part 3: AI doom or boom for jobs? *Global Insights*, February 2, 2024.

González-Pérez, L. I., & Ramírez-Montoya, M. S. (2022). Components of education 4.0 in 21st century skills frameworks: Systematic review. *Sustainability, 14*(3), 1493.

Gray, K. (2022, September 6). University of Redlands' career faculty fellows program embeds career into curriculum. *NACE*. https://www.naceweb.org/career-readiness/best-practices/university-of-redlands-career-faculty-fellows-program-embeds-career-into-curriculum/

Hannan, E., & Liu, S. (2023). AI: new source of competitiveness in higher education. *Competitiveness Review: An International Business Journal, 33*(2), 265–279.

Hlongwane, J., Shava, G. N., Mangena, A., & Muzari, T. (2024). Towards the integration of artificial intelligence in higher education, challenges and opportunities: The African context, a case of Zimbabwe. *International Journal of Research and Innovation in Social Science, 8*(3S), 417–435.

Issa, T., & Hall, M. (2024). A teamwork framework for preventing breaches of academic integrity and improving students' collaborative skills in the AI era. *Heliyon, 10*(19), e38759.

Jackson, E. A., & Jackson, H. F. (2024). Enhancing human knowledge and capabilities with artificial intelligence tools for education. *Educational Challenges, 29*(2). https://doi.org/10.34142/2709-7986.2024.29.2.09

Janjeva, A., Harris, A., Mercer, S., Kasprzyk, A., & Gausen, A. (2023). The rapid rise of generative AI: Assessing risks to safety and security. CETaS Research Reports.

Johanyák, Z., Cserkó, J., & Pásztor, A. (2023). AI-assisted university programming education in practice. *2023 IEEE 35th International Conference on Software Engineering Education and Training (CSEE&T)* (pp. 185–186).

Jones, M. (2022, November 30). *College of Health launches their virtual escape room game, case of the kidnapped practitioners*. College of Health, Ball State University. https://blogs.bsu.edu/coh/2022/11/30/college-of-health-launches-their-virtual-escape-room-game-case-of-the-kidnapped-practitioners/

Kang, E. S., & Lee, J. M. (2022). Artificial intelligence liberal arts curriculum design for non-computer majors. *Journal of Digital Contents Society, 23*(1), 57–66.

Kellner, D., & Gennaro, S. (2022). Critical theory and the transformation of education in the new millennium. In *The Palgrave handbook on critical theories of education* (pp. 21–45). Springer International Publishing.

Kelly, J. (2024, November 1). AI writes over 25% of code at Google- what does the future look like for software engineers? *Forbes*. https://www.forbes.com/sites/jackkelly/2024/11/01/ai-code-and-the-future-of-software-engineers/

Kirova, V. D., Ku, C. S., Laracy, J. R., & Marlowe, T. J. (2024, March). Software engineering education must adapt and evolve for an llm environment. In *Proceedings of the 55th ACM Technical Symposium on Computer Science Education V. 1* (pp. 666–672).

Lee, K. J. (2022). Adaptive expertise, career adaptability, and career success of R&D personnel. *Technology Analysis & Strategic Management, 22*(2), 189–206.

Lee, K. D. (2017). *Foundations of programming languages*. Springer.

Liu, J., & Li, S. (2024). Toward artificial intelligence-human paired programming: A review of the educational applications and research on artificial intelligence code-generation tools. *Journal of Educational Computing Research*, 07356331241240460.

Mabe, K., & Bwalya, K. J. (2022). Critical soft skills for information and knowledge management practitioners in the fourth industrial revolution. *South African Journal of Information Management, 24*(1), 1–11.

Modi, P. (2024, October 17). The future of work: How linkedin is helping you prepare for the ai-driven workforce. *Education Next*. https://www.educationnext.in/posts/the-future-of-work-how-linkedin-is-helping-you-prepare-for-the-ai-driven-workforce?utm_source=chatgpt.com

O'Reilly, T. (2025, February 4). The end of programming as we know it. *O'Reilly*. https://www.oreilly.com/radar/the-end-of-programming-as-we-know-it/

Pugačova, K. (2023). Transforming education with artificial intelligence: Challenges, opportunities, and future directions. *Вісник науки та освіти*.

Rajaram, K. (2023). Cultural intelligence in teaching and learning. In K. Rajaram (Ed.), *Learning intelligence: Innovative and digital transformative learning strategies: Cultural and social engineering perspectives* (pp. 57–118). Springer Nature Singapore.

Risinamhodzi, D. T., & Heymann, R. (2023, May). Community-based hackathon as a problem identification tool for capstone projects. In *2023 IEEE Global Engineering Education Conference (EDUCON)* (pp. 1–8). IEEE.

Ruxiang, L., & Yue, T. (2023). Design and integration of interdisciplinary curriculum based on artificial intelligence. *Journal of Intelligence and Knowledge Engineering (ISSN: 2959-0620), 1*(3), 75.

Tan, X., Long, X., Ni, X., Zhu, Y., Jiang, J., & Zhang, L. (2024). How far are AI-powered programming assistants from meeting developers' needs?. *arXiv preprint arXiv:2404.12000.*

Urhan, B. (2023). Crucial role of soft skills in challenging times: Conceptual analysis of leadership skills. In A. Baytok (Ed.), *Leadership approaches in global hospitality and tourism* (pp. 23–39). IGI Global.

U.S. Copyright Office. (2025). *Copyright and artificial intelligence, Part 2: Copyrightability.* U.S. Copyright Office. https://www.copyright.gov/ai

Walczak, K., & Cellary, W. (2023). Challenges for higher education in the era of widespread access to Generative AI. *Economics and Business Review, 9*(2), 71–100.

Weber, T., Brandmaier, M., Schmidt, A., & Mayer, S. (2024). Significant productivity gains through programming with large language models. *Proceedings of the ACM on Human-Computer Interaction, 8*(EICS), 1–29.

Weller-Newton, J. M., & Burgess, A. (2023). Challenges in early career research scholarship. *Clinical Teacher, 20*(5), e13620.

Werthner, H., Stanger, A., Schiaffonati, V., Knees, P., Hardman, L., & Ghezzi, C. (2023). Digital humanism: The time is now. *Computer, 56*(1), 138–142.

World Economic Forum (WEF). (2025, January 8). Future of Jobs Report 2025: The jobs of the future – and the skills you need to get them. https://www.weforum.org/stories/2025/01/future-of-jobs-report-2025-jobs-of-the-future-and-the-skills-you-need-to-get-them/?utm_source=chatgpt.com

Yegge, S. (2023, May 11). We're gonna need a bigger moat. *Medium.* https://steve-yegge.medium.com/were-gonna-need-a-bigger-moat-478a8df6a0d2

A.1 Glossary of Key Terms and Concepts

Adaptive Curriculum: Educational strategies and content designed to dynamically adjust to learners' individual needs, abilities, and interests.

Agentic Capabilities: The capacity of AI systems to perform tasks autonomously, make decisions independently, and interact proactively with users.

AI-Augmented Analysis: Leveraging artificial intelligence to enhance data analysis by automating tasks such as summarization, theme identification, and preliminary interpretation.

AI-Driven Debugging: Using artificial intelligence to autonomously detect, diagnose, and correct errors in software code, thus streamlining the development process.

AI-Powered Coding Assistants: Software tools such as GitHub Copilot and Cursor, which support programming by providing automated suggestions, completing code fragments, and reducing the cognitive load associated with syntax memorization.

Bloom's Revised Taxonomy: An updated educational model for categorizing educational goals that prioritizes higher-order thinking skills, such as analyzing, evaluating, and creating, over mere memorization.

Coding: The practice of translating instructions into a programming language understandable by computers, emphasizing syntactic accuracy and command execution.

Collaborative AI: Artificial intelligence systems designed not only to automate but also to actively participate as partners in creative and analytical processes.

Computational Thinking: A problem-solving methodology involving logical analysis, pattern recognition, abstraction, and algorithmic processes, central to programming and software literacy.

Conceptual Originality: The innovative capacity to generate novel ideas and approaches independent of the technical aspects of implementation, increasingly prioritized over traditional, syntax-driven methodologies.

Creative Coding: Utilizing programming languages and computational methods as creative mediums, focusing on artistic expression, innovation, and exploratory processes rather than solely technical outcomes.

Curatorial Approach: The strategic selection, organization, and presentation of programming and analytical tools and methods, guided by human judgment, to effectively address research or educational objectives.

Deployment Skills: Abilities related to implementing and managing software applications in practical, real-world environments, prioritized over purely theoretical or syntactical knowledge.

Generative Artificial Intelligence (GAI): AI systems capable of generating original content—textual, visual, auditory—based on patterns learned from extensive data sets, widely applicable in creative, educational, and analytical contexts.

Holistic Understanding: A comprehensive perspective on software development that integrates logical reasoning, high-level design, and project structuring, shifting away from a purely syntax-centered approach.

Inclusive Curricula: Educational structures deliberately designed to accommodate diverse student backgrounds and learning styles, particularly integrating STEM and non-STEM disciplines.

Interdisciplinary Thinking: Cognitive strategies that integrate knowledge and methodologies across multiple academic disciplines, essential for navigating complex, multifaceted challenges in contemporary research and education.

Literate Programming: A programming model where code is written primarily for readability by humans, facilitating clearer documentation, explanation, and pedagogical utility.

Machine-Generated Content: Outputs created autonomously by artificial intelligence, including text, code, and analysis, intended to complement human-generated materials rather than replace them entirely.

Organizational Thinking: Cognitive processes that emphasize planning, structuring, and managing tasks and resources effectively within software projects, identified as foundational skills alongside coding competencies.

Reflective Practice: An educational approach that involves critical reflection on one's experiences, decisions, and outcomes to enhance learning and improve future performance.

Software Literacy: The ability to effectively understand, create, evaluate, and use software, recognized as a foundational competency necessary across all fields in the 21st-century educational and professional landscape.

STEM/Non-STEM Integration: Educational strategies aimed at merging traditionally separate Science, Technology, Engineering, Mathematics (STEM) disciplines with humanities and social sciences, promoting more inclusive, balanced curricula.

Syntax-First Approach: A traditional pedagogical model emphasizing mastery of programming language syntax before broader conceptual understanding or practical application, now increasingly critiqued and supplemented by AI-driven pedagogies.

Systematic Design Approaches: Methodologies emphasizing thorough planning, clear conceptual frameworks, and iterative development processes to ensure software and research quality and efficiency.

Troubleshooting: The analytical process of diagnosing and resolving problems or errors within software, emphasizing critical thinking, logical deduction, and practical problem-solving skills.

Index

5G networks, 202

A

AI literacy, 22–24, 157, 158, 212, 215
Algorithmic bias, 213
Algorithmic planning, 7
API, 123, 126–128, 134, 135, 138, 182–184
Assembly, 2
Assistive code review platforms, 90
Australian Research Council (ARC), 211
AutoDev, 199

B

BASIC, 99, 100
Big data, 9, 18
Bioinformatics, 17
Bloom's Taxonomy, 137, 140, 164, 165
Blooms 2 Sigma problem, 13
Business, 4, 5, 8, 10, 17, 32–35, 38, 39, 45, 46, 48–50, 53, 79, 100, 110, 157, 162, 163, 177–180, 200, 209, 212, 213, 215, 216

C

C, 2, 38, 82, 99
ChatGPT, 19, 38, 40, 42, 45, 51–54, 56, 57, 75, 99, 104, 133, 145, 150, 157, 160, 166, 169–172, 174, 175, 178, 179, 193, 198
Cicero, 6
Claude, 22
COBOL, 2, 99, 100
CodeAid, 44
Codeium, 65–67, 198
CodePen, 54
Codiga, 66, 67

Computational thinking, x, 1–4, 7–10, 12, 19, 20, 24, 31, 32, 34–36, 38, 46–48, 50–53, 63, 65, 71, 76, 79, 84, 88, 101, 102, 108–110, 118, 119, 136, 137, 139, 142, 143, 149, 150, 155–159, 162, 163, 165, 170, 176, 178, 179, 192, 201, 206–210, 217, 218, 223
Computer science, x, xi, 1–3, 5, 10, 13, 19, 20, 30, 36, 38, 39, 42, 47, 50, 55, 78, 79, 91, 100, 109, 114, 163, 201, 207, 214, 217
Computer vision, 15
Continuous Integration/ Continuous Deployment (CI/CD), 114, 199
Corpora, xi, 9, 126, 174
CSS, 44, 53, 54, 102–105, 110–112
Cursor, x, 1, 12, 37, 40, 63, 66, 67, 119, 223

D

Data privacy, 213
Data storytelling, 17
Data visualization, 5, 6, 14, 18, 31, 48, 51, 89, 105, 106, 108, 114, 124, 130, 141, 165–167, 218
Debugging, 4, 9, 12, 19, 21–23, 30, 33–35, 37, 38, 40–53, 55–58, 63–65, 67, 68, 70, 74–76, 78–83, 85, 88, 109, 116, 126–133, 135–139, 142, 145, 146, 149, 153, 157, 158, 191–195, 197, 198–202, 211, 215, 216, 223
Debugging tools, 50, 58, 129, 197
DeepClassic, 196
Deep Research, 182, 197
DeepSeek, 211
DevOps, 66, 69, 99, 101, 114, 199
Digital humanities, 14, 50, 182